ESSENTIAL JAPANESE KANJI

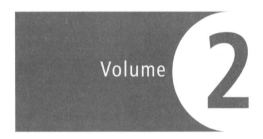

Volume 2

The Kanji Text Research Group **The University of Tokyo**

TUTTLE Publishing

Tokyo │ Rutland, Vermont │ Singapore

About Tuttle
"Books to Span the East and West"

Our core mission at Tuttle Publishing is to create books which bring people together one page at a time. Tuttle was founded in 1832 in the small New England town of Rutland, Vermont (USA). Our fundamental values remain as strong today as they were then—to publish best-in-class books informing the English-speaking world about the countries and peoples of Asia. The world has become a smaller place today and Asia's economic, cultural and political influence has expanded, yet the need for meaningful dialogue and information about this diverse region has never been greater. Since 1948, Tuttle has been a leader in publishing books on the cultures, arts, cuisines, languages and literatures of Asia. Our authors and photographers have won numerous awards and Tuttle has published thousands of books on subjects ranging from martial arts to paper crafts. We welcome you to explore the wealth of information available on Asia at **www.tuttlepublishing.com.**

Published by Tuttle Publishing, an imprint of Periplus Editions (HK) Ltd.

www.tuttlepublishing.com

ISBN 978-4-8053-1379-4

Distributed by

North America, Latin America & Europe
Tuttle Publishing
364 Innovation Drive
North Clarendon, VT 05759-9436 U.S.A.
Tel: 1 (802) 773-8930; Fax: 1 (802) 773-6993
info@tuttlepublishing.com; www.tuttlepublishing.com

Japan
Tuttle Publishing
Yaekari Building, 3rd Floor, 5-4-12 Osaki, Shinagawa-ku, Tokyo 141 0032
Tel: (81) 3 5437-0171; Fax: (81) 3 5437-0755
sales@tuttle.co.jp; www.tuttle.co.jp

Asia Pacific
Berkeley Books Pte. Ltd.
61 Tai Seng Avenue #02-12
Singapore 534167
Tel: (65) 6280-3320; Fax: (65) 6280-6290
inquiries@periplus.com.sg; www.periplus.com

20 19 18 17 16   10 9 8 7 6 5 4 3 2 1

Printed in Singapore   1609MP

TO THE LEARNER

Do you like learning kanji? Or do you wish that kanji would disappear from the face of the earth—or at least from the Japanese language? Well, learning kanji can be fun, *if* you are motivated. And this kanji book was created to motivate you, with practical learning methods that really work, and which will enable you to enjoy studying kanji.

The first edition of this book was published in 1993, and a second volume was published in 1997. Since then, they've helped countless learners master kanji. In later editions, we revised the books to include the 410 kanji required for the College Board Advanced Placement Japanese Language and Culture Course Exam.

Taking an Active Approach

An important feature of this book is the active approach it takes to introducing kanji. By using authentic materials, periodic quizzes, and memory aids, it gradually helps learners acquire the ability to understand and use kanji in natural contexts—that is, in everyday life.

Another key aspect of *Essential Japanese Kanji Volume 2* is the presentation of authentic materials, for instance the business cards you might receive from people you meet in Japan. We also use photographs, many of which were taken by our foreign students during their adventures in Japan. The kanji taught here are, clearly, based on everyday use. (Please note that prices mentioned in these authentic materials may have changed.)

Also, for each kanji we include either etymologies or memory aids, which will help students to understand and memorize the kanji systematically. The list of kanji compounds will also help learners understand how new words are created by combining the familiar kanji, and to realize the power that mastering kanji offers them.

Each lesson helps you master a new group of kanji, and consists of several sections.
- **Introductory Quiz** introduces some familiar, everyday situations where the kanji is likely to be used.
- **Vocabulary** contains the readings and meanings of the kanji that you've encountered in the Quiz.
- **New Characters** teaches you the kanji systematically, by introducing the meaning, the basic **on-kun** readings, the etymologies or memory aids, and compound words.
- **Practice** will help you improve your kanji reading and writing skills.
- **Advanced Placement Exam Practice Questions** will test your competence in reading and writing semi-authentic natural Japanese. These questions reflect the format of the College Board's Japanese Language and Culture examination.

We wish to thank Koichi Maekawa, Michael Handford, Su Di, Sandra Korinchak, Cathy Layne, and June Chong. Junko Ishida, Kazuko Karasawa, Tomoko Kigami, and Akiyo Nishino revised the 2008 edition; Junko Ishida, Kazuko Karasawa, and Akiyo Nishino revised the 2016 edition.

The following books were useful in compiling the kanji charts: *Reikai Gakushu Kanji Jiten*, published by Shogakukan, and *Kanjigen* published by Gakushu Kenkyusha.

We sincerely hope that this book will help all learners—yes, even you who have been stymied by kanji before!—begin to enjoy learning kanji.

The Kanji Text Research Group 漢字教材研究グループ
Japanese Language Class 日本語教室
Department of Civil Engineering 社会基盤学専攻
The University of Tokyo 東京大学大学院

Authors: 2008　　　　　著者:
Junko Ishida　　　　　石田順子
Kazuko Karasawa　　　唐澤和子
Tomoko Kigami　　　　木上伴子
Akiyo Nishino　　　　　西野章代
Illustrator:　　　　イラストレーター:
Hitomi Suzuki　　　　　鈴木ひとみ

CONTENTS

INTRODUCTION

This book contains 21 lessons introducing 250 kanji. Each lesson focuses on an everyday situation in Japan.

There is a short explanation of kanji and kana before the lessons begin. You will also find the Appendices, the **On-Kun** Index and the Vocabulary Index useful to refer to as you learn.

A modified Hepburn system of romanization has been used.

Each lesson is composed of the following sections.

1. Introductory Quiz — This section describes situations that you may encounter in daily life, and is followed by a quiz. By referring first to the words in **Vocabulary**, you'll learn the readings and the meanings of the words that are introduced in the lesson. And by solving the quiz, you will understand the situation that's presented. Try the quiz again *after* the lesson, and you'll find out how much you have learned.

2. Vocabulary — This section contains the readings and meanings of the words used in the **Introductory Quiz**. Refer to it when studying the illustrations or taking the quiz. The numeral above each kanji indicates the lesson where the kanji is introduced.

3. New Characters — This section introduces the kanji of the lesson using **Kanji Charts** with their meanings, basic **on-kun** readings, stroke orders, etymologies or memory-aid hints, and compounds with their English translations.

The compounds essentially consist of newly or previously introduced kanji. (Kanji that are not included in the 500 taught in the two volumes of this series are marked with ×.) More important compounds are shown in the upper part of the list. However, you are encouraged to study those in the lower part of the list as well. When kana is optionally added to kanji (**okurigana**), the most common usage is adopted and formal usages are shown in parentheses.

4. Practice — This section provides practice for reading and writing the kanji found mainly in the upper part of the kanji charts. You should use the practice as a final check for the kanji learned in each lesson. Answers to this section are not provided.

5. Advanced Placement Exam Practice Questions — This section provides an exercise similar in format to the College Board's Advanced Placement examination for Japanese Language and Culture. You can try the exercise after each lesson, or after completing all the lessons.

UNDERSTANDING KANJI

The oldest Chinese characters, the precursors of kanji, originated more than 3,000 years ago. Originally they were simple illustrations of objects and phenomena in everyday life, and developed as a writing tool mainly characterized by pictography and ideography. Thus each of the Chinese characters carries its own meaning within itself.

Chinese characters, or kanji, can be classified according to origin and structure into four main categories:

1. Pictographic characters are derived from the shapes of concrete objects.

   → 木 → 木 ＝ tree

   → θ → 日 ＝ sun

2. Sign characters are composed of points and lines that express abstract ideas.

   → 上 → 上 ＝ above, on, up

   → 下 → 下 ＝ below, down, under

3. Ideographic characters are composed of combinations of other characters.

   木 (tree) ＋ 木 (tree) → 林 ＝ forest
   日 (sun) ＋ 月 (moon) → 明 ＝ bright

4. Phonetic-ideographic characters are composed of combinations of ideographic and phonetic elements. Upper parts or righthand parts often indicate the reading of the kanji. About 90% of all kanji fall into this category.
   先 (セン previous) → 洗 (セン wash)
   安 (アン peaceful) → 案 (アン proposal)

The Japanese had no writing symbols until kanji were introduced from China in the fifth century. Soon after this, kanji were simplified into phonetic symbols known as **hiragana** and **katakana**. Thus the Japanese language came to be written in combinations of **kanji** and **kana** (see page 9).

This kanji-kana writing system is more effective than writing with kana only. As the written Japanese language doesn't leave spaces between words, kanji among kana make it easier for readers to distinguish units of meaning and to understand the context. Readers can easily grasp the rough meaning of written text by following kanji only.

Kanji can usually be read two ways. These readings are referred to as **on-yomi** and **kun-yomi**. **On-yomi** is the Japanese reading taken from the original Chinese pronunciation. **Kun-yomi** is the pronunciation of an original Japanese word applied to a kanji according to its meaning. Hiragana added after **kun-yomi** readings are called **okurigana**. **Okurigana** primarily indicates the inflectional ending of a kanji, though the last part of the stem is occasionally included in the **okurigana**.

Most kanji are composed of two or more elements, and parts of one kanji are often found in different compounds in other kanji. Certain commonly shared parts are called radicals, or **bushu** in Japanese. Radicals are used to classify kanji in dictionaries; thus each kanji is allocated only one radical. Each radical also carries a core meaning. For example, the radical 言 means "word" or "speak." Therefore the kanji 語 (language), 話 (speak, story), 読 (read), 記 (note down), and 論 (discuss) all have something to do with the meaning of 言.

There are 214 radicals altogether. Some frequently seen radicals are listed below.

1. 冫 ice   3. 女 woman   5. 广 slanting roof   7. 禾 grain   9. 門 gate
2. 彳 step   4. 刂 knife   6. 尸 corpse   8. 糸 thread   10. 灬 fire

Kanji strokes are written in a fixed direction and order. There are several fundamental rules for writing the strokes.

1. Horizontal strokes: from left to right

三 (three)   土 (soil)   工 (engineering)

2. Vertical or slanting strokes: from top to bottom

十 (ten)   木 (tree)   人 (man)   八 (eight)

3. Hook strokes: from top left to right or left bottom

日 (day)   手 (hand)   分 (minute)   氏 (surname)

4. The center stroke first, followed by the left and right strokes

小 (small)   山 (mountain)

5. The outside strokes first, followed by the middle strokes

月 (moon)   中 (inside)

6. The horizontal stroke first, followed by the vertical stroke (usually followed by another horizontal stroke)

十 (ten)   土 (soil)

7. The left-hand slanting stroke first, followed by the right-hand side

八 (eight)   六 (six)

As your knowledge of kanji increases, kanji dictionaries become more helpful. There are three ways to refer to a kanji.

1. Look for the kanji by radical in the **bushu** (radical) index.
2. Look for the kanji by stroke number in the **kakusū** (stroke number) index.
3. Look for the kanji by pronunciation in the **on-kun** reading index.

UNDERSTANDING KANA

Japanese Writing Systems

There are four different kinds of characters used for writing Japanese: kanji, hiragana, katakana, and rōmaji (Roman alphabet). Kanji incorporates meanings as well as sounds. Hiragana, katakana, and rōmaji are phonetic characters that express only sounds. However, unlike English, one kana character can be pronounced only one way: 「あ」 or 「ア」 is only pronounced [a].

Japanese sentences are usually written with a combination of kanji, hiragana, and katakana. Katakana is mainly used for foreign words that are adapted to fit Japanese pronunciation. Kanji appears in nouns, verbs, adjectives, and adverbs. Hiragana is primarily used to show the inflectional endings of kanji (**okurigana**). Particles, conjunctions, and interjections are mostly written in hiragana. Although hiragana can substitute for kanji, a combination of kanji and hiragana is much faster to read. For example, compare these four ways of writing the same information:

Kanji and hiragana: 私は毎朝早く起きます。 出かける前にテレビを見ます。
Hiragana only: わたしはまいあさはやくおきます。 でかけるまえにテレビをみます。
Rōmaji: Watashi-wa maiasa hayaku okimasu. Dekakeru mae-ni terebi-o mimasu.
English: I get up early every morning. I watch TV before I leave home.

Japanese Syllabary Chart

Each square in the chart below represents one pronounced syllable.

hiragana — あ **a** / rōmaji — / katakana — ア

	a	i	u	e	o
	あ **a** ア	い **i** イ	う **u** ウ	え **e** エ	お **o** オ
k	か **ka** カ	き **ki** キ	く **ku** ク	け **ke** ケ	こ **ko** コ
s	さ **sa** サ	し **shi** シ	す **su** ス	せ **se** セ	そ **so** ソ
t	た **ta** タ	ち **chi** チ	つ **tsu** ツ	て **te** テ	と **to** ト
n	な **na** ナ	に **ni** ニ	ぬ **nu** ヌ	ね **ne** ネ	の **no** ノ
h	は **ha** ハ	ひ **hi** ヒ	ふ **fu** フ	へ **he** ヘ	ほ **ho** ホ
m	ま **ma** マ	み **mi** ミ	む **mu** ム	め **me** メ	も **mo** モ
y	や **ya** ヤ		ゆ **yu** ユ		よ **yo** ヨ
r	ら **ra** ラ	り **ri** リ	る **ru** ル	れ **re** レ	ろ **ro** ロ
w	わ **wa** ワ				を **o** ヲ

ya	yu	yo
きゃ **kya** キャ	きゅ **kyu** キュ	きょ **kyo** キョ
しゃ **sha** シャ	しゅ **shu** シュ	しょ **sho** ショ
ちゃ **cha** チャ	ちゅ **chu** チュ	ちょ **cho** チョ
にゃ **nya** ニャ	にゅ **nyu** ニュ	にょ **nyo** ニョ
ひゃ **hya** ヒャ	ひゅ **hyu** ヒュ	ひょ **hyo** ヒョ
みゃ **mya** ミャ	みゅ **myu** ミュ	みょ **myo** ミョ

りゃ **rya** リャ	りゅ **ryu** リュ	りょ **ryo** リョ

ん **n** ン

g	が ga ガ	ぎ gi ギ	ぐ gu グ	げ ge ゲ	ご go ゴ
z	ざ za ザ	じ ji ジ	ず zu ズ	ぜ ze ゼ	ぞ zo ゾ
d	だ da ダ	ぢ ji ヂ	づ zu ヅ	で de デ	ど do ド
b	ば ba バ	び bi ビ	ぶ bu ブ	べ be ベ	ぼ bo ボ
p	ぱ pa パ	ぴ pi ピ	ぷ pu プ	ぺ pe ペ	ぽ po ポ

ぎゃ gya ギャ	ぎゅ gyu ギュ	ぎょ gyo ギョ
じゃ ja ジャ	じゅ ju ジュ	じょ jo ジョ

びゃ bya ビャ	びゅ byu ビュ	びょ byo ビョ
ぴゃ pya ピャ	ぴゅ pyu ピュ	ぴょ pyo ピョ

Additional Katakana

Created with small ァ ィ ゥ ェ ォ ュ

	a	i	u	e	o	yu
y				イェ ye		
w		ウィ wi		ウェ we	ウォ wo	
kw	クァ kwa	クィ kwi		クェ kwe	クォ kwo	
gw	グァ gwa	グィ gwi		グェ gwe	グォ gwo	
sh				シェ she		
j				ジェ je		
t		ティ ti	トゥ tu			テュ tyu
d		ディ di	ドゥ du			デュ dyu
ts	ツァ tsa	ツィ tsi		ツェ tse	ツォ tso	
f	ファ fa	フィ fi		フェ fe	フォ fo	フュ fyu
v	ヴァ va	ヴィ vi	ヴ vu	ヴェ ve	ヴォ vo	ヴュ vyu

Derivation of Kana

Hiragana and katakana are Japanese phonetic syllabaries developed from kanji in the eighth century. Hiragana, which are cursive letters, derive from the shapes of entire kanji characters. Katakana, which are combinations of straight lines, derive from various parts of kanji characters. In some cases both hiragana and katakana are derived from the same kanji, such as **ka**, **mo**, **te**, **yu**, **ra**, and **ri**, shown below. Kana derived from some of the kanji introduced in this textbook are also shown.

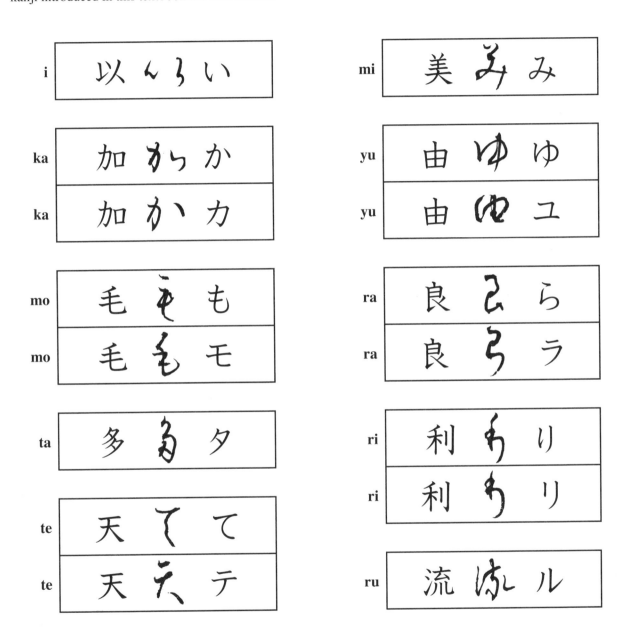

A SAMPLE KANJI CHART

A sample from the kanji charts is explained below.

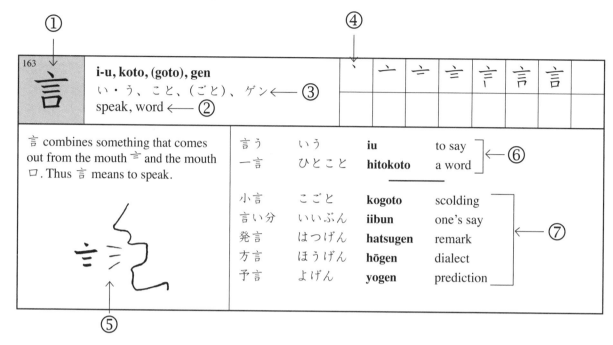

① The kanji and its serial number in this textbook.
② Meanings.
③ Readings: **kun**-readings in hiragana, and **on**-readings in katakana.
   Hiragana following a dot [・う in the sample above] are **okurigana**.
   Readings in parentheses ( ) express euphonic change, i.e., modified readings. [For example, こと、（ごと）]
④ Stroke order.
⑤ Etymology or memory-aid. (The authors have created new derivations for some kanji when the etymology is unclear or confusing.)
⑥ Important compound words, and their readings and meanings.
⑦ Additional compound words, and their readings and meanings.

Note that:

• Kanji marked × are not included in the 500 kanji taught in two volumes of *Essential Japanese Kanji*.
• Kana in parentheses ( ) in kanji compounds is optional when writing. [For example, 終（わ）る can be written 終わる or 終る]. Two sets of ( ) appear for most nouns derived from compound verbs. The kana in both ( ) or in the former ( ) only may be omitted, but the kana in the latter ( ) alone cannot be omitted. [For example, 取（り）消（し）can be written 取り消し、取消し、or 取消、but not 取り消.]
• * indicates exceptional readings.
• Small numbers placed above certain kanji in the Vocabulary sections refer to Lesson numbers in this book.
• "々" is a kanji repetition mark, used like "少々", **shōshō**.

Living in Japan

日本に住みます

Looking for a place to live is one of the most important matters for newcomers to Japan. Three ways are available to search for apartments or houses: using the Internet, looking over a real estate lease information magazine, and visiting a real estate agent. The listings show various kinds of floor plans; among these, the studio and the 1K (one room, plus kitchen) apartment are the most common. In this lesson, you will learn some technical terms commonly used when searching for housing.

1 ▶ Introductory Quiz

Look at the illustrations below and refer to the words in **Vocabulary**. Then try the following quiz.

Which apartment will Ichiro and Kaori choose? Write the appropriate letters (A, B) in the parentheses.

1. さくらマンション （　　　　）

広くてきれい！

交通・生活に便利！

駅まで歩いて3分

洋　室
フローリング
約10帖

収納

洗

家　賃：8万5千円

管理費：5千円

敷　金：2か月分

礼　金：2か月分

必ず身分証明書をおもちください！

2. ふじアパート （　　　　）

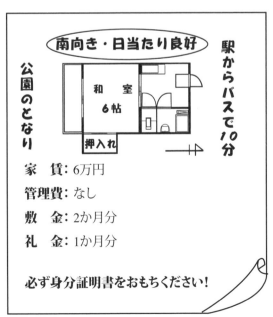

南向き・日当たり良好

駅からバスで10分

公園のとなり

和　室
6帖

押入れ

家　賃：6万円

管理費：なし

敷　金：2か月分

礼　金：1か月分

必ず身分証明書をおもちください！

A ぼくは駅からとおくても安いアパートがいいな。さんぽが好きだから、公園のちかくもいいな。

B 私は高くても、駅からちかくて、便利なところがいいわ。夜一人で歩くのはこわいもの。

Ichiro   Kaori

2 ▶ Vocabulary

Study the readings and meanings of these words to help you understand the **Introductory Quiz**.

1.	広い	ひろ い	**hiroi**	spacious
2.	交通	こう つう	**kōtsū**	transportation
3.	生活	せい かつ	**seikatsu**	living
4.	便利な	べん り な	**benri na**	convenient
5.	～帖／畳	～ じょう	**~jō**	counter for tatami mats
6.	家賃	や ちん	**yachin**	rent (house)
7.	管理費	かん り ひ	**kanrihi**	maintenance fee
8.	敷金	しき きん	**shikikin**	deposit
9.	礼金	れい きん	**reikin**	key money
10.	必ず	かなら ず	**kanarazu**	surely
11.	身分証明書	み ぶん しょう めい しょ	**mibun shōmeisho**	identification card
12.	南向き	みなみ む き	**minamimuki**	facing south
13.	日当たり	ひ あ たり	**hiatari**	sunshine
14.	良好	りょう こう	**ryōkō**	good
15.	公園	こう えん	**kōen**	park
16.	私	わたくし／わたし	**watakushi/watashi**	I
17.	夜	よる	**yoru**	night

3 ▶ New Characters

Twelve characters are introduced in this lesson. Use the explanations to help you understand and remember the characters. Study the compound words to increase your vocabulary.

広 交 活 利 家 賃 理 礼 身 向 好 私

---

1 広   **hiro-i, (biro-i), kō**
ひろ・い、（びろ・い）、コウ
broad, wide, spread

`	亠	广	広	広			

Roof 广 and ム arm combined, 広 means the space in the house where one can stretch arms widely. Thus 広 means wide.

広い	ひろい	**hiroi**	spacious
広場	ひろば	**hiroba**	plaza
広大な	こうだいな	**kōdai na**	vast
広間	ひろま	**hiroma**	hall, spacious room
広義	こうぎ	**kōgi**	broad sense
手広い	てびろい	**tebiroi**	extensive
広々	ひろびろ	**hirobiro**	extensive

---

2 交   **maji-waru, kō**
まじ・わる、コウ
intersection, exchange

`	亠	六	六	亣	交		

Six 六 people are at work and interacting ㄨ. Thus 交 means to cross or exchange.

交わる	まじわる	**majiwaru**	to intersect
交通	こうつう	**kōtsū**	transportation
交番	こうばん	**kōban**	koban, police box
外交	がいこう	**gaikō**	diplomacy
国交	こっこう	**kokkō**	diplomatic relations
社交的	しゃこうてき	**shakōteki**	sociable
交代する	こうたいする	**kōtai suru**	to take turns
交付	こうふ	**kōfu**	deliver

3 活

katsu, (ka')
カツ、（カッ）
life, activity

		`	⁀	⺡	⺡	汗	汗	汗	活
活									

舌 is a pictograph of a tongue. Tongue 舌 and water 氵 combined, 活 suggests wet tongue. Thus 活 means life and by extension activity.

生活	せいかつ	**seikatsu**	living
生活費	せいかつひ	**seikatsuhi**	living expense
活動	かつどう	**katsudō**	activity
活発な	かっぱつな	**kappatsu na**	lively
活用	かつよう	**katsuyō**	practical use
自活する	じかつする	**jikatsu suru**	to support oneself

4 利

ri
リ
advantage, interest

	⸝	⸍	千	禾	禾	利	利

Grain 禾 and a plow 刂 combined, 利 means profitable, because if you plow the earth, you will reap more grain, which is a benefit to you.

便利な	べんりな	**benri na**	convenient
利用する	りようする	**riyō suru**	to use
利用者	りようしゃ	**riyōsha**	user
有利な	ゆうりな	**yūri na**	advantageous
不利な	ふりな	**furi na**	disadvantageous
利子	りし	**rishi**	interest (on a loan)

5 家

ie, ka, ya
いえ、カ、ヤ
house, family, person

	`	⺊	⼧	宀	宁	宇	宇	家
家	家							

Pigs 豕 were important animals in ancient China, and they were kept in the house 宀 where people lived. The original meaning is to roof animals like pigs, but it has changed to mean a building with a roof.

家	いえ	**ie**	house
家内	かない	**kanai**	wife
大家	おおや	**ōya**	landlord/landlady
家計	かけい	**kakei**	house economy
家事	かじ	**kaji**	house work
家出	いえで	**iede**	run away from home

6 — 賃

chin
チン
fare, wages

Stroke order: ノ イ イ 仁 任 任 任 侟 侟 侟 侟 賃 賃

任 is a combination of a person イ and the load 壬 the person is carrying, thus meaning responsibility. 任 combined with money 貝, 賃 means the amount of money one is responsible to pay.

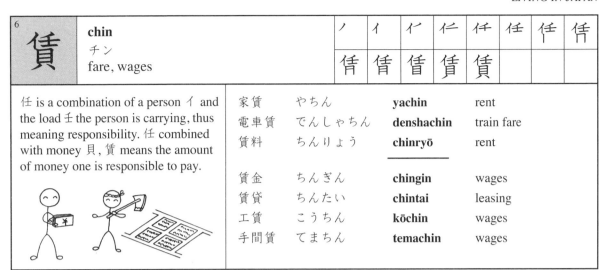

家賃	やちん	**yachin**	rent
電車賃	でんしゃちん	**denshachin**	train fare
賃料	ちんりょう	**chinryō**	rent
賃金	ちんぎん	**chingin**	wages
賃貸	ちんたい	**chintai**	leasing
工賃	こうちん	**kōchin**	wages
手間賃	てまちん	**temachin**	wages

7 — 理

ri
リ
reason, logic, principle

Stroke order: 一 丁 干 王 玕 理 理 理 理 理 理

The king, or ruler, 王 of the village 里 is reasonable.

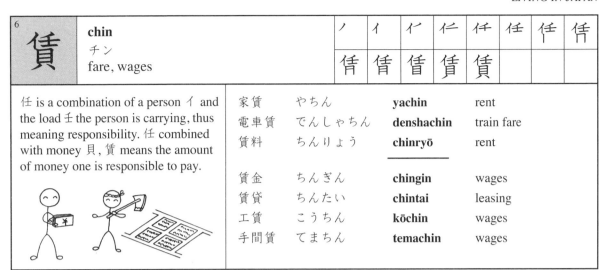

管理費	かんりひ	**kanrihi**	administrative fee
管理	かんり	**kanri**	management
管理人	かんりにん	**kanrinin**	supervisor, caretaker, superintendent
無理な	むりな	**muri na**	impossible
理学部	りがくぶ	**rigakubu**	faculty of science
料理	りょうり	**ryōri**	cooking
修理	しゅうり	**shūri**	repair
理事	りじ	**riji**	director

8 — 礼

rei
レイ
bow, thanks, etiquette

Stroke order: ` ラ ネ ネ 礼

礼 combines shrine ネ, and a line し suggesting to bow. Thus 礼 means bow.

礼	れい	**rei**	bow, thanks, etiquette
礼金	れいきん	**reikin**	key money
お礼	おれい	**orei**	thanks
無礼	ぶれい	**burei**	rudeness
祭礼	さいれい	**sairei**	religious festival
目礼	もくれい	**mokurei**	nod, greet by eyes
非礼	ひれい	**hirei**	impolite
洗礼	せんれい	**senrei**	baptism

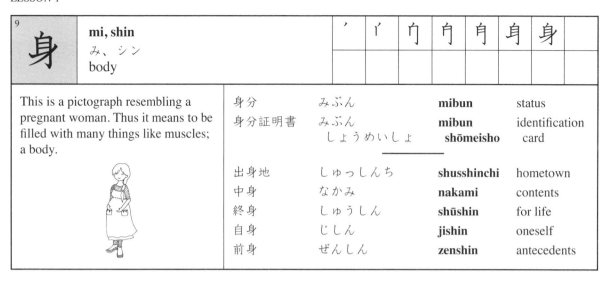

9 身　mi, shin
み、シン
body

｀　丿　冂　白　自　身　身

This is a pictograph resembling a pregnant woman. Thus it means to be filled with many things like muscles; a body.

身分	みぶん	**mibun**	status
身分証明書	みぶん しょうめいしょ	**mibun shōmeisho**	identification card
出身地	しゅっしんち	**shusshinchi**	hometown
中身	なかみ	**nakami**	contents
終身	しゅうしん	**shūshin**	for life
自身	じしん	**jishin**	oneself
前身	ぜんしん	**zenshin**	antecedents

10 向　mu-ku, kō
む・く、コウ
face toward

｀　丿　冂　向　向　向

The air flows out through the window 口 of a house toward one direction.

南向き	みなみむき	**minamimuki**	facing south
方向	ほうこう	**hōkō**	direction
前向きに	まえむきに	**maemuki ni**	positively
外人向け	がいじんむけ	**gaijin muke**	for foreigners
向学心	こうがくしん	**kōgakushin**	love of learning
向上心	こうじょうしん	**kōjōshin**	desire to improve oneself
意向	いこう	**ikō**	intention

11 好　su-ki, kō
す・き、コウ
fond

く　女　女　好　好　好

Women 女 like 好 children 子.

好きな	すきな	**suki na**	fond
好物	こうぶつ	**kōbutsu**	favorite food
好意	こうい	**kōi**	good will
好意的	こういてき	**kōiteki**	friendly
好人物	こうじんぶつ	**kōjimbutsu**	good natured person
好男子	こうだんし	**kōdanshi**	handsome man
好学	こうがく	**kōgaku**	love of learning
好都合	こうつごう	**kōtsugō**	favorable

12 私	watakushi, (watashi), shi わたくし、(わたし)、シ I, private	ノ	二	千	禾	禾	私	私	

禾 is grain. ム is the figure of an arm holding grain. Thus 私 means to take in the grain or whatever belongs to an individual.

私	わたくし／わたし	**watakushi/ watashi**	I
私立	しりつ	**shiritsu**	private (institution)
私語	しご	**shigo**	private talk
私費	しひ	**shihi**	one's own expense
私用	しよう	**shiyō**	private engagement
私生活	しせいかつ	**shiseikatsu**	private life
私室	ししつ	**shishitsu**	private room

4 ▶ Practice

I. Write the readings of the following kanji in hiragana.

1. 交通　　　　　2. 生活　　　　　3. 家賃　　　　　4. 礼金

5. 身分証明書　　6. 方向　　　　　7. 好物　　　　　8. 私立

9. 広くて安いアパートをさがしています。

10. 交番はどこですか。

11. コンビニは便利なので、よく利用します。

12. この家は南向きで明るいです。

13. このアパートは管理（かん）がいいです。　14. 私は子どもが大好きです。

II. Fill in the blanks with appropriate kanji.

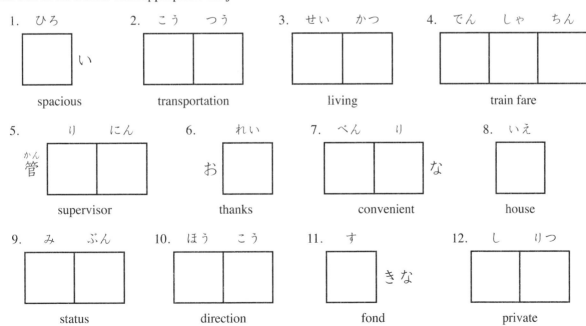

1. ひろ ☐ い — spacious

2. こう つう ☐☐ — transportation

3. せい かつ ☐☐ — living

4. でん しゃ ちん ☐☐☐ — train fare

5. り にん 管（かん）☐☐ — supervisor

6. れい お☐ — thanks

7. べん り ☐☐ な — convenient

8. いえ ☐ — house

9. み ぶん ☐☐ — status

10. ほう こう ☐☐ — direction

11. す ☐ きな — fond

12. し りつ ☐☐ — private

5 ▶ Advanced Placement Exam Practice Questions

You are looking for a studio apartment. Compare two options, #1 and #2, and decide which one you will choose.

Write which option you selected and compare at least THREE aspects (similarities and/or differences) between #1 and #2. Also write reasons for your selection.

Your writing should be 300 to 400 characters or longer. Use the **desu/masu** or **da** (plain) style, but use one style consistently. Also, use kanji wherever kanji from the AP Japanese kanji list is appropriate. You have 20 minutes to write.

#1

#2

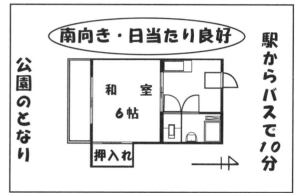

Homestay

ホームステイ

When you come to study in Japan for a while, a homestay is a good way to get to know the daily customs of Japanese life, as well as everyday life and special events in that particular area of the country. You may talk with the neighbors, the family's relatives and their friends, and better understand how the Japanese relate to each other. Taking a trip with your host family is another great opportunity to learn. And, as a homestay provides you with the basic essentials like furniture, you won't have to buy those for yourself. If you would like to set up a homestay, you can consult with the university or company you're affiliated with. In this lesson, you will learn terminology related to homestays and host parents.

1 ▶ Introductory Quiz

Look at the illustrations on page 22 and refer to the words in **Vocabulary**. Then try the following quiz.

You received this letter from your friend who lives with a Japanese host family.

　私は、ホームステイをしています。ホストファミリーの家は、駅から遠いですが、みどりが多くていい所にあります。

　お父さんは、会社で働いています。とても親切な人で、いろいろなことを相談できます。すこし太っています。お母さんは、家にいて、とてもやさしい人です。外国人登録をする時もいっしょについて来てくれました。

　ホストファミリーの家にはかわいい犬がいます。私もひまな時、犬といっしょに近所をさんぽします。

　時々、近所の人も集まってきて、いろいろな話をします。私も短い話なら日本語でできるようになりました。皆さん、とても親切です。

　お会いできるのをたのしみにしています。

　　　　　　　　　　　　　　　　　　　　　　　　　トム リー

Which are the correct contents of the letter? Write ◯ (correct) or ✕ (wrong) in the spaces provided.

1. (   )   2. (   )   3. (   )

4. (   )   5. (   )   6. (   )

---

2 ▶ Vocabulary

Study the readings and meanings of these words to help you understand the **Introductory Quiz**.

1. ホストファミリー		**hosuto famirī**	host family
2. 遠い	とおい	**tōi**	far
3. お父さん	おとうさん	**otō san**	father
4. 働く	はたらく	**hataraku**	to work
5. 親切な	しんせつな	**shinsetsu na**	kind
6. 相談する	そうだんする	**sōdan suru**	to consult with

7. 太っている	ふと っている	**futotteiru**	stout
8. お母さん	お かあ さん	**okā san**	mother
9. 外国人登録	がい こく じん とう ろく	**gaikokujin tōroku**	alien registration
10. かわいい		**kawaii**	cute
11. 犬	いぬ	**inu**	dog
12. 近所	きん じょ	**kinjo**	neighborhood
13. 時々	とき どき	**tokidoki**	sometimes
14. 集まる	あつ まる	**atsumaru**	to get together
15. 短い	みじか い	**mijikai**	short
16. 皆さん	みな さん	**minasan**	everybody

3 ▶ New Characters

Fourteen characters are introduced in this lesson. Use the explanations to help you understand and remember the characters. Study the compound words to increase your vocabulary.

遠 父 母 働 親 相 太 登 録 犬 近 集 短 皆

---

13 遠   **tō-i, en**   とお・い、エン   far

一	十	土	圡	吉	吉	吉	吉
吉	袁	袁	遠	遠			

The loose 袁 way to go 辶 to the destination is a longer way to go. Thus 遠 means far.

destination

short way → ⊃ ← loose way, long way

start

遠い	とおい	**tōi**	far
遠回し	とおまわし	**tōmawashi**	indirect
遠回り	とおまわり	**tōmawari**	roundabout way
遠近法	えんきんほう	**enkinhō**	law of perspective
遠来	えんらい	**enrai**	from afar
遠方	えんぽう	**empō**	afar

14 父	**chichi, fu** ちち、フ father	ノ	ハ	分	父			

As mature men in the family were traditionally responsible for wood cutting, a hand 乂 with an ax signifies father.

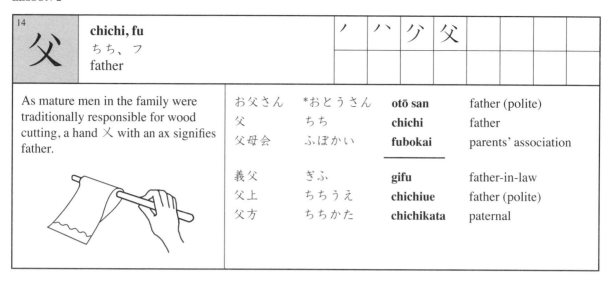

お父さん	*おとうさん	**otō san**	father (polite)
父	ちち	**chichi**	father
父母会	ふぼかい	**fubokai**	parents' association
義父	ぎふ	**gifu**	father-in-law
父上	ちちうえ	**chichiue**	father (polite)
父方	ちちかた	**chichikata**	paternal

15 母	**haha, bo** はは、ボ mother	ㄥ	口	口	母	母		

A human figure with pronounced breasts suggests nursing; thus this kanji means mother.

お母さん	*おかあさん	**okā san**	mother (polite)
母	はは	**haha**	mother
父母	ふぼ	**fubo**	father and mother; parents
母国	ぼこく	**bokoku**	mother land
母国語	ぼこくご	**bokokugo**	mother tongue
生母	せいぼ	**seibo**	one's real mother
母上	ははうえ	**hahaue**	mother (polite)
母方	ははかた	**hahakata**	maternal

16 働	**hatara-ku, dō** はたら・く、ドウ work	ノ	イ	イ	仁	仁	佢	佢	佢
		侢	俥	傽	衝	働			

働 combines a man イ, heavy 重, and power 力, suggesting a man working, moving heavy things.

働く	はたらく	**hataraku**	to work
労働者	ろうどうしゃ	**rōdōsha**	worker
働き口	はたらきぐち	**hatarakiguchi**	job
働き者	はたらきもの	**hatarakimono**	hard worker
働き手	はたらきて	**hatarakite**	worker

17 親	**oya, shin** おや、シン parent	`	亠	ㅗ	立	立	立	辛	辛
		亲	亲	新	新	新	親	親	親

Parents 親 stand 立 on a tree 木 and watch 見 the children.

親	おや	**oya**	parent
親切な	しんせつな	**shinsetsu na**	kind
母親	ははおや	**hahaoya**	mother
		———	
親子	おやこ	**oyako**	parent and child
親日	しんにち	**shinnichi**	pro-Japanese
親日家	しんにちか	**shinnichika**	pro-Japanese person

18 相	**ai, sō, shō** あい、ソウ、ショウ mutual, aspect, minister	一	十	才	木	朾	机	机	相
		相							

相 combines eyes 目 and a tree 木, suggesting the idea of looking carefully from behind a tree. Thus it means aspect.

相談する	そうだんする	**sōdan suru**	to consult with
相手	あいて	**aite**	partner
		———	
人相	にんそう	**ninsō**	physiognomy, looks
手相	てそう	**tesō**	lines of the palm
相場	そうば	**sōba**	market price
外相	がいしょう	**gaishō**	minister of foreign affairs
相次いで	あいついで	**aitsuide**	one after another

19 太	**futo-i, futo-ru, tai, ta** ふと・い、ふと・る、タイ、タ fat, thick, big	一	ナ	大	太				

Big 大 is even further emphasized with a dot.

太い	ふとい	**futoi**	fat, thick
太平洋	たいへいよう	**Taiheiyō**	the Pacific Ocean
		———	
太鼓	たいこ	**taiko**	drum
太平	たいへい	**taihei**	peace
丸太	まるた	**maruta**	log
丸太小屋	まるたごや	**maruta goya**	log cabin

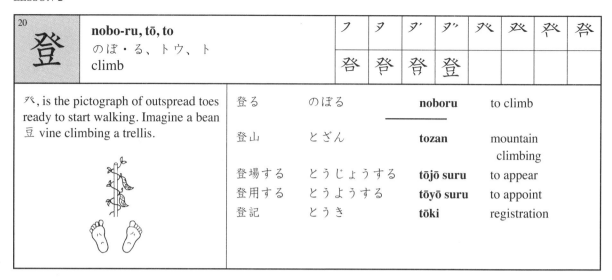

20 登	nobo-ru, tō, to のぼ・る、トウ、ト climb	フ	ヲ	ヺ	ヺ	癶	癶	癶	癶
		咎	咎	登	登				

癶, is the pictograph of outspread toes ready to start walking. Imagine a bean 豆 vine climbing a trellis.	登る	のぼる	**noboru**	to climb
	登山	とざん	**tozan**	mountain climbing
	登場する	とうじょうする	**tōjō suru**	to appear
	登用する	とうようする	**tōyō suru**	to appoint
	登記	とうき	**tōki**	registration

21 録	roku ロク record	ノ	𠂉	厶	牟	牟	牟	釒	金
		釘	釘	釖	鈩	鉰	錄	錄	録

录 indicates the green rust of corroded metal (copper) 金. Both the form and the meaning have been modified to mean engrave. Combined with metal 金, the kanji means to engrave metal to keep a record.	登録する	とうろくする	**tōroku suru**	to register
	外国人登録	がいこくじん とうろく	**gaikokujin tōroku**	alien registration
	記録する	きろくする	**kiroku suru**	to record
	新記録	しんきろく	**shinkiroku**	new record
	議事録	ぎじろく	**gijiroku**	proceedings
	住所録	じゅうしょろく	**jūshoroku**	address book
	語録	ごろく	**goroku**	sayings

22 犬	inu, ken いぬ、ケン dog	一	ナ	大	犬				

犬 is a pictograph of a dog. The dot is the tail.	犬	いぬ	**inu**	dog
	子犬	こいぬ	**koinu**	puppy
	番犬	ばんけん	**banken**	watchdog
	犬小屋	いぬごや	**inu goya**	kennel

| 23 近 | chika-i, (jika-i), kin
ちか・い、（ぢか・い）、キン
near | ノ | ア | ヂ | 斤 | 斤 | 近 | 近 | |

斤 is a pictograph of an ax about to cut the target object. Thus 斤 means close to something. Road 辶 is added, so 近 means near.

近い	ちかい	**chikai**	near
近所	きんじょ	**kinjo**	neighborhood
近道	ちかみち	**chikamichi**	shortcut
近代	きんだい	**kindai**	modern times
中近東	ちゅうきんとう	**chūkintō**	the Near and Middle East
近日	きんじつ	**kinjitsu**	in a few days
手近な	てぢかな	**tejika na**	handy
身近な	みぢかな	**mijika na**	familiar

| 24 集 | atsu-maru, atsu-meru, shū
あつ・まる、あつ・める、シュウ
gather, meet | ノ | イ | イ' | 仁 | 什 | 什 | 什 | 隹 |
| | | 隹 | 隼 | 集 | 集 | | | | |

Birds 隹 of a feather flock together (to a tree 木).

集まる	あつまる	**atsumaru**	to get together
集める	あつめる	**atsumeru**	to collect
集会所	しゅうかいしょ／じょ	**shūkaisho/jo**	meeting place
集会室	しゅうかいしつ	**shūkaishitsu**	meeting room
特集	とくしゅう	**tokushū**	special issue
集中する	しゅうちゅうする	**shūchū suru**	to concentrate
集金	しゅうきん	**shūkin**	collecting money
全集	ぜんしゅう	**zenshū**	complete works

| 25 短 | mijika-i, tan
みじか・い、タン
short | ノ | ト | ヒ | 矢 | 矢 | 矢 | 矢 | 矢 |
| | | 矩 | 矩 | 短 | 短 | | | | |

An arrow 矢 reaches the target in a short time, and a bean 豆 is short.

短い	みじかい	**mijikai**	short
短期	たんき	**tanki**	short term
短大	たんだい	**tandai**	junior college
短所	たんしょ	**tansho**	defect

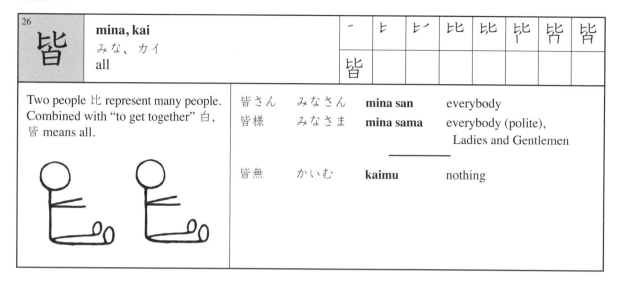

26 皆	mina, kai みな、カイ all	一	ヒ	ヒ′	比	比	毕	皆	皆
		皆							

Two people 比 represent many people. Combined with "to get together" 白, 皆 means all.

皆さん	みなさん	**mina san**	everybody
皆様	みなさま	**mina sama**	everybody (polite), Ladies and Gentlemen
皆無	かいむ	**kaimu**	nothing

4 Practice

I. Write the readings of the following kanji in hiragana.

1. 近道
2. 皆様
3. 登る
4. 太平洋
5. 外国人登録
6. この犬は、太っています。
7. 集会所で集まりましょう。
8. お母さんは、とても親切です。
9. お父さんと相談します。

II. Fill in the blanks with appropriate kanji.

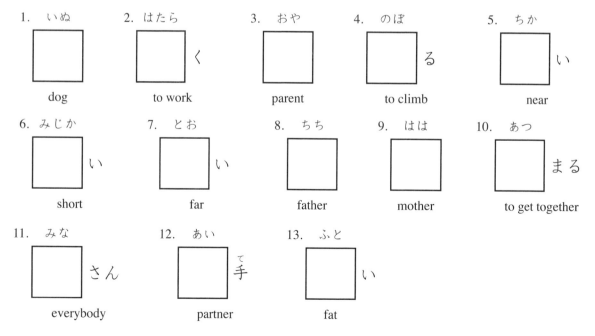

1. いぬ
dog

2. はたら
く
to work

3. おや
parent

4. のぼ
る
to climb

5. ちか
い
near

6. みじか
い
short

7. とお
い
far

8. ちち
father

9. はは
mother

10. あつ
まる
to get together

11. みな
さん
everybody

12. あい
て手
partner

13. ふと
い
fat

5 ▶ Advanced Placement Exam Practice Questions

Read these suggestions from a woman who has had the experience of hosting a foreign student.

　　日本に来て、短い間でもホームステイをし、実際に日本人といっしょに住むことにより、日本人の生活を体験できることは、とてもいいことだと思います。もちろん家族によってちがいますが、普通の日本人の¹生活習慣、考え方、²礼儀、年中行事などを経験することができます。ホームステイをする時、家族の皆さんに、親類の家や近所の家、近くのお祭りなどに、どんどん連れて行ってもらって、いろいろなことを知りましょう。きっと学ぶことがたくさんあると思います。自分のへやは、自分でそうじをしましょう。日本にはまだ³食洗機が少ないないので、みんながいやがる食後の⁴後かたづけを引き受けると、一番よろこばれます。食事の準備を手伝うのもいいです。日本人が口にする料理の作り方が分かります。時には、自分の国の料理を作って家族を⁵もてなすと、家族もあなたの国について関心を持つでしょう。夜おそくなる時は、かならず伝えること。交通事故にあったのではないかなどと、日本人のお母さんは心配をするからです。お父さんに、何でも相談するといいです。よろこんでいろいろ話してくれるでしょう。

¹生活習慣: a way of life　　²礼儀:etiquette　　³食洗機: dishwasher

⁴後かたづけ: clearing the table, washing the dishes after meal

⁵もてなす: to offer one's hospitality

1. According to the suggestions, what is the best way to learn the Japanese lifestyle, way of thinking, and so on with your host family?
   A. watching the TV together
   B. playing together at the park
   C. going out together for various activities or events
   D. studying Japanese together

2. According to the suggestions, what is the best way you should help the family?
   A. holding a party
   B. preparing their dinner
   C. washing clothes
   D. washing the dishes of the family

3. According to the suggestions, why is the homestay a good approach to staying in Japan?
   A. Because they serve meals for you.
   B. Because you are able to understand Japanese people's customs.
   C. Because you are able to understand Japanese history.
   D. Because it is enjoyable to have fun with the host family.

4. According to the suggestions, why is it good for you to help the family to prepare the meal?
   A. Because that way you can eat a delicious meal.
   B. Because you know how to make Japanese dishes.
   C. Because the family are happy to have your help.
   D. Because you can enjoy time with the family.

5. According to the suggestions, why is it good for the family to prepare your own country's dishes?
   A. Because the family members show interest in your country.
   B. Because the family members enjoy your dishes.
   C. Because the family members do not have to prepare the meal.
   D. Because you can demonstrate your attitude to the family.

Host in Family

ホストファミリー

The lifestyle of Japanese families is very different from family to family. Some people embrace Japanese style in most aspects of their lives, but many prefer western style. The average number of children per family used to be between three and five, about 60 years ago. The average now is less than two children per family; if someone has three children, Japanese view that as many.

About half of all wives stay at home and focus on their families. After their children have grown up, they start to enjoy themselves with hobbies or friends. Some do volunteer work, and others begin to work on a part-time basis. Nowadays many women work at companies or other firms (compared with several decades ago). A few wives continue to work on a full-time basis, while they bring up children. In this lesson you will learn kanji related to the family.

1 ▶ Introductory Quiz

Look at the illustrations below and refer to the words in **Vocabulary**. Then try the following quiz.

You introduce your host family.

私のホストファミリーは、とてもいい家族です。

お父さんは、自分の会社を持っています。
社長です。

お母さんは、病院で働いています。
お医者さんです。

お姉さんは、主婦です。
ボランティア活動をしています。

お姉さんのご主人は、大学で英語を教えてい
ます。アメリカへ行った経験もあります。

お兄さんは、去年大学を出て、
お母さんと同じ病院で
仕事をしています。

弟さんは、今アメリカの大学
の学生です。アメリカ文学を
勉強しています。ワシント
ン州にいます。

妹さんは、高校生です。
数学が好きです。スポーツ
はテニスをしています。

Based on the explanations above, answer true (○) or false (×) for each statement by filling in the (   )
provided.

1. The elder sister's husband has stayed in France to teach at a university. (   )
2. The father has his own company. (   )
3. The elder brother works for his father's company. (   )
4. The younger sister does not like mathematics. (   )
5. The younger brother lives in the United States now. (   )
6. The elder sister does volunteer work. (   )
7. The mother works at her husband's company. (   )
8. The elder sister's husband teaches English at a university. (   )
9. The younger brother studies Spanish literature at a university. (   )
10. The elder brother graduated from a university last year. (   )

2 ▶ Vocabulary

Study the readings and meanings of these words to help you understand the **Introductory Quiz**.

1.	家族	か ぞ く	**kazoku**	family
2.	自分	じ ぶん	**jibun**	oneself
3.	会社	かい しゃ	**kaisha**	company
4.	持つ	も つ	**motsu**	to have, to hold
5.	社長	しゃ ちょう	**shachō**	president of the company
6.	病院	びょう いん	**byōin**	hospital
7.	医者	い しゃ	**isha**	medical doctor
8.	お姉さん	お ねえ さん	**onē san**	elder sister (polite)
9.	主婦	しゅ ふ	**shufu**	housewife
10.	活動	かつ どう	**katsudō**	activity
11.	主人	しゅ じん	**shujin**	husband
12.	英語	えい ご	**eigo**	English
13.	経験	けい けん	**keiken**	experience
14.	お兄さん	お にい さん	**onii san**	elder brother (polite)
15.	去年	きょ ねん	**kyonen**	last year
16.	同じ	お な じ	**onaji**	the same
17.	仕事	し ごと	**shigoto**	work, job
18.	弟さん	おとうと さん	**otōto san**	younger brother (polite)
19.	今	いま	**ima**	now
20.	勉強	べん きょう	**benkyō**	study
21.	州	しゅう	**shū**	state
22.	妹さん	いもうと さん	**imōto san**	younger sister (polite)
23.	高校生	こう こう せい	**kōkōsei**	high school student
24.	数学	すう がく	**sūgaku**	mathematics

3 ▶ New Characters

Sixteen characters are introduced in this lesson. Use the explanations to help you understand and remember the characters. Study the compound words to increase your vocabulary.

族 持 姉 主 婦 経 兄 去 同 仕 弟 今 州 妹 校 数

27 族

zoku
ゾク
family, tribe

ヽ	ユ	う	方	方	扩	扩	扩
萨	族	族					

族 combines a flag 扩 and an arrow 矢, meaning tribe. Tribes get together to fight with arrows under a flag.

家族	かぞく	**kazoku**	family
親族	しんぞく	**shinzoku**	relatives
一族	いちぞく	**ichizoku**	kin
部族	ぶぞく	**buzoku**	tribe
氏族	しぞく	**shizoku**	clan
士族	しぞく	**shizoku**	a descendant of a **samurai**
水族館	すいぞくかん	**suizokukan**	aquarium

28 持

mo-tsu, ji
も・つ、ジ
have, possess, hold

一	十	扌	扩	扩	扩	拌	持
持							

Soil 土 and hand 寸 suggest work. A place where priests work is a temple 寺. Temple combined with hand 扌 means to hold or possess, because temples possessed power and wealth.

持つ	もつ	**motsu**	to hold
気持ち	きもち	**kimochi**	feeling
持ち物	もちもの	**mochimono**	belongings
金持ち	かねもち	**kanemochi**	rich people
支持する	しじする	**shiji suru**	to support
持ち家	もちいえ	**mochiie**	one's own house
手持ち	てもち	**temochi**	goods on hand
受け持つ	うけもつ	**ukemotsu**	to be in charge

29 姉

ane, shi
あね、シ
elder sister

く	女	女	女	扩	扩	姉	姉

姉 combines a woman 女 and a market 市. It is the elder sister who goes to market.

お姉さん	*おねえさん	**onē san**	elder sister (polite)
姉	あね	**ane**	elder sister

30 主	**omo, nushi, shu, su** おも、ぬし、シュ、ス main, master, lord	丶	二	十	干	主		

主 is the pictograph of a lighted candle. The flame stays still. In ancient China, the master of the house stayed at one place in the house like the candle, and made a command. Thus 主 means the master.

主な	おもな	**omo na**	main
主人	しゅじん	**shujin**	husband
主語	しゅご	**shugo**	subject (grammar)
主人公	しゅじんこう	**shujinkō**	hero/heroine
店主	てんしゅ	**tenshu**	shopkeeper
主食	しゅしょく	**shushoku**	staple food

31 婦	**fu** フ woman, wife	く	女	女	女ㄱ	女ㄥ	女ㅋ	女ㅋ	婦
		婦	婦	婦					

A woman 女 with a broom 帚 is an adult woman.

主婦	しゅふ	**shufu**	housewife
婦人	ふじん	**fujin**	lady
婦人会	ふじんかい	**fujinkai**	ladies' society
婦人用	ふじんよう	**fujinyō**	for ladies
婦人科	ふじんか	**fujinka**	gynecology

32 経	**he-ru, kei, kyō** へ・る、ケイ、キョウ longitude, passage of time	く	幺	幺	幺	糸	糸	糸	紅	終
		経	経	経						

経 combines the warp of a loom and thread 糸, and means longitude.

経験	けいけん	**keiken**	experience
経済	けいざい	**keizai**	economy
経営	けいえい	**keiei**	management
経理	けいり	**keiri**	accounting
経常	けいじょう	**keijō**	current
経費	けいひ	**keihi**	cost

33 兄	**ani, kyō, kei** あに、キョウ、ケイ elder brother	ノ	口	口	尸	兄			

Traditionally, a big brother had power. Thus 兄 combines big mouth 口, meaning a lot of power, and a person with legs 儿 emphasized.	お兄さん	*おにいさん	**onii san**	elder brother (polite)
	兄	あに	**ani**	elder brother
	兄弟	きょうだい	**kyōdai**	brothers and sisters
	兄弟子	あにでし	**ani deshi**	senior fellow student
	実兄	じっけい	**jikkei**	one's real elder brother
	義兄	ぎけい	**gikei**	one's elder brother-in-law

34 去	**sa-ru, kyo, ko** さ・る、キョ、コ leave	一	十	土	去	去			

去 is a pictograph of a container ム with a lid 土. By extension, 去 means to leave, take off or pass. Past is the sealed (or covered) time.	去年	きょねん	**kyonen**	last year
	去る	さる	**saru**	to leave
	去来	きょらい	**kyorai**	coming and going

35 同	**ona-ji, dō** おな・じ、ドウ same	一	冂	冂	同	同	同		

同 is a pictograph of one of the cut-off sides of a pipe, all of which look the same.	同じ	おなじ	**onaji**	same
	同時に	どうじに	**dōji ni**	at the same time
	同好会	どうこうかい	**dōkōkai**	association of like-minded people
	同様	どうよう	**dōyō**	same
	同意	どうい	**dōi**	agreement
	一同	いちどう	**ichidō**	all (of us)

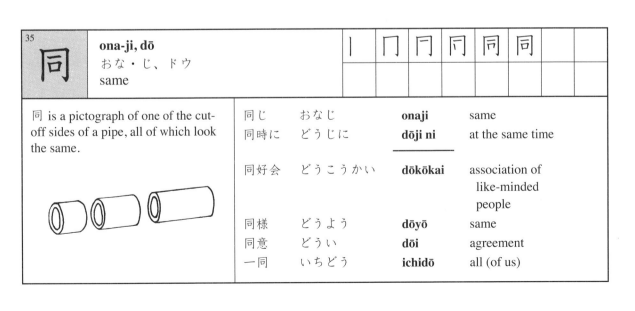

36 仕	**tsuka-eru, shi** つか・える、シ serve	ノ	イ	仁	仕	仕			

仕 combines a high rank officer 士 and a man イ serving him. Thus 仕 means to serve, or work.

仕える	つかえる	**tsukaeru**	to serve
仕事	しごと	**shigoto**	work, job
仕方	しかた	**shikata**	way, method
仕立て屋	したてや	**shitateya**	tailor
仕上げる	しあげる	**shiageru**	to finish up, to complete

37 弟	**otōto, dai, de, tei** おとうと、ダイ、デ、テイ younger brother; disciple	丶	ソ	丷	当	弟	弟	弟	

弟 is a pictograph of a climbing vine with the lowest part emphasized with "ノ", suggesting a younger brother.

弟さん	おとうとさん	**otōto san**	younger brother (polite)
弟	おとうと	**otōto**	younger brother
義兄弟	ぎきょうだい	**gikyōdai**	brothers- and sisters-in-law
弟子	でし	**deshi**	pupil
子弟	してい	**shitei**	children
門弟	もんてい	**montei**	follower
高弟	こうてい	**kōtei**	leading disciple

38 今	**ima, kon, kin** いま、コン、キン now	ノ	人	今	今				

今 combines to conceal something フ underneath a cover 亼, and means to keep "time" inside the cover lest it should escape. Thus 今 means "now".

今	いま	**ima**	now
今日	*きょう	**kyō**	today
今週	こんしゅう	**konshū**	this week
今月	こんげつ	**kongetsu**	this month
今年	*ことし	**kotoshi**	this year
今後	こんご	**kongo**	after this
今期	こんき	**konki**	present term

past ← now → future

39 州	su, shū す、シュウ state, a sandbar	`	ﾘ	ﾘ	州	外	州		

Originally written with a circle on each line, indicating the sand rising out of the shallow river. Thus 州 means an island in the river. By extension, 州 also means a state.	州	しゅう	**shū**	state, province
	本州	ほんしゅう	**Honshū**	the mainland (of Japan)
	九州	きゅうしゅう	**Kyūshū**	Kyushu Island
	中州	なかす	**nakasu**	sand bank in a river

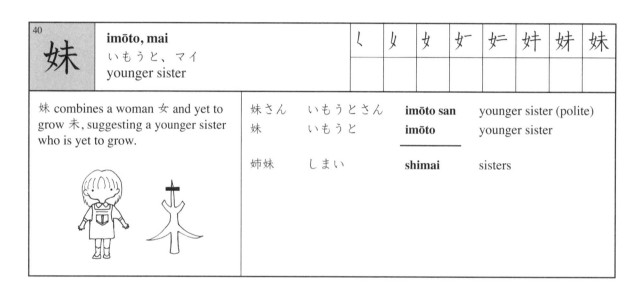

40 妹	imōto, mai いもうと、マイ younger sister	く	タ	女	女‐	妇	妌	妹	妹

妹 combines a woman 女 and yet to grow 未, suggesting a younger sister who is yet to grow.	妹さん	いもうとさん	**imōto san**	younger sister (polite)
	妹	いもうと	**imōto**	younger sister
	姉妹	しまい	**shimai**	sisters

41 校	kō コウ school, proof	一	十	才	木	朩゙	朳	朳	栌
		朳	校						

School houses in ancient China were built with crossed 交 logs 木, like a log cabin.	小学校	しょうがっこう	**shōgakkō**	elementary school
	中学校	ちゅうがっこう	**chūgakkō**	junior high school
	高校生	こうこうせい	**kōkōsei**	high school student
	母校	ぼこう	**bokō**	alma mater
	校正する	こうせいする	**kōsei suru**	to read proofs
	登校する	とうこうする	**tōkō suru**	to go to school
	下校する	げこうする	**gekō suru**	to come home from school

38

42 数	kazu, kazo-eru, sū, (zū) かず、かぞ・える、スウ、(ズウ) number, count	丶	丷	丷	半	米	米	类
		类	类	数	数	数		

Eighty eight 八十八 = 米 women 女 are engaged in a number 数 of actions 攵.

数	かず	**kazu**	number
数学	すうがく	**sūgaku**	mathematics
人数	にんずう	**ninzū**	number of people
手数料	てすうりょう	**tesūryō**	commission
無数の	むすうの	**musū no**	numerous
分数	ぶんすう	**bunsū**	fraction
半数	はんすう	**hansū**	half the number
回数券	かいすうけん	**kaisūken**	coupon ticket

4 ▶ Practice

I. Write the readings of the following kanji in hiragana.

1. 気持ち　　　　2. 主語　　　　　　3. 去年　　　　　　4. 仕事

5. 九州　　　　　6. 数学　　　　　　7. 主婦　　　　　　8. 経験

9. わたしの家族は、イリノイ州に住んでいます。

10. お姉さんは、今ボランティアをしています。

11. お兄さんは、お父さんと同じ仕事をしています。

12. 弟は、去年中学生になりました。

13. 妹は、アメリカに行った経験があります。

II. Fill in the blanks with appropriate kanji.

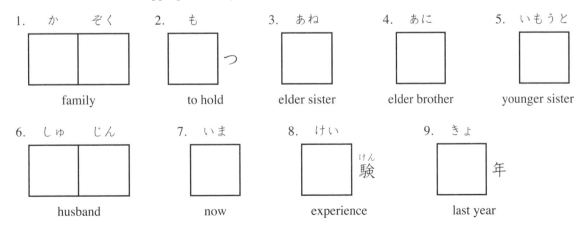

1. か　ぞく　　　　2. も　　　　　3. あね　　　　4. あに　　　　5. いもうと

□□　　　　　□つ　　　　□　　　　□　　　　□

family　　　　　to hold　　　elder sister　　elder brother　　younger sister

6. しゅ　じん　　　7. いま　　　　8. けい　　　　9. きょ

□□　　　　　□　　　　□ 験　　　　□ 年
　　　　　　　　　　　　　 けん

husband　　　　　now　　　experience　　　last year

10.　ワシントン〔しゅう〕

State of Washington

11.　〔こう〕〔こう〕生

high school

12.　〔すう〕〔がく〕学

mathematics

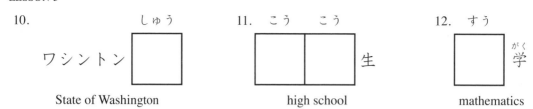

5 ▸ Advanced Placement Exam Practice Questions

Read the passage below and answer the questions.

　以前、日本では専業主婦が多かった。しかし、今はフルタイム、あるいはパートタイムで仕事をする主婦がふえている。前者は、医者、会社員、店員、銀行員、教員、[1]公務員などいろいろな[2]分野で働いている。後者は、コンビニの店員から大学の講師まで、広く[3]活躍している。家庭の主婦の半数が仕事を持っていることになる。学校を卒業後[4]就職し、結婚して定年まで同じ会社で働き続ける人もいるが、まだあまり多くない。[5]育児のために仕事をやめると、もう一度同じ会社で働くのが難しいからだ。しかし、[6]少子化のため、少しずつ[7]産休制度も広がり、会社によっては家で仕事ができるシステムも始めている。今までは、女性が外で仕事をしていても、家事・育児をやるべきだという考えが強かった。[8]共働きをしている夫が家事・育児をしないからであったが、今、若い人の中には、家事・育児を夫と妻がいっしょにやろうという考えも少しずつふえてきた。「女は家事を、男は仕事を」という、昔からの考えは、変わってきている。

[1]公務員: government officer, civil servant
[2]分野: field of …
[3]活躍する: to be active
[4]就職する: to get a job
[5]育児: raising a child
[6]少子化: trend towards having fewer children
[7]産休制度: maternity/paternity leave
[8]共働き: working couple

1. According to this article, what field do women work in?
   A. universities
   B. various fields
   C. convenience stores
   D. companies

2. According to this article, how many wives work outside the home, including wives who work on a part-time basis?
   A. a few
   B. half
   C. many
   D. all

3. According to this article, how do companies support women who work?
   A. Companies take care of the women's children.
   B. Government provides the proper system for them.
   C. The women's parents take care of their children.
   D. Companies give them various working options.

4. According to this article, when have husbands and wives begun to share housework?
   A. since a long time ago
   B. since 30 years ago
   C. very recently
   D. from now on

5. According to this article, which sentence of the following is correct?
   A. Wives do not like to work outside the home.
   B. Old-fashioned Japanese ideas are changed by the younger generation, little by little.
   C. The Japanese government does not allow wives to work outside the home.
   D. Husbands do not like wives to work outside the home.

Airport Procedures and Facilities

国際空港

Narita International Airport is one of the busiest airports in the world. Although you can get by at the airport using only English, it is a convenient place to learn kanji. There are many services available to help you get through the airport smoothly, and if you know kanji it is easier to take advantage of these services. For example, knowing kanji can help you to plan the route and means of transportation to reach the airport. You can also take advantage of a service that will deliver your baggage directly to the airport, so you don't have to carry it yourself. And check the signs, so that you don't forget to declare your valuables at the customs desk! In this lesson, you will learn terms for these and other facilities at the airport.

1 ▶ Introductory Quiz

Look at the illustrations below and refer to the words in **Vocabulary**. Then try the following quiz.

I. You are leaving Japan for your home country. You have just arrived at Narita International Airport Terminal 2. There are various facilities at the airport, as shown. Fill in the spaces for each statement with the correct letters (a–f).

a.

b.

c.

d.

e.

f.

1. いろいろなものを、安く買うことができます。（　　　）

2. 日本のお金をほかの国のお金にかえます。（　　　）

3. くうこうで、分からないことがあったら、ここで聞きましょう。（　　　）

4. ここで、日本を出るために、てつづきをします。（　　　）

5. シャトルにのるまで、ここでまちます。（　　　）

6. まっすぐ行くと、だい2りょきゃくターミナルがあります。（　　　）

II. You are returning to Japan. To enter Japan, follow the course (page 44).

成田空港では、たくさんの飛行機が飛び立ったり、着いたりします。

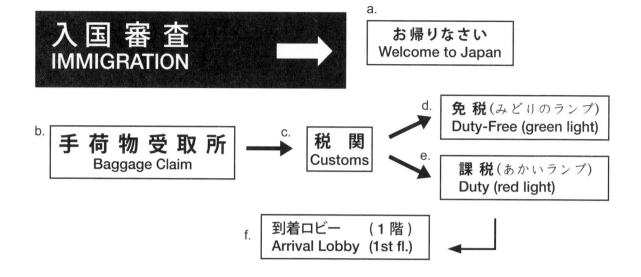

Fill in the spaces with the correct letters (**a–f**).

1. 入国審査の後、（　　　）で、自分のにもつを受け取ります。

2. ぜいきんをはらうとき、（　　　）へ行きます。

3. ともだちが、（　　　）で待っています。

4. にもつを受け取ってから、（　　　）へ行きます。

5. ぜいきんをはらわないとき、（　　　）へ行きます。

6. このことば（　　　）を見ると、日本人は*ほっとします。(*feel relieved)

2 ▶ Vocabulary

Study the readings and meanings of these words to help you understand the **Introductory Quiz**.

1. 空港	くう こう	**kūkō**	airport
2. 成田国際空港	なり た こく さい くう こう	**Narita kokusai kūkō**	Narita International Airport
3. 第2旅客ターミナル	だい に りょ きゃく ターミナル	**Dai ni ryokyaku tāminaru**	Airport Terminal 2
4. ご案内	ご あん ない	**goannai**	information
5. 免税売店 (免税店	めん ぜい ばい てん めん ぜい てん	**menzei baiten** **menzeiten**	duty-free shop commonly used orally)
6. 両替	りょう がえ	**ryōgae**	currency exchange
7. 出国手続	しゅっ こく て つづき	**shukkoku tetsuzuki**	passport control/ procedure for departure

8. 本館	ほん かん	**honkan**	main building
9. 待合所	まち あい しょ／じょ	**machiaisho/jo**	waiting place
10. 入国審査	にゅう こく しん さ	**nyūkoku shinsa**	Immigration
11. お帰りなさい	お かえ りなさい	**Okaerinasai**	Welcome back to Japan
12. 荷物	に もつ	**nimotsu**	baggage
13. 手荷物受取所	て に もつ うけ とり しょ／じょ	**tenimotsu uketorisho/jo**	baggage claim area
14. 税金	ぜい きん	**zeikin**	tax
15. 税関	ぜい かん	**zeikan**	customs
16. 免税	めん ぜい	**menzei**	duty-free
17. 課税	か ぜい	**kazei**	duty
18. 到着ロビー	とう ちゃく ロビー	**tōchaku robī**	arrival lobby
19. 飛行機	ひ こう き	**hikōki**	airplane
20. 飛ぶ	と ぶ	**tobu**	to fly

3 ▷ New Characters

Fifteen characters are introduced in this lesson. Use the explanations to help you understand and remember the characters. Study the compound words to increase your vocabulary.

港 第 旅 客 免 税 両 続 待 合 帰 荷 関 飛 機

43 港	minato, kō みなと、コウ harbor, port	丶	氵	氵	氵	氵	氵	洪	洪
		洪	洪	港	港				

巷 is a pictograph of streets. 氵 means water. 港 thus refers to shipping lanes and a port.

巷

港	みなと	**minato**	harbor
空港	くうこう	**kūkō**	airport
成田国際 空港	なりた こくさい くうこう	**Narita kokusai kūkō**	Narita International Airport
入港	にゅうこう	**nyūkō**	entering port
開港	かいこう	**kaikō**	opening the port
母港	ぼこう	**bokō**	home port

44 第 — dai / ダイ / counter for numbers

Stroke order: ノ ト ト ト ゲ ゲ 竺 竺 竺 第 第

第 combines bamboo 竹, and the horizontal lines representing bamboo joints 弟, suggesting the order.

第2 ターミナル	だいに ターミナル	**Dai ni tāminaru**	Airport Terminal 2
第二	だいに	**dai ni**	the second
第一人者	だいいち にんしゃ	**dai ichi ninsha**	leading person
第一線	だいいっせん	**dai issen**	front line

45 旅 — tabi, ryo / たび、リョ / trip, travel

Stroke order: ` 亠 ゔ 方 方 ゲ ゲ 斿 旅 旅

方, is the pictograph of a flag flying in the wind. 从 suggests that two men are walking in a row under the flag like travelers in a caravan. It means journey.

旅	たび	**tabi**	trip
旅行	りょこう	**ryokō**	trip
旅券	りょけん	**ryoken**	passport
旅費	りょひ	**ryohi**	travel expenses
旅館	りょかん	**ryokan**	Japanese-style inn

46 客 — kyaku, kaku / キャク、カク / guest, customer

Stroke order: ` 宀 宀 ゔ 宮 宓 客 客

Someone who stops 各 at a house 宀 is a guest 客.

客	きゃく	**kyaku**	guest
旅客	りょきゃく	**ryokyaku**	traveler
第2旅客 ターミナル	だいに りょきゃく ターミナル	**Dai ni ryokyaku tāminaru**	Airport Terminal 2
お客様	おきゃくさま	**okyaku sama**	guest (polite)
客間	きゃくま	**kyakuma**	guest room
客車	きゃくしゃ	**kyakusha**	passenger coach

47 免

manuka-reru, men
まぬか・れる、メン
escape, exempt

ノ	ク	⼾	⼧	凸	岱	孕	免

免 depicts a woman giving birth.

免税	めんぜい	**menzei**	duty-free
ご免	ごめん	**gomen**	Excuse me. (casual)
ご免なさい	ごめんなさい	**gomen nasai**	Excuse me. (polite)
免税店	めんぜいてん	**menzeiten**	duty-free shop
免税品	めんぜいひん	**menzeihin**	tax-free goods

48 税

zei
ゼイ
tax

⼀	⼆	千	禾	禾	禾	利	利
秒	秒	秒	税				

Government 兄 or big brother with two horns ソ on the head collects grain 禾 as taxes.

税金	ぜいきん	**zeikin**	tax
税込み	ぜいこみ	**zeikomi**	including tax
税引き	ぜいびき	**zeibiki**	after taxes
無税	むぜい	**muzei**	tax free
地方税	ちほうぜい	**chihōzei**	local taxes

49 両

ryō
リョウ
both

⼀	⼚	丆	市	両	両		

This is the pictograph of a scale with the weight equally balanced on the right and left sides. Thus it means both or two.

両替	りょうがえ	**ryōgae**	currency exchange
両方	りょうほう	**ryōhō**	both
両手	りょうて	**ryōte**	both hands
両親	りょうしん	**ryōshin**	parents
両立する	りょうりつする	**ryōritsu suru**	to coexist
両者	りょうしゃ	**ryōsha**	both persons
両面	りょうめん	**ryōmen**	both sides

| 50 続 | tsuzu-ku, tsuzu-keru, zoku
つづ・く、つづ・ける、ゾク
continue | く | 幺 | 幺 | 糸 | 糸 | 糸 | 紵 | 約 |
| | | 紵 | 結 | 紵 | 続 | 続 | | | |

Thread 糸 and sell 売 combined, 続 means that one must continue to sell thread (to stay in business).

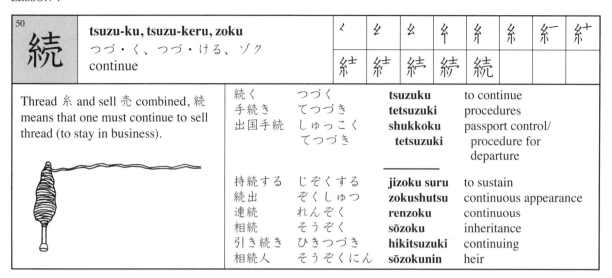

続く	つづく	**tsuzuku**	to continue
手続き	てつづき	**tetsuzuki**	procedures
出国手続	しゅっこく てつづき	**shukkoku tetsuzuki**	passport control/ procedure for departure
持続する	じぞくする	**jizoku suru**	to sustain
続出	ぞくしゅつ	**zokushutsu**	continuous appearance
連続	れんぞく	**renzoku**	continuous
相続	そうぞく	**sōzoku**	inheritance
引き続き	ひきつづき	**hikitsuzuki**	continuing
相続人	そうぞくにん	**sōzokunin**	heir

| 51 待 | ma-tsu, tai
ま・つ、タイ
wait | ノ | ク | 彳 | 彳 | 彳 | 往 | 往 | 待 |
| | | 待 | | | | | | | |

When in trouble, one goes 彳 to the temple 寺 every day, waiting for one's prayer to be answered.

待つ	まつ	**matsu**	to wait
待合所	まちあいしょ／じょ	**machiaisho/jo**	waiting place
待合室	まちあいしつ	**machiaishitsu**	waiting room
期待	きたい	**kitai**	expectation
待機する	たいきする	**taiki suru**	to stand by

| 52 合 | a-u, a-wasu, a-waseru, gō, ga'
あ・う、あ・わす、あ・わせる、
ゴウ、ガッ
fit, put together | ノ | 人 | 스 | 合 | 合 | 合 | | |

△ is a pictograph of a lid, and 口 is a hole. Thus 合 means to put together or fit.

合う	あう	**au**	to fit
話し合う	はなしあう	**hanashiau**	to discuss
合計	ごうけい	**gōkei**	total
集合	しゅうごう	**shūgō**	getting together
会合	かいごう	**kaigō**	meeting
都合	つごう	**tsugō**	convenience
問い合わせ	といあわせ	**toiawase**	inquiry
付き合う	つきあう	**tsukiau**	to be friends with
合意	ごうい	**gōi**	mutual consent

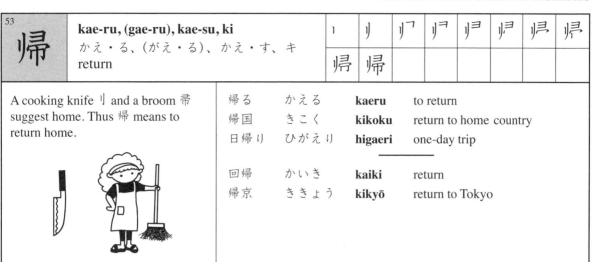

53 帰 kae-ru, (gae-ru), kae-su, ki
かえ・る、（がえ・る）、かえ・す、キ
return

丿	刂	刂⁷	刂ㄱ	刂ㅋ	刂ㅋ	帰	帰
帰	帰						

A cooking knife 刂 and a broom 帚 suggest home. Thus 帰 means to return home.

帰る	かえる	**kaeru**	to return
帰国	きこく	**kikoku**	return to home country
日帰り	ひがえり	**higaeri**	one-day trip
回帰	かいき	**kaiki**	return
帰京	ききょう	**kikyō**	return to Tokyo

54 荷 ni, ka
に、カ
load, luggage, cargo

一	十	艹	产	芢	芢	荷	
荷	荷						

A man 亻 carrying a balance 可 and 艹 plant, 荷 means a load or luggage.

荷物	にもつ	**nimotsu**	luggage, baggage
手荷物	てにもつ	**tenimotsu**	luggage, baggage
入荷	にゅうか	**nyūka**	arrival of goods
出荷	しゅっか	**shukka**	shipment
初荷	はつに	**hatsuni**	first cargo
荷車	にぐるま	**niguruma**	cart

55 関 seki, kan
せき、カン
barrier

丨	冂	冂	門	門	門	門	門
門	閂	関	関	関	関		

Gate 門 and barricade 关 combined, 関 means a barrier or barrier station.

税関	ぜいかん	**zeikan**	customs
関東	かんとう	**Kantō**	Kanto (region)
関税	かんぜい	**kanzei**	customs duty
関西	かんさい	**Kansai**	Kansai (region)
関所	せきしょ	**sekisho**	border station (old)
関取	せきとり	**sekitori**	ranking sumo wrestler

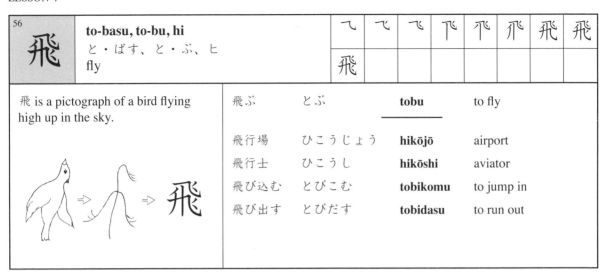

56 飛	to-basu, to-bu, hi と・ばす、と・ぶ、ヒ fly	乀	乁	乁	乫	乸	飛	飛	飛
		飛							

飛 is a pictograph of a bird flying high up in the sky.

飛ぶ	とぶ	**tobu**	to fly
飛行場	ひこうじょう	**hikōjō**	airport
飛行士	ひこうし	**hikōshi**	aviator
飛び込む	とびこむ	**tobikomu**	to jump in
飛び出す	とびだす	**tobidasu**	to run out

57 機	hata, ki はた、キ opportunity, machine, loom	一	十	才	木	术	材	松	松
		松	松	檆	楼	楼	機	機	機

Two threads 糸糸, a pike or tool 戈, a woman 人 and wood 木 combined suggest a wooden tool, a loom used by women. 機 also came to mean machine.

飛行機	ひこうき	**hikōki**	airplane
一機	いっき	**ikki**	one airplane
機会	きかい	**kikai**	opportunity
無機	むき	**muki**	inorganic
有機	ゆうき	**yūki**	organic
動機	どうき	**dōki**	motivation
機知	きち	**kichi**	wit

4 ▶ Practice

I. Write the readings of the following kanji in hiragana.

1. 空港
2. 旅客
3. 税金
4. 関税
5. 手荷物
6. 免税
7. ここで、出国手続をします。
8. ここは、第2旅客ターミナルです。
9. 待合所で、すこしシャトルを待ちます。
10. 何番ゲートから、飛行機は出ますか。
11. 旅を続けます。
12. 日本に帰ってきました。

II. Fill in the blanks with appropriate kanji.

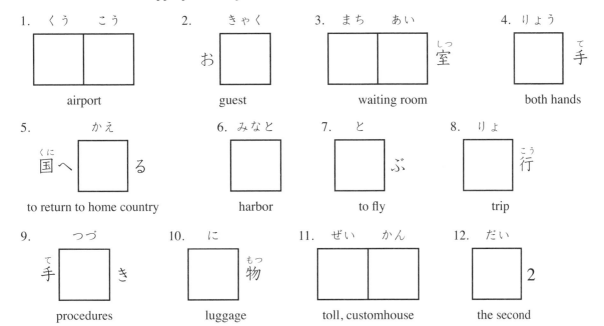

1. くう こう — airport
2. きゃく — お［　］ guest
3. まち あい — ［　］［　］室 waiting room
4. りょう — ［　］手 both hands
5. かえ — 国へ［　］る to return to home country
6. みなと — harbor
7. と — ［　］ぶ to fly
8. りょ — ［　］行 trip
9. つづ — 手［　］き procedures
10. に — ［　］物 luggage
11. ぜい かん — toll, customhouse
12. だい — ［　］2 the second

5 ▶ Advanced Placement Exam Practice Questions

You will participate in a simulated exchange of text-chat messages. Each time it is your turn to write in Japanese, you will have 90 seconds to respond. You should respond as fully and as appropriately as possible.

You saw a Japanese girl, Akiko Tanaka, on the high school campus. You are interested in Japan and are about to go to Japan for study. Try to talk to her. She is also interested in talking in Japanese with an American.

1. How do you begin speaking to her?

   You: _____

2. Introduce yourself to her.

   Tanaka: はい、何でしょうか。

   You: _____

3. Respond.

Tanaka: ああ、こんにちは。はじめまして。私は、東京から来た田中明子です。アメリカの大学で
アメリカ文学を勉強したくて、準備のために、今アメリカの高校に1年間の留学をしてい
ます。どうぞよろしく。日本の何に関心があるんですか。

You: _____

4. Describe your idea.

Tanaka: そうですか。どこで、その勉強をする予定ですか。

You: _____

5. Describe precisely.

Tanaka: そのために、今、どんな準備をしているんですか。飛行機のチケットなども、もう用意し
たんですか。荷物は少ない方がいいですよ。

You: _____

6. Respond and ask a specific question.

Tanaka: 日本についてほかに何か質問はありませんか。

You: _____

7. Respond.

Tanaka: 今日は、声をかけてくださってありがとう。これから授業があるんです。また会いまし
ょう。メールアドレスを教えてください。

You: _____

Going to a Convenience Store

LESSON 5

コンビニへ行きます

Kombini is the abbreviated term for "convenience store." They appeared in Japan early in the 1970s. **Kombini** sells a wide variety of goods: packed lunches (**bentō**), side dishes, sweets, drinks (including alcohol), magazines, stationery, domestic items, and so on. The **kombini** is like a small supermarket, but its business hours are different. **Kombini** is open 24 hours a day throughout the year, and they're widespread. Therefore, **kombini** is very convenient for people who are busy or cannot go shopping in the daytime. Now you can even pay public utility charges or reserve tickets for concerts in **kombini**. In this lesson, you will learn some kanji which can be seen in a **kombini**.

1 Introductory Quiz

Look at the illustrations below and refer to the words in **Vocabulary**. Then try the following quiz.

Fill in the space for the item from 1 to 8 with the correct sign (**a–h**).

1. Frozen pizza (   ) 2. Salt (   ) 3. Ice (   ) 4. Vegetables (   )
5. Dish liquid (   ) 6. Envelopes (   ) 7. White socks (   ) 8. Send a parcel (   )

a. 台所用洗剤

b. 調味料

c. 野菜
レタス・きゅうり・トマト

d. 氷 ✉ e. 10枚入り封筒

f. 2足組白

g. 冷凍食品

h. 荷物・書類を送る
お客さまはこちらです

2 ▶ Vocabulary

Study the readings and meanings of these words to help you understand the **Introductory Quiz**.

1.	台所用	だい どころ よう	**daidokoroyō**	for the kitchen
2.	洗剤	せん ざい	**senzai**	detergent
3.	調味料	ちょう み りょう	**chōmiryō**	seasoning
4.	野菜	や さい	**yasai**	vegetable
5.	氷	こおり	**kōri**	ice
6.	〜枚	〜まい	**〜mai**	counter for thin and flat things
7.	封筒	ふう とう	**fūtō**	envelope
8.	2足組	に そく ぐみ	**ni soku gumi**	set of two pairs
9.	白	しろ	**shiro**	white
10.	冷凍食品	れい とう しょく ひん	**reitō shokuhin**	frozen food
11.	荷物	に もつ	**nimotsu**	parcel
12.	書類	しょ るい	**shorui**	papers, documents
13.	送る	おく る	**okuru**	to send
14.	お客様	お きゃく さま	**okyaku sama**	customer (polite)

3 ▶ New Characters

Ten characters are introduced in this lesson. Use the explanations to help you understand and remember the characters. Study the compound words to increase your vocabulary.

台 調 味 野 氷 枚 組 白 冷 送

58 台	**dai, tai** ダイ、タイ table, stool, counter for cars and machines	㇛	㇛	台	台	台			

台 combines a stick to plough with ㇛ and word 口, meaning to do something good with tools and words. Later 台 came to mean a table. Another version says there are many things ㇛ to eat 口 on the table.	台	だい	**dai**	table
	台所	だいどころ	**daidokoro**	kitchen
	台所用	だいどころよう	**daidokoroyō**	for the kitchen
	三台	さんだい	**san dai**	three (cars)
	土台	どだい	**dodai**	foundation
	台地	だいち	**daichi**	plateau
	台無し にする	だいなし にする	**dainashi ni suru**	to ruin
	台本	だいほん	**daihon**	scenario

59 調

shira-beru, totono-u, totono-eru, chō
しら・べる、ととの・う、ととの・える、チョウ
investigate, check, arrange

、　ニ　ニ　言　言　言　言　訂
訂　訂　訝　調　調　調　調

周 is the pictograph of a field full of rice plants. Together with 言, 調 means to ask and examine fully.

調べる	しらべる	**shiraberu**	to check
調子	ちょうし	**chōshi**	condition
調和する	ちょうわする	**chōwa suru**	to harmonize
好調な	こうちょうな	**kōchō na**	in good condition
空調機	くうちょうき	**kūchōki**	air conditioner
調理する	ちょうりする	**chōri suru**	to cook

60 味

aji, aji-wau, mi
あじ、あじ・わう、ミ
taste

丿　口　口　口一　口二　吀　味　味

未 is the figure of top twigs not fully grown. Thus the potential is unknown. The combination of 口 mouth and 未 unknown means taste. Everyone likes to try the taste of the unknown.

味	あじ	**aji**	taste
調味料	ちょうみりょう	**chōmiryō**	seasoning
意味	いみ	**imi**	meaning
趣味	しゅみ	**shumi**	hobby
正味	しょうみ	**shōmi**	net weight
中味	なかみ	**nakami**	contents
人間味	にんげんみ	**ningemmi**	human touch
味方	みかた	**mikata**	friend

61 野

no, ya
の、ヤ
field, plain

丿　口　日　日　甲　甲　里　野
野　野　野

里 village and 予 previous combine to mean 野 a previous state of the village, or a wild field.

野菜	やさい	**yasai**	vegetable
平野	へいや	**heiya**	a plain
野生	やせい	**yasei**	wild (animal, plant)
分野	ぶんや	**bun'ya**	field (of endeavor)
野山	のやま	**noyama**	hills and fields
上野	うえの	**Ueno**	Ueno (place)

62 氷	**kōri, hi, hyō** こおり、ヒ、ヒョウ ice	丿	丬	汀	汳	氷			

氷 combines water 水 and a dot, suggesting ice.	氷	こおり	**kōri**	ice
	氷水	こおりみず	**kōrimizu**	ice water
	氷山	ひょうざん	**hyōzan**	iceberg
	氷上	ひょうじょう	**hyōjō**	on ice
	氷結	ひょうけつ	**hyōketsu**	freezing

63 枚	**mai** マイ counter for thin and flat things	一	十	才	木	朾	枚	枚	枚

枚 combines tree 木, and a hand holding a plank 攵.	一枚	いちまい	**ichi mai**	one sheet
	枚数	まいすう	**maisū**	number of sheets
	大枚	たいまい	**taimai**	large sum of money

64 組	**kumi, (gumi), ku-mu, so** くみ、(ぐみ)、く・む、ソ group, put together	乊	纟	纟	糹	糸	糸	約	紀
		絅	組	組					

By combining thread 糸 and to pile up 且, 組 means to form something larger by making a cord out of many threads.	A組	エーぐみ	**ē gumi**	class A
	二足組	にそくぐみ	**ni soku gumi**	set of two pairs
	大木組	おおきぐみ	**Ōki gumi**	Oki Corporation
	番組	ばんぐみ	**bangumi**	(TV) program
	組み立てる	くみたてる	**kumitateru**	to assemble
	組み合わせる	くみあわせる	**kumiawaseru**	to combine
	組合	くみあい	**kumiai**	union

65

白

shiro, shiro-i, shira, haku, byaku
しろ、しろ・い、しら、ハク、ビャク
white

Stroke order: ノ 丨 白 白 白

白 is a simplified form of white rice.

白い	しろい	**shiroi**	white
白線	はくせん	**hakusen**	white line
白紙	はくし	**hakushi**	blank paper
空白	くうはく	**kūhaku**	blank
白書	はくしょ	**hakusho**	white paper (official paper)
自白	じはく	**jihaku**	confession

66

冷

tsume-tai, hi-eru, sa-meru, rei
つめ・たい、ひ・える、さ・める、レイ
cold, chill

Stroke order: 丶 冫 冫 冷 冷 冷 冷

冫 means ice. 令 is added for pronunciation. Thus 冷 means icy cold, or chilly.

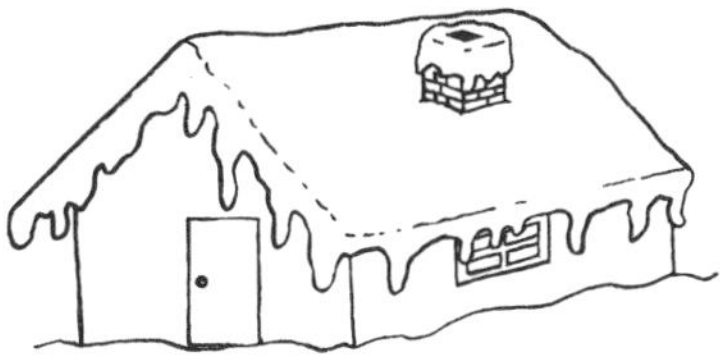

冷たい	つめたい	**tsumetai**	cold
冷凍	れいとう	**reitō**	frozen
冷房	れいぼう	**reibō**	air conditioning
冷水	れいすい	**reisui**	cold water
冷蔵する	れいぞうする	**reizō suru**	to keep (food) cool

67

送

oku-ru, sō
おく・る、ソウ
send

Stroke order: 丶 丷 䒑 兰 关 关 关 送 送

关 is the pictograph of holding things with both hands. With to move onward 辶, 送 means to send.

送る	おくる	**okuru**	to send
見送る	みおくる	**miokuru**	to see off
送料	そうりょう	**sōryō**	delivery charge
送金	そうきん	**sōkin**	remittance
郵送	ゆうそう	**yūsō**	mail
回送	かいそう	**kaisō**	out of service
電送	でんそう	**densō**	electrical transmission

4 ▶ **Practice**

I. Write the readings of the following kanji in hiragana.

1. 調 味 料
2. 野 菜
3. 氷
4. 二 枚 組
5. 白
6. 一 台
7. 冷 た い 水 を 飲 み ま す 。
8. 駅 ま で と も だ ち を 見 送 り に 行 き ま す 。
9. こ れ は い い 味 で す ね 。

II. Fill in the blanks with appropriate kanji.

1. だい　どころ

kitchen

2. しら
べ る
to check

3. ちょう　み　りょう
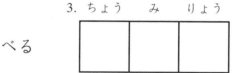
seasoning

4. へい　や
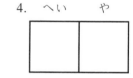
plain

5. こおり

ice

6. に　まい　ぐみ

set of two

7. はく　せん

white line

8. れい　しょく　ひん
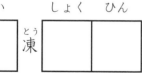
frozen food

9. おく
る
to send

5 ▶ Advanced Placement Exam Practice Questions

You are being interviewed by a manager of ABC Convenience Store to get a part time job.

1. Introduce yourself.

    Manager: 次の方、どうぞ。

    You: _____

2. Respond.

    Manager: はじめまして。マネージャーの山川です。今、早朝と夕方働ける人をさがしているんですが、時間はだいじょうぶですか。来られる曜日と時間を教えてください。

    You: _____

3. Respond.

    Manager: こちらでアルバイトをしたいと思った理由は何ですか。

    You: _____

4. Respond.

    Manager: 今までコンビニやスーパーなどでアルバイトをしたことがありますか。あなたのアルバイトの経験を教えてください。

    You: _____

5. Respond.

    Manager: それでは最後にコンビニの仕事について何でもきいてください。

    You: _____

Strolling Along a Shopping Street

LESSON 6

近くの商店街で買います

Shopping streets surround most neighborhoods and supplement the goods offered by supermarkets. In the small stores that line the shopping streets, shop owners are happy to talk with you and answer questions about their goods as well as about activities in the area in general. Shopkeepers usually belong to a community organization called the **shōtenkai**, which promotes their business. Special sale events are often held on shopping streets, especially during the summer and at the end of the year. Shopkeepers are likely to offer frequent-shopper coupons or discounts to encourage residents to shop in the neighborhood regularly. **Kome** and **sake** were at one time sold only at the special licensed stores but convenience stores are also allowed to sell these items nowadays. In this lesson, you will learn the names of many specialty shops likely to be found on a shopping street.

1 ▶ Introductory Quiz

Look at the illustrations (page 61) and refer to the words in **Vocabulary**. Then try the following quiz. Your Japanese friend took you around a shopping street in the neighborhood and showed you the services available from a wide range of specialty stores.

Where should you go for the following services? Fill in the spaces with the correct letters (a–i) of shops.

1. おこめを買う　　　　　　　　　　　　　　　　（　　,　　）
2. *かみをシャンプー、カット、セットする (*hair)　（　　　　）
3. このよこで、はなを買う　　　　　　　　　　　（　　　　）
4. ふるい本を売る　　　　　　　　　　　　　　　（　　　　）
5. おさけを買う　　　　　　　　　　　　　　　　（　　,　　）
6. しゃしんをとる　　　　　　　　　　　　　　　（　　　　）
7. 落とし物を届ける　　　　　　　　　　　　　　（　　　　）
8. ともだちと、おさけをのむ　　　　　　　　　　（　　　　）

Shopping Street
商 店 街

a.

b.

c.

d.

e.

f.

g.

h.

i.

61

2 ▶ Vocabulary

Study the readings and meanings of these words to help you understand the **Introductory Quiz**.

1. 商店街	しょう てん がい	**shōtengai**	shopping street
2. 写真	しゃ しん	**shashin**	photograph
3. 証明写真	しょう めい しゃ しん	**shōmei shashin**	photograph for certification
4. 酒	さけ	**sake**	liquor
5. 米	こめ	**kome**	rice
6. 居酒屋	い ざ か や	**izakaya**	bar, pub
7. 花	はな	**hana**	flower
8. 横	よこ	**yoko**	side
9. 美容室	び よう しつ	**biyōshitsu**	beauty salon/parlor
10. 古本	ふる ほん	**furuhon**	secondhand book
11. 交番	こう ばん	**kōban**	koban, police box
12. 落とし物	お とし もの	**otoshimono**	lost article, lost property
13. 届ける	とど ける	**todokeru**	to report, forward

3 ▶ New Characters

Eleven characters are introduced in this lesson. Use the explanations to help you understand and remember the characters. Study the compound words to increase your vocabulary.

商 写 真 酒 米 花 横 美 容 古 落

68 商	akina-u, shō あきな・う、ショウ commerce	＼	亠	产	产	产	芦	芮	芮
		商	商	商					

商 depicts a merchant's two storied house. He lives on the second floor and works at his shop downstairs.

商店	しょうてん	**shōten**	shop
商店街	しょうてんがい	**shōtengai**	shopping street
商品	しょうひん	**shōhin**	merchandise
商人	しょうにん	**shōnin**	merchant
商業	しょうぎょう	**shōgyō**	commerce
商売	しょうばい	**shōbai**	trade

69 写

utsu-su, sha
うつ・す、シャ
copy, duplicate

Stroke order: ゙ 一 冖 写 写

Cover 冖, joined with the figure of a crane 与, leads to the kanji for copy 写. How it came to mean "copy" or "take photo" is not clear.

写す	うつす	**utsusu**	to copy
写真	しゃしん	**shashin**	photo
写実	しゃじつ	**shajitsu**	realism
写生する	しゃせいする	**shasei suru**	to sketch
写本	しゃほん	**shahon**	handwritten copy

70 真

ma, shin
ま、シン
truth, reality, exactly

Stroke order: 一 十 广 市 古 肖 盲 直 真 真

Antenna 十, eyes 目, and table 宀 combined resemble a TV set which shows real and true pictures or images.

真上	まうえ	**maue**	right above
写真店	しゃしんてん	**shashinten**	photo studio
真理	しんり	**shinri**	truth
真空	しんくう	**shinkū**	vacuum
真実	しんじつ	**shinjitsu**	truth
真相	しんそう	**shinsō**	truth
真っ正面	まっしょうめん	**masshōmen**	right in front of

71 酒

sake, saka, (zaka), shu
さけ、さか、（ざか）、シュ
wine, rice wine (sake), liquor

Stroke order: 丶 氵 氵 汀 汀 沂 沔 酒 酒 酒

酉 is the pictograph of a wine jar with water 氵 added for emphasis.

酒	さけ	**sake**	liquor
酒屋	さかや	**sakaya**	liquor shop
日本酒	にほんしゅ	**nihonshu**	Japanese rice wine (sake)
居酒屋	いざかや	**izakaya**	bar, pub
禁酒	きんしゅ	**kinshu**	abstinence from alcohol
酒場	さかば	**sakaba**	bar

| 72 米 | **kome, bei, mai**
 こめ、ベイ、マイ <br> rice, America (short form) | 丶 | 丷 | 丷 | 半 | 半 | 米 | |

It takes 八十八 eighty-eight processes before we can eat rice. Another explanation says that 米 is the pictograph of a grain.

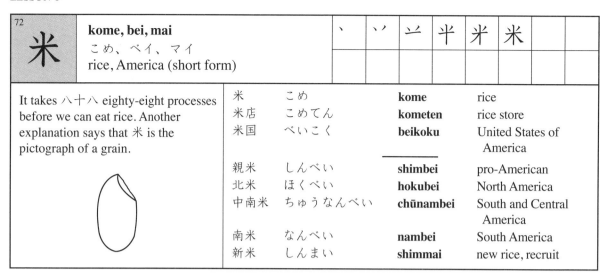

米	こめ	**kome**	rice
米店	こめてん	**kometen**	rice store
米国	べいこく	**beikoku**	United States of America
親米	しんべい	**shimbei**	pro-American
北米	ほくべい	**hokubei**	North America
中南米	ちゅうなんべい	**chūnambei**	South and Central America
南米	なんべい	**nambei**	South America
新米	しんまい	**shimmai**	new rice, recruit

| 73 花 | **hana, (bana), ka**
 はな、(ばな)、カ <br> flower | 一 | 十 | 艹 | 艹 | 艾 | 芢 | 花 |

化 means change and plant 艹 is added to get 花 which means flower that will eventually change into seed.

花	はな	**hana**	flower
花屋	はなや	**hanaya**	florist
花火	はなび	**hanabi**	firework
火花	ひばな	**hibana**	sparks
国花	こっか	**kokka**	national flower
お花見	おはなみ	**ohanami**	cherry blossom viewing

| 74 横 | **yoko, ō**
 よこ、オウ <br> side | 一 | 十 | 才 | 木 | 杧 | 杧 | 杧 | 杧 |
| | | 杧 | 栉 | 椪 | 横 | 横 | 横 | 横 | |

黄 is a pictograph of a burning oil-tipped arrowhead with the bright yellow color of the flame spreading out towards all sides. Combined with wood 木, 横 means a wood spreading out towards all sides, and came to mean side or width.

横	よこ	**yoko**	side
横着	おうちゃく	**ōchaku**	lazy
横切る	よこぎる	**yokogiru**	to cross
横道	よこみち	**yokomichi**	side street
横目	よこめ	**yokome**	side glance

75 美

utsuku-shii, bi
うつく・しい、ビ
beautiful

`	゛	⸜	⸝	⸞	羊	羊	美
美							

Sheep 羊 and big 大 together means beautiful, because sheep were very important for the ancient Chinese. Big sheep are thought to be very beautiful.

美しい	うつくしい	**utsukushii**	beautiful
美人	びじん	**bijin**	beautiful woman
人工美	じんこうび	**jinkōbi**	manmade beauty
美男	びなん	**binan**	handsome man
美学	びがく	**bigaku**	aesthetics
美食家	びしょくか	**bishokuka**	gourmet

76 容

yō
ヨウ
contain; form, appearance

`	`	宀	宀	穴	宛	突	突
容	容						

House 宀 and valley 谷 together 容 means to put something in place.

美容	びよう	**biyō**	aesthetics
美容室	びようしつ	**biyōshitsu**	beauty parlor
美容院	びよういん	**biyōin**	beauty parlor
内容	ないよう	**naiyō**	content
全容	ぜんよう	**zen'yō**	the full picture

77 古

furu-i, ko
ふる・い、コ
old

一	十	十	古	古			

To help you remember this kanji imagine an old tombstone and a cross on top.

古い	ふるい	**furui**	old
古本	ふるほん	**furuhon**	secondhand book
古本屋	ふるほんや	**furuhon'ya**	secondhand book-store
中古車	ちゅうこしゃ	**chūkosha**	used car
古都	こと	**koto**	ancient city, old city
古代	こだい	**kodai**	ancient times
古事	こじ	**koji**	ancient event
古語	こご	**kogo**	archaic word
古来	こらい	**korai**	from ancient times

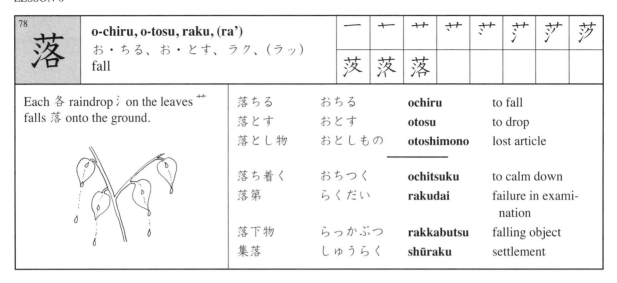

78 落	**o-chiru, o-tosu, raku, (ra')** お・ちる、お・とす、ラク、(ラッ) fall	一	十	艹	艹	艹	艹	艻	莎
		茨	莈	落					

Each 各 raindrop ⺡ on the leaves 艹 falls 落 onto the ground.	落ちる	おちる	**ochiru**	to fall
	落とす	おとす	**otosu**	to drop
	落とし物	おとしもの	**otoshimono**	lost article
	落ち着く	おちつく	**ochitsuku**	to calm down
	落第	らくだい	**rakudai**	failure in exami-nation
	落下物	らっかぶつ	**rakkabutsu**	falling object
	集落	しゅうらく	**shūraku**	settlement

4 ▶ Practice

I. Write the readings of the following kanji in hiragana.

1. 米国　　　　2. 酒　　　　3. 商品　　　　4. 古本

5. 内容　　　　6. 花　　　　7. 美しい

8. 写真を三枚、写しました。

9. 日本酒は、米からつくられます。

10. 中古車は、新車より安いです。

11. 酒屋の横に、美容室があります。

12. 落とし物をひろったら、交番へ届けましょう。

II. Fill in the blanks with appropriate kanji.

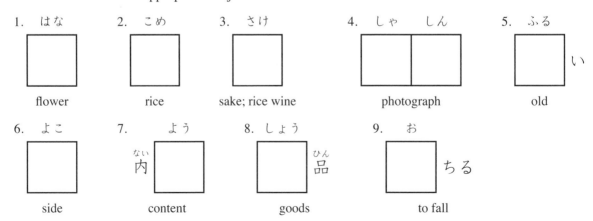

1. はな
□
flower

2. こめ
□
rice

3. さけ
□
sake; rice wine

4. しゃ　しん
□□
photograph

5. ふる
□い
old

6. よこ
□
side

7. よう
内□
ない
content

8. しょう
□品
ひん
goods

9. お
□ちる
to fall

10.

こ

^{ちゅう}中 [　　] 車^{しゃ}

used car

11.

しゅ

日本 [　　]

Japanese rice wine

12.

び

[　　] 人^{じん}

beautiful woman

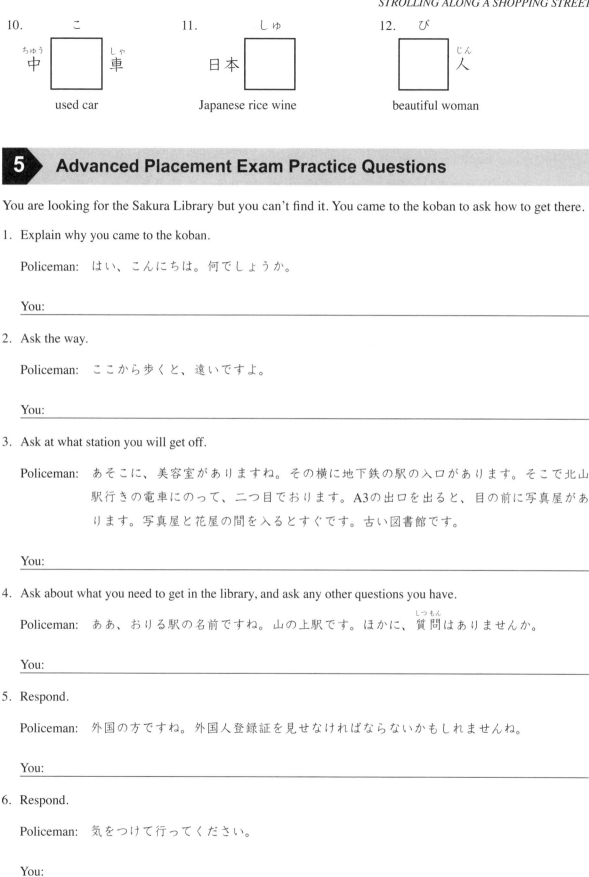

---

5 ▶ Advanced Placement Exam Practice Questions

You are looking for the Sakura Library but you can't find it. You came to the koban to ask how to get there.

1. Explain why you came to the koban.

   Policeman: はい、こんにちは。何でしょうか。

   You: _____

2. Ask the way.

   Policeman: ここから歩くと、遠いですよ。

   You: _____

3. Ask at what station you will get off.

   Policeman: あそこに、美容室がありますね。その横に地下鉄の駅の入口があります。そこで北山駅行きの電車にのって、二つ目でおります。A3の出口を出ると、目の前に写真屋があります。写真屋と花屋の間を入るとすぐです。古い図書館です。

   You: _____

4. Ask about what you need to get in the library, and ask any other questions you have.

   Policeman: ああ、おりる駅の名前ですね。山の上駅です。ほかに、質問^{しつもん}はありませんか。

   You: _____

5. Respond.

   Policeman: 外国の方ですね。外国人登録証を見せなければならないかもしれませんね。

   You: _____

6. Respond.

   Policeman: 気をつけて行ってください。

   You: _____

Recycle

リサイクル

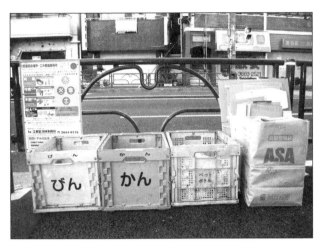

Garbage collection is regulated by the local governmental garbage collection department, **Seisō jimusho**. In Tokyo, combustible garbage is collected twice a week and noncombustible garbage is collected once a week. Collection days are decided by a local office. Large items like furniture are collected through arrangement by the local office. Recycling is encouraged; cans, bottles and paper are collected on certain days of the week, while big supermarkets and convenience stores often provide recycling bins near the front entrance for the disposal of plastic wrappings and milk cartons. These recycling programs are sponsored by the local governmental office or by volunteer groups. In this lesson, you will learn the kanji related to garbage disposal and recycling.

1 ▶ Introductory Quiz

Look at the illustrations and information below and refer to the words in **Vocabulary**. Then try the following questionnaire.

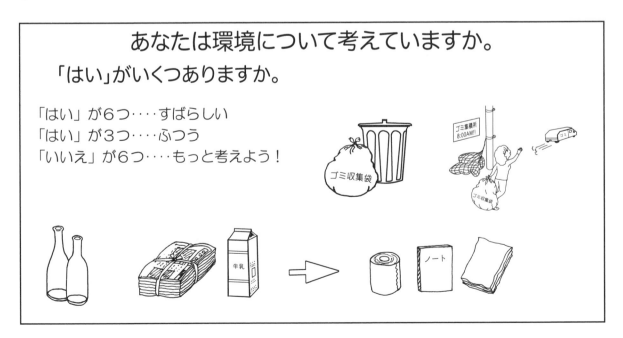

あなたは環境について考えていますか。

「はい」がいくつありますか。

「はい」が6つ‥‥すばらしい
「はい」が3つ‥‥ふつう
「いいえ」が6つ‥‥もっと考えよう！

問1　ごみは分別して出しています。　　　　　　　　　はい・いいえ

問2　指定日以外にごみを出していません。　　　　　　はい・いいえ

問3　きまった時間に遅れないように出しています。　　はい・いいえ

問4　新聞紙や牛乳パックはリサイクルできます。　　　はい・いいえ

問5　びん類は何回も使えます。　　　　　　　　　　　はい・いいえ

問6　粗大ごみは申込み制です。　　　　　　　　　　　はい・いいえ

環境のために個人ができることはたくさんあります。

ご協力をお願いします。

2 ▷ Vocabulary

Study the readings and meanings of these words to help you understand the **Introductory Quiz**.

1. 環境	かん きょう	**kankyō**	the environment
2. 考える	かん が える	**kangaeru**	to think, think about
3. 分別する	ぶん べつ する	**bumbetsu suru**	to separate
4. 指定日以外	し てい び い がい	**shiteibi igai**	noncollection days
5. 遅れる	おく れる	**okureru**	to be late
6. 新聞紙	しん ぶん し	**shimbunshi**	a piece of newspaper
7. 牛乳パック	ぎゅう にゅう パック	**gyūnyū pakku**	milk carton
8. びん類	びん るい	**binrui**	all kind of bottles
9. 粗大ごみ	そ だい ごみ	**sodai gomi**	outsized trash
10. 申込み制	もうし こ み せい	**mōshikomi sei**	contact the garbage collection
11. 個人	こ じん	**kojin**	individual
12. ご協力	ご きょう りょく	**gokyōryoku**	cooperation (polite)
13. お願いします	お ね が い します	**onegai shimasu**	please

3 ▷ New Characters

Eleven characters are introduced in this lesson. Use the explanations to help you understand and remember the characters. Study the compound words to increase your vocabulary.

考　別　指　以　遅　聞　紙　類　制　個　願

79 考	kanga-eru, kō かんが・える、コウ think	一	十	土	耂	耂	考		

考 combines an old man 耂, whose back is bending, and "to bend" 与. Thus, 考 means to think, suggesting that good ideas do not come up so easily and directly.

考える	かんがえる	**kangaeru**	to think
考え方	かんがえかた	**kangaekata**	way of thinking
考案	こうあん	**kōan**	conception
考古学	こうこがく	**kōkogaku**	archaeology
考証	こうしょう	**kōshō**	historical research

80 別	waka-reru, betsu, (be') わか・れる、ベツ、(ベッ) part from	丶	冖	口	弔	뭐	別	別	

別 combines the left side, a joint of a leg, and a sword 刂, suggesting separating the joint with the sword.

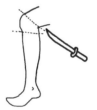

別れる	わかれる	**wakareru**	to part from
分別する	ぶんべつする	**bumbetsu suru**	to separate
特別	とくべつ	**tokubetsu**	special
区別	くべつ	**kubetsu**	distinction
分別	ふんべつ	**fumbetsu**	discretion
無分別	むふんべつ	**mufumbetsu**	imprudence
別館	べっかん	**bekkan**	annex

81 指	yubi, sa-su, (za-su), shi ゆび、さ・す、(ざ・す)、シ finger; point to	一	十	扌	扩	担	指	指	指
		指							

旨 is a simplified form of sweet 甘 and a ladle ヒ. Thus 旨 means tasty. By extension, 旨 means good or important. The most important parts of a hand are fingers.

指	ゆび	**yubi**	finger
指定日	していび	**shiteibi**	appointed day
指定席	していせき	**shiteiseki**	reserved seat
小指	こゆび	**koyubi**	little finger
指名する	しめいする	**shimei suru**	to nominate
指す	さす	**sasu**	to point to
目指す	めざす	**mezasu**	to aim at
指数	しすう	**shisū**	index

82	**i**			ヽ	↓	↓	↓	以		
以	イ									
	~than (prefix), by means of									

Two people 从 can do better than one.

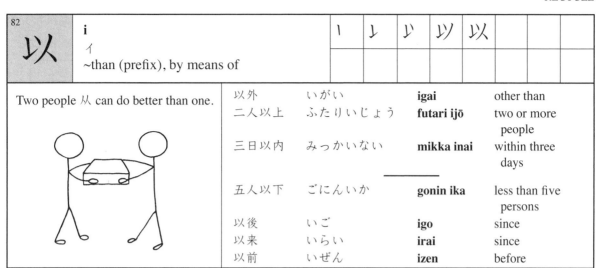

以外	いがい	**igai**	other than
二人以上	ふたりいじょう	**futari ijō**	two or more people
三日以内	みっかいない	**mikka inai**	within three days
———			
五人以下	ごにんいか	**gonin ika**	less than five persons
以後	いご	**igo**	since
以来	いらい	**irai**	since
以前	いぜん	**izen**	before

83	**oso-i, oku-reru, chi**		ｱ	ｺ	尸	尺	尸	尺	犀	屖
遅	おそ・い、おく・れる、チ		犀	犀	遲	遅				
	late, tardy, slow									

Originally the character 犀 meant a rhinoceros, which moves 辶 slowly.

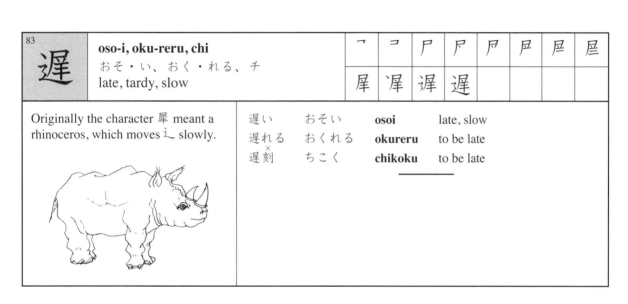

遅い	おそい	**osoi**	late, slow
遅れる	おくれる	**okureru**	to be late
遅刻	ちこく	**chikoku**	to be late
———			

84	**ki-ku, ki-koeru, bun, mon**		丨	冂	冂	冃	冃	門	門	門
聞	き・く、き・こえる、ブン、モン		門	閂	閆	間	聞	聞		
	listen, hear									

An ear 耳 at a gate 門 means to listen, because a person listens carefully to someone out of sight behind a gate.

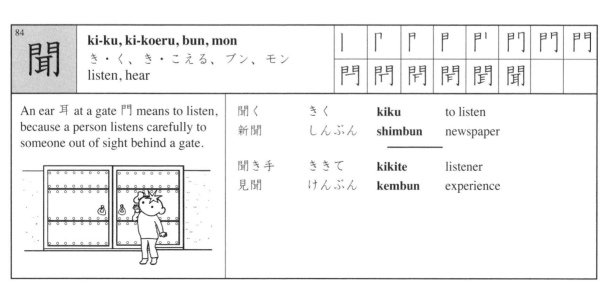

聞く	きく	**kiku**	to listen
新聞	しんぶん	**shimbun**	newspaper
———			
聞き手	ききて	**kikite**	listener
見聞	けんぶん	**kembun**	experience

85 紙

kami, (gami), shi
かみ、(がみ)、シ
paper

く	幺	幺	糸	糸	糸	糸	紙
紙	紙						

紙 combines thread 糸 or fiber, and flat spoon 氏. Thus 紙 means paper which is made of fiber and is flat.

新聞紙	しんぶんし	**shimbunshi**	a piece of news-paper
手紙	てがみ	**tegami**	letter
和紙	わし	**washi**	Japanese paper
紙コップ	かみコップ	**kami koppu**	paper cup
洋紙	ようし	**yōshi**	western paper
表紙	ひょうし	**hyōshi**	cover

86 類

rui
ルイ
category

丶	丷	丷	半	米	米	米	类
类	类	类	類	類	類	類	類	類

Rice 米 is categorized according to the size (大 or 小) of the grain head 頁.

缶類	かんるい	**kanrui**	cans
人類	じんるい	**jinrui**	mankind
書類	しょるい	**shorui**	papers, documents
親類	しんるい	**shinrui**	relative
紙類	かみるい	**kamirui**	papers
分類する	ぶんるいする	**bunrui suru**	to categorize
類義語	るいぎご	**ruigigo**	synonym

87 制

sei
セイ
system, regulate

ノ	⺧	⺧	产	与	制	制	制

朱 is a pictograph of a tree being cut in the middle to make lumber, and when sword 刂 is added, they combine to mean to regulate or system.

申込み制	もうしこみせい	**mōshikomi sei**	upon application
制作	せいさく	**seisaku**	production
税制	ぜいせい	**zeisei**	taxation system
制止	せいし	**seishi**	control
制約	せいやく	**seiyaku**	restriction

88 個	**ko** コ individual	ノ	イ	彳	们	们	伵	伵	個
		個	個						

古 is a pictograph of an old and dried skull with a decoration, meaning old. Enclosed in a frame 口, 固 means solid. Person 亻 is added, and 個 means an individual.	個人	こじん	**kojin**	individual
	一個	いっこ	**ikko**	one (counter for things)
			————	
	個人主義	こじんしゅぎ	**kojin shugi**	individualism
	個数	こすう	**kosū**	number of things
	個室	こしつ	**koshitsu**	private room
	個別	こべつ	**kobetsu**	individual

89 願	**nega-u, gan** ねが・う、ガン wish	一	厂	厂	厂	斤	斦	盾	原	原	原
		原	原	原	願	願	願	願	願	願	

原 is the figure of white 白 clear spring water 小=水, running at the foot of a cliff 厂. 原 means original, because a spring is the origin of water. Head 頁 is added to mean wish, because the original 原 function of head 頁 is to wish to gods for something.	お願い します	おねがい します	**onegai shimasu**	please
	お願い	おねがい	**onegai**	request
	願書	がんしょ	**gansho**	application for admission
			————	
	出願	しゅつがん	**shutsugan**	application

4 ▶ Practice

I. Write the readings of the following kanji in hiragana.

1. 考え方   2. 分別する   3. 指   4. 以外

5. 遅れる   6. 聞く   7. 手紙   8. 人類

9. 申込み制   10. 個人   11. 願書

12. 今日は特別な日です。

13. 土曜日は遅くまであそびます。

II. Fill in the blanks with appropriate kanji.

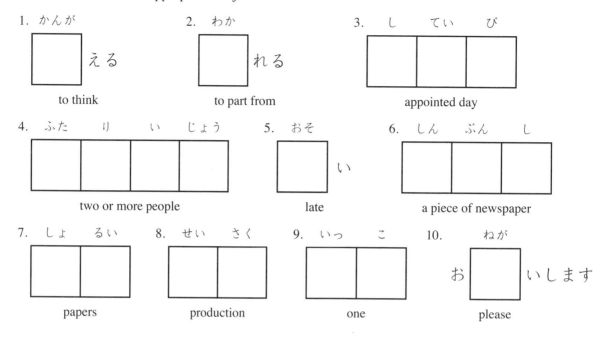

1. かんが
□ える
to think

2. わか
□ れる
to part from

3. し　てい　び
□ □ □
appointed day

4. ふた　り　い　じょう
□ □ □ □
two or more people

5. おそ
□ い
late

6. しん　ぶん　し
□ □ □
a piece of newspaper

7. しょ　るい
□ □
papers

8. せい　さく
□ □
production

9. いっ　こ
□ □
one

10. ねが
お □ いします
please

5 ▶ Advanced Placement Exam Practice Questions

This is the contribution of a high school student to a newspaper. Read the article in Japanese and answer the following questions.

高校生 山下 京子（東京都文京区　17歳）

　私たちのクラスでは10月の1週間を手作り弁当週間にした。コンビニなどで弁当を買わないで自分で作って来るのだ。最初は朝早く起きて弁当を作るのは大変だった。でも3日目ぐらいから、作るのが楽しくなった。それに何よりおいしい。昼休みには友だちとお弁当のおかずをとりかえて、家では食べたことのない料理の味も知った。1週間弁当を作って、とてもいいものだと思った。[1]栄養的には、肉や野菜のバランスがいいこと、[2]添加物がないこと、カロリーを自分で管理できることなどがあげられる。前日の夕食の残りを利用することもできるから、[3]経済的でもある。クラスのみんなが一番おどろいたのはゴミの量だ。手作り弁当はすてるものがない。弁当箱やはしは洗って何回も使える。だから、手作り弁当週間の間、教室のゴミ箱にはほどんどゴミがなかった。コンビニで弁当を買えば、弁当のパックやラップ、はし、[4]ポリ袋など食べたもの以外は全部ゴミになる。もえるゴミともえないゴミの分別もできていなかった。

　「環境について考えよう！ゴミをへらそう！」とよく言われるが、私たちには関係がないと思っていた。しかし、手作り弁当週間は一人ひとりが毎日の生活の中の小さなことから始められるのだということを、私たちに教えてくれた。私はこれからも毎日弁当を作ろうと思う。

1 栄養: nutrition
2 添加物: added substance
3 経済的: economical
4 ポリ袋 : plastic bag

1. According to the article, a homemade **bentō** is
   A. economical and healthy.
   B. economical, but it is hard to prepare.
   C. tasty and convenient.
   D. tasty but expensive.

2. According to the article, the homemade **bentō** week was
   A. one of the best opportunities to learn how to cook.
   B. a good experience for learning about the environ-mental problem.
   C. useful training to keep the classroom clean.
   D. nice, because everybody in the class ate lunch together.

3. According to the article, why is homemade **bentō** good for the environment?
   A. Because a lunch box and chopsticks can be used repeatedly.
   B. Because it is a balanced diet.
   C. Because it is combustible garbage.
   D. Because students have to get up early in the morning.

4. According to the article, what surprised the students of the class?
   A. They were surprised that it is easy to prepare a homemade **bentō**.
   B. They were surprised that they could reduce garbage.
   C. They were surprised that a homemade **bentō** was healthy and economical.
   D. They were surprised that the reduction of garbage was the most important problem.

5. What will the writer of the article do from now on?
   A. She will make an effort to reduce garbage.
   B. She will have lunch with her friends.
   C. She will prepare a homemade **bentō** sometimes.
   D. She will continue to prepare a homemade **bentō** every day.

Visiting Friends

友だちの家へ行きます

When visiting a friend's house by car, the car navigation system is a great help. You need only to input the telephone number of your friend and the car navigation system will guide you there.

Mobile phones are also very useful in helping you find your way around in Japan. Not only can you check train times but there are many mobile phone enabled sites which compute the cheapest or fastest train and metro routes for you. Your mobile phone can also show your present location on the map.

If you prefer more traditional means of finding your way around, there are many map boards around Tokyo outside train and metro stations, bus stops, and koban (police booths). You should be aware that there are not many road names and it is common to navigate by landmarks or shops, such as **kombini**.

In this lesson you will learn some of the kanji used for the names of public buildings.

1 ▶ Introductory Quiz

Look at the illustrations below and on page 77, and refer to the words in **Vocabulary**. Then try the following quiz.

a.

b.

c.

d.

e.

f.

g.

h.

i.

j.

What are these buildings or objects for? Choose from the signs shown in the photos, and fill in the spaces below (   ) with the correct letters (a–j).

1. 3歳のこどもが毎日行きます。 (   )
2. 日曜日こどもとあそんだり、さんぽしたりします。 (   )
3. 車を止めます。 (   )
4. あなたはここにいます。 (   )
5. 自転車を止めます。 (   )
6. 私学の学校のパーティーをします。 (   )
7. 川をわたります。 (   )

2 ▶ Vocabulary

Study the readings and meanings of these words to help you understand the **Introductory Quiz**.

1. 友だち	とも だち	**tomodachi**	friend
2. 現在位置	げん ざい いち	**genzai ichi**	you are here
3. 私学	し がく	**shigaku**	private school
4. 会館	かい かん	**kaikan**	hall, union
5. 吾妻橋	あ づま ばし	**Azumabashi**	Azuma bridge
6. すみだ川	すみだ がわ	**Sumidagawa**	Sumida river
7. 三四郎池	さん し ろう いけ	**Sanshirōike**	Sanshirō pond
8. 一番町	いち ばん ちょう	**Ichibanchō**	Ichiban Town (place)
9. 自転車	じ てん しゃ	**jitensha**	bicycle
10. 自転車置場	じ てん しゃ おきば	**jitensha okiba**	bicycle shed

77

11. 公園	こう えん	**kōen**	park
12. 駐車場	ちゅう しゃ じょう	**chūshajō**	parking area
13. 保育園	ほ いく えん	**hoikuen**	nursery school

3 ▶ New Characters

Twelve characters are introduced in this lesson. Use the explanations to help you understand and remember the characters. Study the compound words to increase your vocabulary.

友 現 橋 川 池 町 転 置 公 園 駐 育

90

友 **tomo, yū**
とも、ユウ
friend

一 ナ 方 友

友 is a pictograph of two friends shaking hands ナ and 又.

友だち	ともだち	**tomodachi**	friend
親友	しんゆう	**shin'yū**	intimate friend
友人	ゆうじん	**yūjin**	friend
学友	がくゆう	**gakuyū**	classmate
友好	ゆうこう	**yūkō**	friendship

91

現 **arawa-su, arawa-reru, gen**
あらわ・す、あらわ・れる、ゲン
appear

一 丁 壬 王 玑 玑 玥 玥
珇 玥 現

The king 王 emerges so the people can see 見 him.

現す	あらわす	**arawasu**	to show
現れる	あらわれる	**arawareru**	to appear
現在	げんざい	**genzai**	the present, now
現在位置	げんざいいち	**genzai ichi**	you are here
現住所	げんじゅうしょ	**genjūsho**	present address
現代	げんだい	**gendai**	present age
現場	げんば	**gemba**	field, site, scene
現実	げんじつ	**genjitsu**	reality

92 橋

hashi, (bashi), kyō
はし、（ばし）、キョウ
bridge

| 一 | 十 | 才 | 木 | 栌 | 杧 | 杧 | 柿 |
| 柿 | 桥 | 桥 | 栌 | 橋 | 橋 | 橋 | 橋 |

橋 combines tree 木 and a tall Chinese style house 喬 with a warped roof. The warped form suggests bridge.

橋	はし	**hashi**	bridge
歩道橋	ほどうきょう	**hodōkyō**	pedestrian overpass
鉄橋	てっきょう	**tekkyō**	iron bridge
八つ橋	やつはし	**yatsuhashi**	zigzag bridge
二重橋	にじゅうばし	**Nijūbashi**	the Double Bridge (at the Imperial Palace in Tokyo)

93 川

kawa, (gawa), sen
かわ、（がわ）、セン
river

| ノ | 川 | 川 | | | | | |

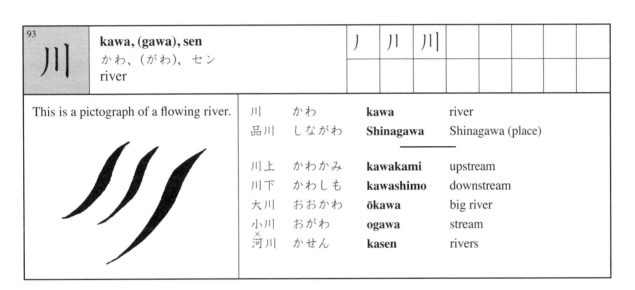

This is a pictograph of a flowing river.

川	かわ	**kawa**	river
品川	しながわ	**Shinagawa**	Shinagawa (place)
川上	かわかみ	**kawakami**	upstream
川下	かわしも	**kawashimo**	downstream
大川	おおかわ	**ōkawa**	big river
小川	おがわ	**ogawa**	stream
×河川	かせん	**kasen**	rivers

94 池

ike, chi
いけ、チ
pond

| 丶 | 氵 | 氵 | 氿 | 沖 | 池 | | |

池 combines water 氵 and a snake 也, suggesting a pond where the snakes live.

池	いけ	**ike**	pond
電池	でんち	**denchi**	battery
用水池	ようすいち	**yōsuichi**	water reservoir
古池	ふるいけ	**furuike**	old pond

95 町	machi, chō まち、チョウ town, quarter	一	冂	冂	日	田	田	町	

A rice field 田 and a road 丁 formed a town.				
	町	まち	**machi**	town, quarter
	一番町	いちばんちょう	**Ichibanchō**	Ichiban Town (place)
	下町	したまち	**shitamachi**	downtown
	横町	よこちょう	**yokochō**	side street
	大手町	おおてまち	**Ōtemachi**	Otemachi (place)
	町内会	ちょうないかい	**chōnaikai**	neighborhood association
	町家	まちや	**machiya**	tradesman's house
	港町	みなとまち	**minatomachi**	port city

96 転	koro-garu, koro-bu, koro-gasu, ten ころ・がる、ころ・ぶ、ころ・がす、テン roll, turn	一	厂	厅	戸	亘	亘	車	車
		車	転	転					

Wheels 車 make sound, or speak 云, while rolling along.				
	転がる	ころがる	**korogaru**	to roll
	自転車	じてんしゃ	**jitensha**	bicycle
	転校する	てんこうする	**tenkō suru**	to change to another school
	回転する	かいてんする	**kaiten suru**	to rotate
	転機	てんき	**tenki**	turning point
	空転	くうてん	**kūten**	getting nowhere
	転用	てんよう	**ten'yō**	divert

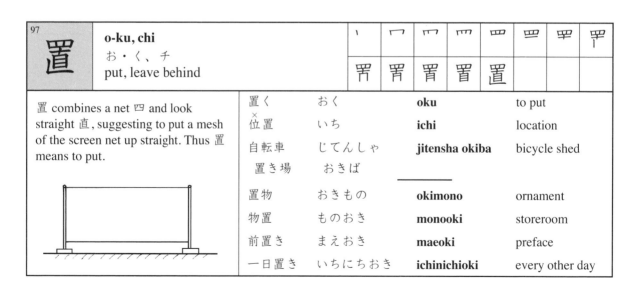

97 置	o-ku, chi お・く、チ put, leave behind	丶	冖	罒	罒	罒	罒	罒	罒
		罒	罒	罒	置	置			

置 combines a net 四 and look straight 直, suggesting to put a mesh of the screen net up straight. Thus 置 means to put.				
	置く	おく	**oku**	to put
	位置	いち	**ichi**	location
	自転車 置き場	じてんしゃ おきば	**jitensha okiba**	bicycle shed
	置物	おきもの	**okimono**	ornament
	物置	ものおき	**monooki**	storeroom
	前置き	まえおき	**maeoki**	preface
	一日置き	いちにちおき	**ichinichioki**	every other day

98 公	**ōyake, kō** おおやけ、コウ public	ノ	ハ	公	公				

Eight ハ and individual area ム combined, 公 means public.	公平な	こうへいな	**kōhei na**	fair
	不公平な	ふこうへいな	**fukōhei na**	unfair
	公表	こうひょう	**kōhyō**	official announcement
	公開	こうかい	**kōkai**	open to the public
	公式	こうしき	**kōshiki**	official
	公立	こうりつ	**kōritsu**	public (institution)
	公約	こうやく	**kōyaku**	pledge, public commitment
	公用	こうよう	**kōyō**	official business
	公文書	こうぶんしょ	**kōbunsho**	official document
	公正	こうせい	**kōsei**	fair

99 園	**sono, en** その、エン garden	丨	冂	冂	冃	串	吊	肙	周
		声	序	菒	園	園			

園 is the pictograph of old fashioned clothing which is very loose and extends a distance from the body. Combined with 囗, it means a round, enclosed area or a garden.

公園	こうえん	**kōen**	park
動物園	どうぶつえん	**dōbutsuen**	zoo
学園	がくえん	**gakuen**	educational institution
楽園	らくえん	**rakuen**	paradise
田園	でんえん	**den'en**	the country

100 駐	**chū** チュウ stop, reside	丨	厂	冂	圧	圧	馬	馬	馬
		馬	馬	馬	馿	駐	駐	駐	

Horse 馬 and master 主 combined, 駐 refers to a place where ancient Chinese people kept horses. Now 駐 means to park cars or bicycles.

駐車場	ちゅうしゃ じょう	**chūshajō**	parking lot
駐日大使	ちゅうにち たいし	**chūnichi taishi**	ambassador to Japan
常駐	じょうちゅう	**jōchū**	permanent stationing

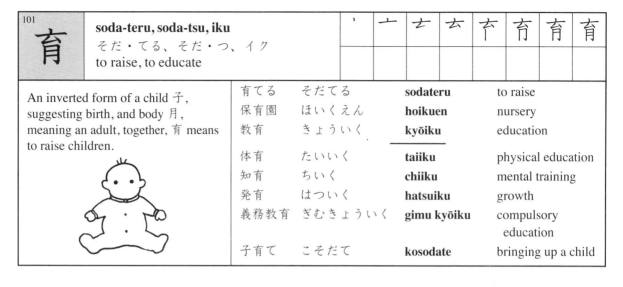

101 育	soda-teru, soda-tsu, iku そだ・てる、そだ・つ、イク to raise, to educate	' 一 ナ 女 玄 育 育 育

An inverted form of a child 子, suggesting birth, and body 月, meaning an adult, together, 育 means to raise children.

育てる	そだてる	**sodateru**	to raise
保育園	ほいくえん	**hoikuen**	nursery
教育	きょういく	**kyōiku**	education
体育	たいいく	**taiiku**	physical education
知育	ちいく	**chiiku**	mental training
発育	はついく	**hatsuiku**	growth
義務教育	ぎむきょういく	**gimu kyōiku**	compulsory education
子育て	こそだて	**kosodate**	bringing up a child

4 ▸ Practice

I. Write the readings of the following kanji in hiragana.

1. 親友
2. 現す
3. 歩道橋
4. 転がる
5. 位置
6. 動物園
7. 駐車場
8. 電池
9. 育てる
10. 公園に大きな池があります。
11. 町の北に大きな川があります。
12. 保育園の前に、自転車置き場があります。
13. 友だちは、現在、一番町に住んでいます。

II. Fill in the blanks with appropriate kanji.

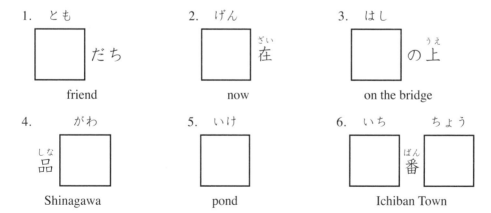

1. とも ☐ だち
friend

2. げん ☐ 在 (ざい)
now

3. はし ☐ の上 (うえ)
on the bridge

4. がわ 品 (しな) ☐
Shinagawa

5. いけ ☐
pond

6. いち ☐ 番 (ばん) ちょう ☐
Ichiban Town

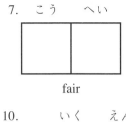

7.
こう　　へい
fair

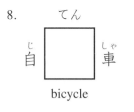

8.
てん
自［ ］車
bicycle

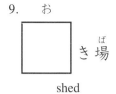

9.
お
［ ］き場
shed

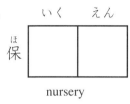

10.
いく　えん
保［ ］
nursery

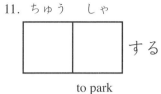

11.
ちゅう　しゃ
［ ］する
to park

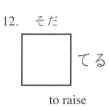

12.
そだ
［ ］てる
to raise

5 ▶ Advanced Placement Exam Practice Questions

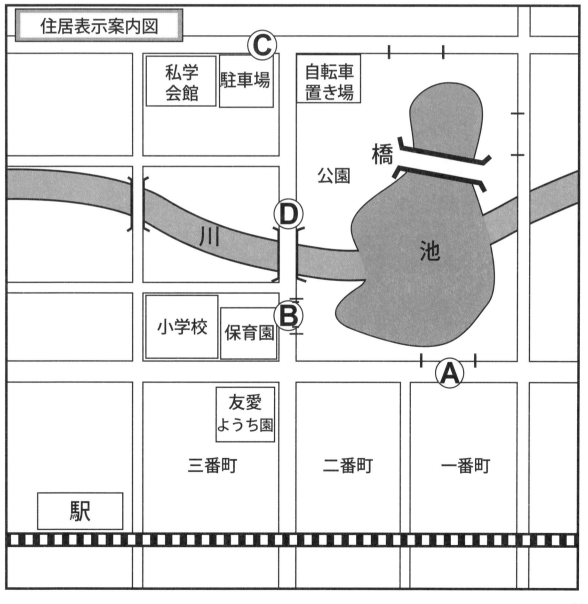

住居表示案内図

私学会館　駐車場　自転車置き場

公園　橋　池　川

小学校　保育園

友愛ようち園

三番町　二番町　一番町

駅

Four high school girls are standing at different places—the locations A, B, C, and D marked on the map—and are talking on their mobile phones. They are going to meet at Shigakukaikan. Yukiko, Naomi and Yoko are talking to Hiromi.

Based on the conversation, answer where each of them is now standing.

Yukiko: ひろみさん、私は今、駐車場と自転車置き場の角を左へまがりました。あっ、私学会館見えて来ました。

Naomi: もしもし、ひろみ。私の現在地は公園の門のところです。前に保育園と¹友愛ようち園っていうのがあるんだけど。

Yoko: あっ、ひろみ。公園の門に着いたけど、全然保育園もようち園もないよ。ここは、一番町だって。公園の中に大きな池があるよ。

Hiromi: もしもし、ようこ。門の前の道を公園に²沿って歩いて来て。もう少し歩くと右に保育園があるから、その手前を右にまがってまっすぐ来て。保育園の少し先に川があるんだけど、私は今その橋をわたったところよ。

¹友愛ようち園: a name of a kindergarten
²沿って: along

1. Where is Yukiko standing?　　(A　B　C　D)

2. Where is Naomi standing?　　(A　B　C　D)

3. Where is Yoko standing?　　(A　B　C　D)

4. Where is Hiromi standing?　　(A　B　C　D)

Let's Go to a Library

図書館へ行きましょう

Public libraries were developed considerably in Japan during the 1980s. But they are still behind western countries with respect to their hours and services. Despite this, libraries are still popular with the people of Tokyo. In Tokyo, you can borrow more than 5 books at a time from each different library. If you can't find the book you want at your nearest library, the librarian will search and is able to get it from another public library within a few days. There is also a private library which specializes in comic books, and houses more than 100,000 comic books from the 1930s to the present. In this lesson, you will learn kanji relating to dictionaries and books.

1 ▶ Introductory Quiz

Look at the illustrations (page 86) and refer to the words in **Vocabulary**. Then try the following quiz. What book does each of these people, 1–6, choose? Fill in the spaces with the correct letters (a–h).

1. 大学院で漢字を勉強している人 　　　　　(　　　)
2. 世界のニュースを知りたい人 　　　　　　(　　　)
3. 毎日の生活でみる漢字を知りたい人 　　　(　　　)
4. 今の政治について知りたい人 　　　　　　(　　　)
5. 浮世絵やかぶきについて知りたい人 　　　(　　　)
6. 英語のことばをたくさん知りたい人 　　　(　　　)

辞書・事典コーナー

雑誌コーナー

c.

モータークラブ

6月号

a.

漢英大辞典

初心者から
研究者まで
必要な10万語

b.

漢英学習辞典

多くの学習者が
選んでいます!

2万語

d.

和英大辞典

単語の力がつく!

e.

生活の中の漢字
５００

初心者用!
すぐに役に立つ
漢字 500

f.

現代思想
5月号

最新の社会
政治を知る!

g.

現代百科事典

困ったときは
この一冊を

h.

NEWSTIME

5/15

東京

2 ▶ Vocabulary

Study the readings and meanings of these words to help you understand the **Introductory Quiz**.

1.	辞書	じしょ	**jisho**	dictionary
2.	事典	じてん	**jiten**	encyclopedia
3.	雑誌	ざっし	**zasshi**	magazine
4.	漢英	かんえい	**kan'ei**	kanji (Chinese character)-English
5.	辞典	じてん	**jiten**	dictionary
6.	初心者	しょしんしゃ	**shoshinsha**	beginner
7.	研究者	けんきゅうしゃ	**kenkyūsha**	researcher
8.	必要な	ひつような	**hitsuyō na**	necessary
9.	学習者	がくしゅうしゃ	**gakushūsha**	learner
10.	選ぶ	えらぶ	**erabu**	to choose
11.	単語	たんご	**tango**	word
12.	力	ちから	**chikara**	ability; power
13.	役に立つ	やくにたつ	**yaku ni tatsu**	useful; helpful
14.	漢字	かんじ	**kanji**	Chinese character
15.	現代	げんだい	**gendai**	modern, present-day
16.	思想	しそう	**shisō**	thinking, thought
17.	最新の	さいしんの	**saishin no**	latest
18.	社会	しゃかい	**shakai**	society
19.	政治	せいじ	**seiji**	politics
20.	百科事典	ひゃっかじてん	**hyakkajiten**	encyclopedia
21.	困る	こまる	**komaru**	to be in trouble, to have a problem
22.	一冊	いっさつ	**issatsu**	one book (counter for books)
23.	浮世絵	うきよえ	**ukiyoe**	Japanese woodblock print
24.	かぶき		**kabuki**	kabuki (Japanese traditional drama)
25.	勉強する	べんきょうする	**benkyō suru**	to study

3 | New Characters

Fourteen characters are introduced in this lesson. Use the explanations to help you understand and remember the characters. Study the compound words to increase your vocabulary.

辞 雑 漢 英 初 心 必 要 選 単 力 字 思 困

---

102 辞

ya-meru, ji
や・める、ジ
word, resignation

ノ	ニ	チ	チ	舌	舌	舌′	舌⸍
舌⸍	舌⸍	辞⸍	辞⸍	辞			

辞 combines tongue 舌, or words, rise up 立, and ten 十. Thus 辞 means a word.

辞める	やめる	**yameru**	to resign
辞書	じしょ	**jisho**	dictionary
辞典	じてん	**jiten**	dictionary
祝辞	しゅくじ	**shukuji**	speech of congratulations
修辞	しゅうじ	**shūji**	figure of speech
美辞	びじ	**biji**	flowery language

---

103 雑

zatsu, (za'), zō
ザツ、（ザッ）、ゾウ
miscellany, a mix

ノ	九	九	卆	卆	杂	朵	杂
雑′	雑′	雑⸍	雑	雑	雑		

雑 combines nine 九, trees 木 and birds 隹, suggesting there are many different trees and birds in the woods. By extension, it means a mix.

雑誌	ざっし	**zasshi**	magazine
雑用	ざつよう	**zatsuyō**	miscellaneous things to do
雑学	ざつがく	**zatsugaku**	knowledge of various subjects
雑音	ざつおん	**zatsuon**	noise
雑木	ぞうき	**zōki**	miscellaneous small trees

104 漢

kan
カン
Chinese; fellow

`ヽ　ミ　氵　氵　氵　氵　氵　氵`
`氵　氵　氵　漢　漢`

People 夫 living in the green ⁺⁺ area at the mouth 口 of a river or water 氵, founded the country of China.

漢字	かんじ	**kanji**	Chinese character, kanji
漢和×辞典	かんわ じてん	**kanwa jiten**	Japanese kanji dictionary
常用 漢字	じょうよう かんじ	**jōyō kanji**	kanji recommended for general use
漢語	かんご	**kango**	Chinese words
漢文	かんぶん	**kambun**	Chinese classics
漢方薬	かんぽうやく	**kampōyaku**	Chinese herbal medicine
門外漢	もんがいかん	**mongaikan**	outsider, layman

105 英

ei
エイ
brilliant, English

`一　十　艹　艹　苎　苎　英　英`

Plant ⁺⁺ and center 央 means exceptionally beautiful flower. Thus 英 now means talented, or brave.

漢英	かんえい	**kan'ei**	kanji-English
英語	えいご	**eigo**	English
英会話	えいかいわ	**eikaiwa**	English conversation
英文	えいぶん	**eibun**	English sentence
英国	えいこく	**eikoku**	England

106 初

haji-me, hatsu, ui, so-meru, sho
はじ・め、はつ、うい、そ・める、ショ
beginning, first

`ヽ　ラ　ネ　ネ　ネ　初　初`

ネ the same as 衣, the pictograph of the kimono's V-shaped neckline, means clothes. Imagine a tape-cutting ceremony celebrating the start of something. Cloth ネ and scissors 刀 are to start something.

初め	はじめ	**hajime**	the beginning
初めて	はじめて	**hajimete**	for the first time
初×級	しょきゅう	**shokyū**	basic course
初歩	しょほ	**shoho**	the first step
初日	しょにち	**shonichi**	opening day
初代	しょだい	**shodai**	the founder

107 心	kokoro, (gokoro), shin, (jin) こころ、（ごころ）、シン、（ジン） mind, heart, core	＼	心	心	心				

This is the pictograph of a heart. 	心	こころ	**kokoro**	heart
	関心	かんしん	**kanshin**	interest
	初心者	しょしんしゃ	**shoshinsha**	beginner
	中心	ちゅうしん	**chūshin**	center
	安心	あんしん	**anshin**	feel relieved
	真心	まごころ	**magokoro**	sincerity
	小心	しょうしん	**shōshin**	timid
	野心	やしん	**yashin**	ambition
	不用心な	ぶようじんな	**buyōjin na**	unsafe
	身心	しんしん	**shinshin**	body and mind

108 必	kanara-zu, hitsu, (hi') かなら・ず、ヒツ、（ヒッ） necessary	＼	ソ	义	必	必			

必 combines a heart 心 and an emphasis ノ, suggesting necessity. 	必ず	かならず	**kanarazu**	surely, to be sure
	必要な	ひつような	**hitsuyō na**	necessary
	必読	ひつどく	**hitsudoku**	required reading
	必然	ひつぜん	**hitsuzen**	inevitability
	必修	ひっしゅう	**hisshū**	required subject
	科目	かもく	**kamoku**	
	必要品	ひつようひん	**hitsuyōhin**	necessities

109 要	i-ru, yō い・る、ヨウ main point, necessity	一	厂	〒	西	两	两	要	要
		要							

Traditionally a woman's 女 waist was a central physical feature and by extension 要 has come to mean important. 	主要な	しゅような	**shuyō na**	main
	要約	ようやく	**yōyaku**	summary
	要人	ようじん	**yōjin**	VIP
	所要時間	しょようじかん	**shoyō jikan**	required time
	要注意	ようちゅうい	**yōchūi**	requiring care
	不要な	ふような	**fuyō na**	not necessary

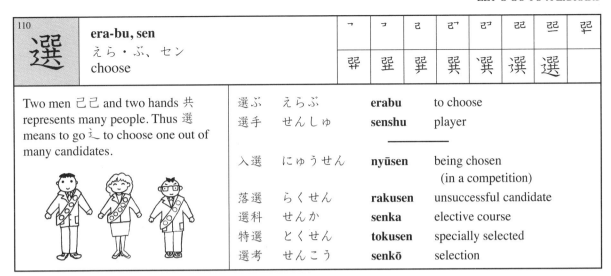

110 選	**era-bu, sen** えら・ぶ、セン choose	フ	コ	己	已	己ʼ	己己	己己	罪
		罪	翌	巽	巽	巽	選	選	

選ぶ	えらぶ	**erabu**	to choose
選手	せんしゅ	**senshu**	player
入選	にゅうせん	**nyūsen**	being chosen (in a competition)
落選	らくせん	**rakusen**	unsuccessful candidate
選科	せんか	**senka**	elective course
特選	とくせん	**tokusen**	specially selected
選考	せんこう	**senkō**	selection

Two men 己己 and two hands 共 represents many people. Thus 選 means to go 辶 to choose one out of many candidates.

111 単	**tan** タン simple, single	ヽ	ヾ	ツ	バ	并	肖	当	単
		単							

単語	たんご	**tango**	word
単身	たんしん	**tanshin**	alone
単位	たんい	**tan'i**	credit
単数	たんすう	**tansū**	singular (in grammar)
単一	たんいつ	**tan'itsu**	single
単元	たんげん	**tangen**	unit of academic credit
単調	たんちょう	**tanchō**	monotonous
単線	たんせん	**tansen**	single track

単 is a pictograph of a single shaped beater.

112 力	**chikara, riki, ryoku** ちから、リキ、リョク power	フ	力						

力	ちから	**chikara**	power
電力	でんりょく	**denryoku**	electric power
人力車	じんりきしゃ	**jinrikisha**	rickshaw
風力	ふうりょく	**fūryoku**	wind power
水力	すいりょく	**suiryoku**	water power
全力	ぜんりょく	**zenryoku**	utmost effort
動力	どうりょく	**dōryoku**	power
主力	しゅりょく	**shuryoku**	main power
力学	りきがく	**rikigaku**	dynamics
力士	りきし	**rikishi**	sumo wrestler

力 depicts a strong man's arm, which indicates power.

113 字

aza, ji
あざ、ジ
character, letter

`	`	宀	字	宀	字		

A child 子 is practicing writing letters in the house 宀.

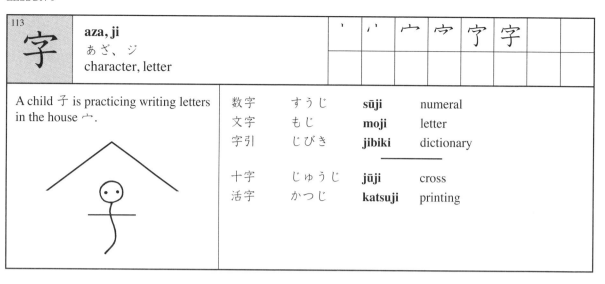

数字	すうじ	**sūji**	numeral
文字	もじ	**moji**	letter
字引	じびき	**jibiki**	dictionary
十字	じゅうじ	**jūji**	cross
活字	かつじ	**katsuji**	printing

114 思

omo-u, shi
おも・う、シ
think

`	冂	冂	田	田	甼	思	思
思							

思 combines heart 心 and rice paddy 田. A farmer always thinks of his rice paddy.

思う	おもう	**omou**	to think
不思議	ふしぎ	**fushigi**	wonder
思い出	おもいで	**omoide**	memory
思い込む	おもいこむ	**omoikomu**	to have the idea that
思案	しあん	**shian**	thought
意思	いし	**ishi**	intent
親思い	おやおもい	**oya omoi**	affection for one's parents
思考	しこう	**shikō**	thinking
思い付く	おもいつく	**omoitsuku**	to think of

115 困

koma-ru, kon
こま・る、コン
be distressed, difficulty, trouble

｜	冂	冂	田	困	困	困	

Imagine a tree growing in a box. The tree is in difficulty.

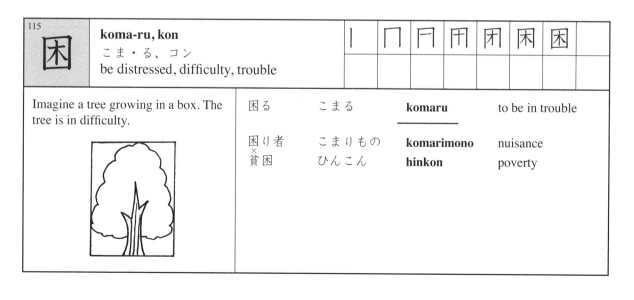

困る	こまる	**komaru**	to be in trouble
困り者	こまりもの	**komarimono**	nuisance
貧困	ひんこん	**hinkon**	poverty

4 Practice

I. Write the readings of the following kanji in hiragana.

1. 辞書　　　　　2. 雑用　　　　　3. 心　　　　　4. 選手
5. 電力　　　　　6. 文字　　　　　7. 困る　　　　8. 主要
9. 初めて漢和辞典を選びました。
10. 英会話はむずかしいと思います。
11. 必ず単語をおぼえましょう。

II. Fill in the blanks with appropriate kanji.

1. じ
典
dictionary

2. ざっ
誌
magazine

3. かん　じ
Chinese character

4. えい
語
English

5. しょ　しん
者
beginner

6. ひつ　よう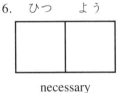
necessary

7. たん
身
alone

8. ちから
power

9. し
不　議
wonder

10. こま
る
to be in trouble

11. えら
ぶ
to choose

5 Advanced Placement Exam Practice Questions

A student studying Japanese is talking to a librarian. He wants to choose a dictionary. Read the dialogue below and answer the questions.

S: Student
L: Librarian

S: 使いやすい漢英辞書を選びたいんですが、どれがいいですか。

L: 漢字をどのくらい勉強しているんですか。

S: 週に2回、もう6か月になります。

L: 初心者用の「漢英小辞典」(Kanji dictionary 2,000 words)はどうですか。

S: これはちょっと単語が少ないですね。

L: どんな時に辞書が必要ですか。

S: 教科書を読んだり、問題集をしたりするときに使います。漢字を勉強していると、1熟語もいろいろ調べたくなるし。

L: 一番2詳しいのは「漢英熟語大辞典」(Kanji dictionary 50,000 words) だけど、、。

S: これは持って歩けませんね。

L: それなら「漢英中辞典」(Kanji dictionary 20,000 words) はどうですか。これなら重くなくていいですよ。

S: ああいいですね。でも、この本は漢字の3成り立ちはのっていませんね。

L: 初心者が漢字の成り立ちを知りたいときは、「必修漢字500」(Essential kanji 500) がいいですよ。

S: そうですね。このチャートは見やすいですね。じゃあ、辞典は自分用に買って、この本を借りて行くことにします。

1熟語: kanji compounds　2詳しい: particular　3成り立ち: etymology

1. Why didn't the student choose "Kanji dictionary 2,000 words"?
   A. Because it is too big.
   B. Because it is heavy.
   C. Because the characters are too small.
   D. Because it has few entries.

2. When does the student think he needs a dictionary most?
   A. When he reads his textbook.
   B. When he doesn't understand what the teacher says.
   C. When he wants to look up a kanji character.
   D. When he does his homework.

3. Why didn't the student choose "Kanji dictionary 50,000 words"?
   A. Because it is too big.
   B. Because it is hard to read.
   C. Because he cannot put it in his pocket.
   D. Because it is too big to carry.

4. The student eventually
   A. bought "Essential kanji 500" and borrowed "Kanji dictionary 20,000 words."
   B. bought "Essential kanji 500" and borrowed "Kanji dictionary 50,000 words."
   C. borrowed "Essential kanji 500" and bought "Kanji dictionary 20,000 words."
   D. borrowed "Essential kanji 500" and bought "Kanji dictionary 50,000 words."

5. The librarian said that
   A. the student may refer to a book for the etymology of a Chinese character.
   B. the student should study the etymology of a Chinese character first.
   C. a beginner should use a big dictionary from the beginning.
   D. a beginner had better begin with a small dictionary.

Learning Japanese

日本語を勉強しています

More than 100,000 overseas students have come to study in Japan since 2003. Most of them—93 percent—come from Asia, including China (61%), Korea (14%), and other Asian countries. As one example of this general trend, in 2006 the University of Tokyo enrolled 2,269 foreign students from 95 countries. Of those students 1,800 were from Asia, 220 from Europe, 68 from South America, and 60 students were from Canada and the U.S.A.

The increase of foreign students in Japan's educational system will likely continue to bring various merits to the Japanese students and Japanese society, through communicating with people from other cultures. And for the foreign students as well, the experience in Japan will enrich and color their lives. Why not consider studying Japanese in Japan? Meanwhile, in this lesson we will learn some related kanji.

1 ▶ Introductory Quiz

Look at the illustrations below and refer to the words in **Vocabulary**. Then try the following quiz.

第十課～二十課　学期末試験

SAMPLE TEST

（　　　　）点

名前 _____

問題 1. 反対のことばを線で結びなさい。

Ex.	大きい ———————	遅い
1.	新しい	小さい
2.	難しい	短い
3.	早(はや)い	やさしい
4.	近い	古い
5.	長(なが)い	遠い

問題 2. 漢字の読み方を書きなさい。答は（　　）に書きなさい。

1. 勉強　　　　　　（　　　　　）
2. 忘れる　　　　　（　　　　　）
3. ＿＿＿＿　　　　（　　　　　）

Choose the correct meaning for the kanji from a–k.

1. 課　（　）　　2. 試験　（　）　　3. 点　（　）　　4. 問題　（　）
5. 反対　（　）　　6. 難しい（　）　　7. 読み方（　）　　8. 答　（　）
9. 勉強　（　）　　10. 忘れる（　）　　11. 練習　（　）

a. examination　　b. practice　　c. scores　　d. study　　e. how to read　　f. lesson
g. forget　　h. difficult　　i. answer　　j. opposite　　k. question

2 ▶ Vocabulary

Study the readings and meanings of these words to help you understand the **Introductory Quiz**.

1. 第十課	だい じゅっ か	**daijukka**	lesson 10
2. 学期末	がっ き まつ	**gakkimatsu**	final term
3. 試験	し けん	**shiken**	examination
4. 点	てん	**ten**	score
5. 問題	もん だい	**mondai**	question
6. 反対	はん たい	**hantai**	opposite
7. 難しい	むずか しい	**muzukashii**	difficult
8. 漢字	かん じ	**kanji**	Chinese character
9. 読み方	よ み かた	**yomikata**	how to read
10. 答	こたえ	**kotae**	answer
11. 書く	か く	**kaku**	to write
12. 勉強	べん きょう	**benkyō**	study
13. 忘れる	わす れる	**wasureru**	to forget
14. 練習	れん しゅう	**renshū**	practice

3 ▶ New Characters

Fifteen characters are introduced in this lesson. Use the explanations to help you understand and remember the characters. Study the compound words to increase your vocabulary.

課　試　点　問　題　反　対　難　読　勉　強　忘　練　習　答

116 課

ka
カ
lesson, section

丶	二	三	言	言	言	言	言
訂	訳	訳	誤	課	課	課	

The boss tells 言 someone to work to bear fruit 果. Thus 課 means to assign someone a task.

課	か	**ka**	lesson, section
第十課	だいじゅっか	**daijukka**	lesson 10
学生課	がくせいか	**gakuseika**	student affairs section
教務課	きょうむか	**kyōmuka**	academic affairs section
課外	かがい	**kagai**	extracurricular
課税	かぜい	**kazei**	duty
課目	かもく	**kamoku**	subject

117 試

tame-su, kokoro-miru, shi
ため・す、こころ・みる、シ
give it a try, attempt

丶	二	三	言	言	言	言	言
言	訂	証	試	試			

試 combines ceremony 式 and speak 言, suggesting to try to speak at a ceremony according to a model.

試す	ためす	**tamesu**	to try out
試験	しけん	**shiken**	test, examination
入試	にゅうし	**nyūshi**	abbreviation of 入学試験, entrance examination
試合	しあい	**shiai**	game
試食	ししょく	**shishoku**	sample food
試案	しあん	**shian**	tentative plan
無試験	むしけん	**mushiken**	without an examination

118 点

ten
テン
point

丨	卜	占	占	占	点	点	点
点							

Fortune tellers 占 burn 灬 bones 占 leaving black points or spots, by which they make a prediction.

点	てん	**ten**	score
百点	ひゃくてん	**hyakuten**	perfect score
点数	てんすう	**tensū**	score
要点	ようてん	**yōten**	gist
問題点	もんだいてん	**mondaiten**	the point of issue
終点	しゅうてん	**shūten**	terminal
出発点	しゅっぱつてん	**shuppatsuten**	starting point
点線	てんせん	**tensen**	dotted line
点火する	てんかする	**tenka suru**	to ignite
利点	りてん	**riten**	advantage

97

119 問

to-u, to-i, ton, mon
と・う、と・い、とん、モン
question, problem

丨	冂	冂	冂	冂	門	門	門
門	問	問					

Mouth 口 and gate 門 combined, 問 means to ask, because people can't see what is behind the closed gate and they ask about it.

問い	とい	**toi**	question
問い合わせる	といあわせる	**toiawaseru**	to inquire
×質問	しつもん	**shitsumon**	question
―――――			
学問	がくもん	**gakumon**	studies
反問する	はんもんする	**hammon suru**	to ask back
問屋	とんや	**ton'ya**	wholesaler
自問する	じもんする	**jimon suru**	to ask oneself

120 題

dai
ダイ
subject, title

丨	冂	日	日	旦	早	早	昰	是
是	是	是	題	題	題	題	題	題

是 combines a flat spoon with a long straight handle 日 and feet 疋, suggesting go straight. 是 combined with 頁 head, 題 came to mean title.

題	だい	**dai**	title
問題	もんだい	**mondai**	question, problem
話題	わだい	**wadai**	topic
題名	だいめい	**daimei**	title
出題	しゅつだい	**shutsudai**	giving a question
議題	ぎだい	**gidai**	topic for discussion
課題	かだい	**kadai**	subject, assignment

121 反

so-ru, so-rasu, han, hon, tan
そ・る、そ・らす、ハン、ホン、タン
opposite, anti, reverse

一	厂	反	反				

反 is the pictograph of a hand 又 bending a sheet of material 厂. The sheet bends back easily to an "opposite" direction. Thus 反 means opposite.

反する	はんする	**han suru**	to be contrary
反面	はんめん	**hammen**	on the other hand
反発	はんぱつ	**hampatsu**	repulsion
反転	はんてん	**hanten**	reversal
反動	はんどう	**handō**	reaction
反語	はんご	**hango**	rhetorical question

122 対

tai, tsui
タイ、ツイ
against, pair

'	亠	ナ	文	文-	対	対		

文 is a simplified form of 業, which represented a tool to hang two musical instruments. Combined with a hand 寸, 対 came to mean the action of facing towards each other.

反対	はんたい	**hantai**	opposite
反対する	はんたいする	**hantai suru**	to oppose
反対語	はんたいご	**hantaigo**	antonym
正反対	せいはんたい	**seihantai**	exact opposite
対話	たいわ	**taiwa**	dialogue
対立	たいりつ	**tairitsu**	confrontation
相対	そうたい	**sōtai**	relativity

123 難

muzuka-shii, kata-i, nan
むずか・しい、かた・い、ナン
difficult

一	十	艹	艹	苫	苫	苫	苣	蓳
蓳	嘆	嘆	嘆	難	難	難	難	難

難 combines to burn animal fat 堇 and a bird 隹. The situation was difficult for the bird. Thus, 難 means difficult.

難しい	むずかしい	**muzukashii**	difficult
困難	こんなん	**konnan**	difficulty
難問	なんもん	**nammon**	difficult problem
難題	なんだい	**nandai**	difficult problem
非難	ひなん	**hinan**	adverse criticism
難関	なんかん	**nankan**	barrier
難病	なんびょう	**nambyō**	incurable disease

124 読

yo-mu, doku, toku, tō
よ・む、ドク、トク、トウ
read

'	亠	二	亖	言	言	言	言	
言	訪	訪	読	読	読			

読 combines words 言 and to sell, meaning to read. In ancient times when most people were illiterate, to read for other people was a way to earn money.

読む	よむ	**yomu**	to read
読み方	よみかた	**yomikata**	pronunciation (of a word), way of reading
読書	どくしょ	**dokusho**	reading
読み物	よみもの	**yomimono**	reading matter
多読	たどく	**tadoku**	extensive reading
読点	とうてん	**tōten**	comma

125 勉	**ben** ベン effort, hard work	ノ	ク	ク	免	角	备	多	免
		免	勉						

勉 combines a woman giving birth 免, which is hard, and power 力, leading to a meaning of hard work.

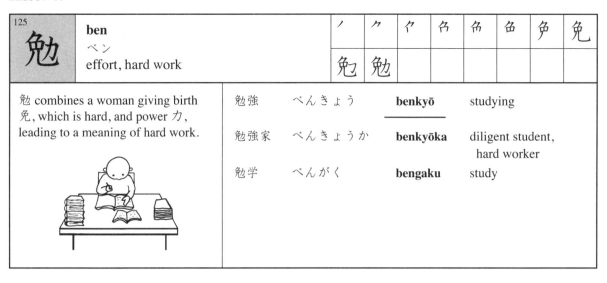

勉強	べんきょう	**benkyō**	studying
勉強家	べんきょうか	**benkyōka**	diligent student, hard worker
勉学	べんがく	**bengaku**	study

---

126 強	**tsuyo-i, shi-iru, kyō, gō** つよ・い、し・いる、キョウ、ゴウ strong	¬	ㄱ	弓	弘	殆	弘	殆	弪
		弴	強	強					

弓 means a strong bow. ㄙ and a worm 虫 together suggest a strong insect. Together they refer to a strong hard insect, like a beetle. Now this kanji means strong.

強い	つよい	**tsuyoi**	strong
強力	きょうりょく	**kyōryoku**	strength
強気	つよき	**tsuyoki**	bullish
強大	きょうだい	**kyōdai**	powerful
強行	きょうこう	**kyōkō**	ram through
強制	きょうせい	**kyōsei**	compulsion
強調	きょうちょう	**kyōchō**	emphasis

---

127 忘	**wasu-reru, bō** わす・れる、ボウ forget	`	亠	亡	亡	忘	忘	忘	

忘 combines a mind 心 and die or "do not exist" 亡, and means to forget.

忘れる	わすれる	**wasureru**	to forget
忘れ物	わすれもの	**wasuremono**	articles left behind
忘年会	ぼうねんかい	**bōnenkai**	year-end party

128 練

ne-ru, ren
ね・る、レン
refine, train

く	幺	幺	幺	糸	糸	紅	紵
紵	紵	紳	紳	練	練		

練 combines thread 糸 and a bundle 東, suggesting to refine the bundle of silk thread. Thus 練 means to refine. By extension, it means to train.

練る	ねる	**neru**	to refine
練習	れんしゅう	**renshū**	practice
		———	
試練	しれん	**shiren**	ordeal
洗練	せんれん	**senren**	refine
修練	しゅうれん	**shūren**	training

129 習

nara-u, shū
なら・う、シュウ
learn

コ	ヲ	ヨ	羽	羽	羽	羽	羽
習	習	習					

習 combines a feather 羽, which was used as a pen, and a sheet of white paper 白. Thus 習 means to learn.

習う	ならう	**narau**	to learn
学習	がくしゅう	**gakushū**	learning
予習	よしゅう	**yoshū**	preparation of lessons
自習	じしゅう	**jishū**	study by oneself
		———	
自習室	じしゅうしつ	**jishūshitsu**	study hall
習字	しゅうじ	**shūji**	penmanship, calligraphy

130 答

kota-eru, kota-e, tō, (dō)
こた・える、こた・え、トウ、（ドウ）
answer

ノ	𠂉	欠	竹	竹	竹	竹	答
答	答	答	答				

答 combines bamboo 竹 and to fit 合, suggesting the answer that corresponds to a question, like a bamboo basket and its cover.

答え	こたえ	**kotae**	answer
口答	こうとう	**kōtō**	oral answer
		———	
回答	かいとう	**kaitō**	answer
問答	もんどう	**mondō**	question and answer
答案用紙	とうあんようし	**tōan'yōshi**	examination paper

4 ▶ Practice

I. Write the readings of the following kanji in hiragana.

1. 学 生 課　　　　2. 点 数　　　　3. 題 名　　　　4. 反 対

5. 困 難　　　　　6. 読 書　　　　7. 忘 年 会　　　　8. 勉 強

9. 口 答　　　　10. 問 題

11. テ ニ ス を 練 習 し て 強 く な り ま し た 。

12. 日 本 語 を 習 い ま す 。

13. 新 し い ゴ ル フ ク ラ ブ を 試 し ま し た 。

II. Fill in the blanks with appropriate kanji.

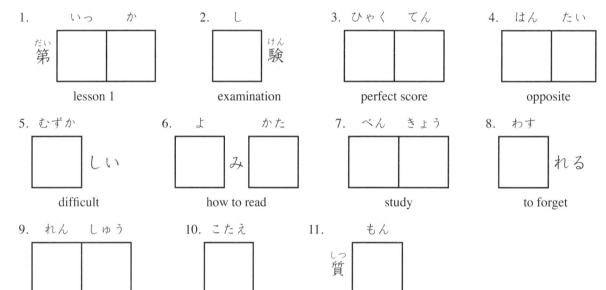

1. いっ　か — 第[だい]☐☐ — lesson 1
2. し　けん[けん] — ☐験 — examination
3. ひゃく　てん — ☐☐ — perfect score
4. はん　たい — ☐☐ — opposite
5. むずか — ☐しい — difficult
6. よ　かた — ☐み☐ — how to read
7. べん　きょう — ☐☐ — study
8. わす — ☐れる — to forget
9. れん　しゅう — ☐☐ — practice
10. こたえ — ☐ — answer
11. もん — 質[しっ]☐ — question

5 ▶ Advanced Placement Exam Practice Questions

Three teachers are talking about the exam which they have just given. Read the dialogue below and answer the questions.

すずき：　今日は先日の日本語の試験について話し合いたいと思います。

たむら：　まず私が点数を読みます。[1]平均点[へいきんてん]は82点でした。

やまもと：　なかなかよかったですね。みんな勉強したんですね。

すずき：　内容[ないよう]は、どうでしたか。

たむら：　　²聴解は90点でとてもよかったんです。³文法とことばは85点でした。でも漢字が悪かっ

たんです。

やまもと：　どれぐらいですか。

たむら：　　一番よくて70点でほとんどの人が40点か50点でした。

やまもと：　去年よりずっと悪いですね。問題が難しかったんですか。

たむら：　　いいえ、問題は去年と同じくらいですが、点数が悪いんです。

すずき：　　そうですか。どうすればよいでしょうね。

やまもと：　漢字はすぐ忘れますから、⁴宿題を毎日出すのがいいですね。

たむら：　　それなら文法も毎日宿題を出したらどうですか。

すずき：　　私は反対ですね。あまり宿題が多いと⁵やる気がなくなりますよ。

たむら：　　いや、私は語学では練習が第一だと思いますよ。

やまもと：　じゃあ漢字の宿題を毎日少しずつ出すことにしてはどうですか。

たむら：　　そうですね。

すずき：　　そうして、後は教師がクラスをみて考えましょう。

¹平均点 : the average mark
²聴解: listening
³文法: grammar
⁴宿題: homework
⁵やる気: motivation

1. The average score was
   A. excellent.
   B. the same as last year.
   C. pretty good.
   D. not good.

2. The best score was on
   A. vocabulary and grammar.
   B. listening.
   C. kanji.
   D. reading.

3. They decided they would give homework for
   A. kanji.
   B. vocabulary.
   C. nothing.
   D. kanji and vocabulary.

4. Who thinks practice is the most important thing?
    A. Suzuki does.
    B. Tamura does.
    C. Yamamoto does.
    D. Tamura and Yamamoto do.

5. Choose the sentence that is correct, according to the discussion.
    A. Listening was easier than last year, but kanji questions were more difficult than last year.
    B. Kanji questions were easier than last year but the scores were bad.
    C. Kanji questions were more difficult than last year so the scores were bad.
    D. Kanji questions were at the same level as last year but the scores were bad.

Seasons in Japan

日本の季節

Japan has four seasons. Spring is a time when cherry blossoms and various colorful flowers are in full bloom and the trees are covered with fresh green leaves. Summer comes after the rainy season called **Tsuyu**. It is hot and humid enough that people may feel uncomfortable. Autumn follows summer. It is cool and refreshing, and the Japanese archipelago is decorated with the red and yellow leaves of trees. Autumn is also the harvest time; fresh delicious fruits are enjoyed. Winter arrives with the first snowfall of the season in Hokkaido. It snows heavily on the Japan Sea side of the country, while it is generally fairer weather on the Pacific Coast side. In this lesson, you will learn some kanji concerning seasons.

1 Introductory Quiz

Look at the illustrations below and refer to the words in **Vocabulary**. Then try the following quiz.

Fill in the below spaces with the appropriate letters (a–h).

a. 暑い   b. 寒い   c. 暖かい   d. 涼しい   e. スキー   f. お花見   g. 海水浴   h. 紅葉

1. Spring (   ) (   )   2. Summer (   ) (   )   3. Autumn (   ) (   )   4. Winter (   ) (   )

2 ► Vocabulary

Study the readings and meanings of these words to help you understand the **Introductory Quiz**.

1.	季節	き せつ	**kisetsu**	season
2.	風	かぜ	**kaze**	wind
3.	運ぶ	はこ ぶ	**hakobu**	to carry
4.	春	はる	**haru**	spring
5.	夏	なつ	**natsu**	summer
6.	秋	あき	**aki**	autumn
7.	冬	ふゆ	**fuyu**	winter
8.	暖かい	あたた かい	**atatakai**	warm
9.	涼しい	すず しい	**suzushii**	cool
10.	暑い	あつ い	**atsui**	hot
11.	寒い	さむ い	**samui**	cold
12.	気温	き おん	**kion**	temperature
13.	～度	～ど	**~do**	~ degree(s)
14.	お花見	お はな み	**ohanami**	cherry blossom viewing
15.	海水浴	かい すい よく	**kaisuiyoku**	swimming in the sea
16.	紅葉	こう よう	**kōyō**	autumn colors

3 ► New Characters

Twelve characters are introduced in this lesson. Use the explanations to help you understand and remember the characters. Study the compound words to increase your vocabulary

節　風　運　春　夏　秋　冬　暖　暑　寒　温　度

131 節

fushi, setsu, sechi
ふし、セツ、セチ
season, section, joint

ノ ト ヒ ヒ 竹 竹 竺 竺
笁 笁 笁 笁 節

節 combines bamboo 竹 and a man kneeling to eat food 即. The knee is a joint. By extension, it also means section. A season is a section of a year.

節	ふし	**fushi**	knot
季節	きせつ	**kisetsu**	season
調節	ちょうせつ	**chōsetsu**	adjustment
節約	せつやく	**setsuyaku**	economizing
音節	おんせつ	**onsetsu**	syllable
使節	しせつ	**shisetsu**	mission
節分	せつぶん	**Setsubun**	Setsubun Festival (day before the beginning of spring)
節目	ふしめ	**fushime**	turning point

132 風

kaze, kaza, fū, fu
かぜ、かざ、フウ、フ
wind, appearance, style

ノ 几 几 凡 凡 凨 風 風
風

Combining a sail 几 and a worm 虫 coming out from the ground 一 in spring when spring winds start blowing, 風 means wind.

風	かぜ	**kaze**	wind
台風	たいふう	**taifū**	typhoon
風邪	かぜ	**kaze**	a cold
風呂場	ふろば	**furoba**	bathroom
和風	わふう	**wafū**	Japanese style
洋風	ようふう	**yōfū**	Western style
校風	こうふう	**kōfū**	school tradition
風習	ふうしゅう	**fūshū**	custom
風車	ふうしゃ	**fūsha**	windmill
強風	きょうふう	**kyōfū**	strong wind

133 運

hako-bu, un
はこ・ぶ、ウン
carry, transport, fate, luck

丶 冖 冖 尸 冝 冝 冒 亘
軍 軍 運 運

軍, a combination of roof 冖 and vehicle 車, means armed forces. Imagine tanks used for battle. To go 辶 is added to mean to carry. By extension, 運 also means luck, because luck is a vehicle that carries a person along without the person's efforts or initiative.

運ぶ	はこぶ	**hakobu**	to carry
運転する	うんてんする	**unten suru**	to drive
運転手	うんてんしゅ	**untenshu**	driver
運動する	うんどうする	**undō suru**	to move, to campaign
運送会社	うんそうがいしゃ	**unsō gaisha gaisha**	shipping agency
運用	うんよう	**un'yō**	put into practice
運行	うんこう	**unkō**	run (trains)
運休	うんきゅう	**unkyū**	not running (trains)
運	うん	**un**	luck
不運な	ふうんな	**fuun na**	unlucky

134 春

haru , shun
はる、シュン
spring

一	二	三	声	夫	夫	春	春
春							

春 depicts a plant that is about to grow and the sun 日 combined, thus spring 春 is a season when trees and plants grow.

春	はる	**haru**	spring
春休み	はるやすみ	**haru yasumi**	spring vacation
新春	しんしゅん	**shinshun**	the New Year
春分の日	しゅんぶんのひ	**shumbun no hi**	Vernal Equinox Day
春風	はるかぜ	**harukaze**	spring breeze
思春期	ししゅんき	**shishunki**	puberty

135 夏

natsu, ka, ge
なつ、カ、ゲ
summer

一	一	厂	丏	百	百	百	頁
頁	夏						

Head 首 and legs 夂 suggest the dance of a summer festival.

夏	なつ	**natsu**	summer
夏休み	なつやすみ	**natsu yasumi**	summer vacation
初夏	しょか	**shoka**	early summer
真夏	まなつ	**manatsu**	midsummer
夏期	かき	**kaki**	summer period
夏物	なつもの	**natsumono**	summer clothing

136 秋

aki, shū
あき、シュウ
autumn, fall

ノ	ニ	千	禾	禾	禾	和	秋
秋							

禾 is grain. People harvest grain and dry it with sunshine and fire 火 to store it. Thus 秋 is harvest time, autumn. Another version is that the color of grain turns into the color of 火 fire. Thus 秋 means autumn.

秋	あき	**aki**	autumn
秋分の日	しゅうぶんのひ	**shūbun no hi**	Autumnal Equinox Day
初秋	しょしゅう	**shoshū**	early autumn
秋田	あきた	**Akita**	Akita (prefecture)

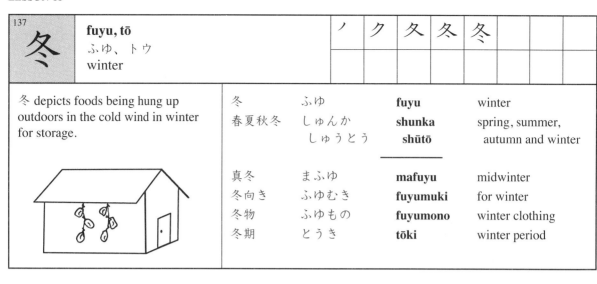

137

冬

fuyu, tō
ふゆ、トウ
winter

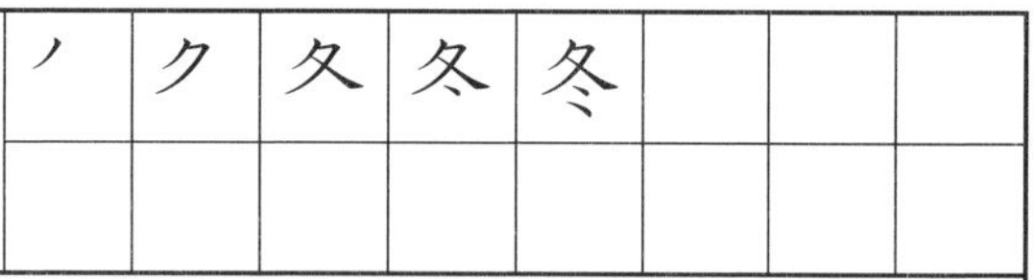

冬 depicts foods being hung up outdoors in the cold wind in winter for storage.

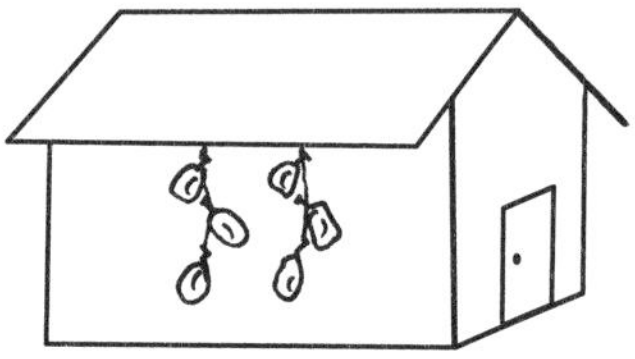

冬	ふゆ	**fuyu**	winter
春夏秋冬	しゅんか しゅうとう	**shunka shūtō**	spring, summer, autumn and winter
真冬	まふゆ	**mafuyu**	midwinter
冬向き	ふゆむき	**fuyumuki**	for winter
冬物	ふゆもの	**fuyumono**	winter clothing
冬期	とうき	**tōki**	winter period

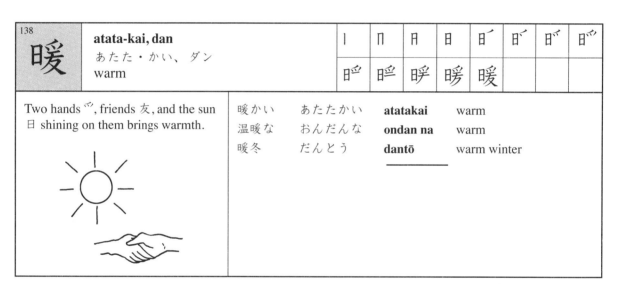

138

暖

atata-kai, dan
あたた・かい、ダン
warm

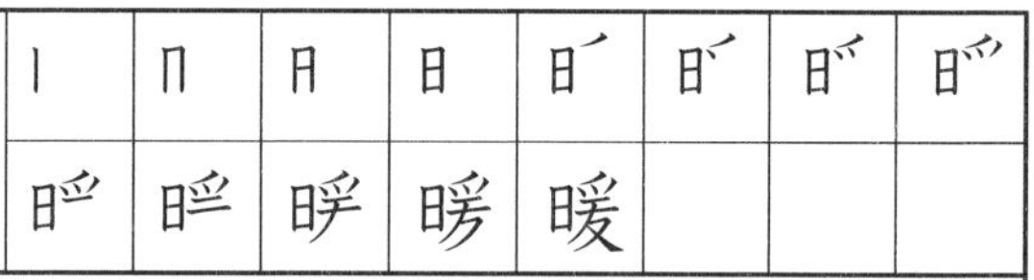

Two hands 爫, friends 友, and the sun 日 shining on them brings warmth.

暖かい	あたたかい	**atatakai**	warm
温暖な	おんだんな	**ondan na**	warm
暖冬	だんとう	**dantō**	warm winter

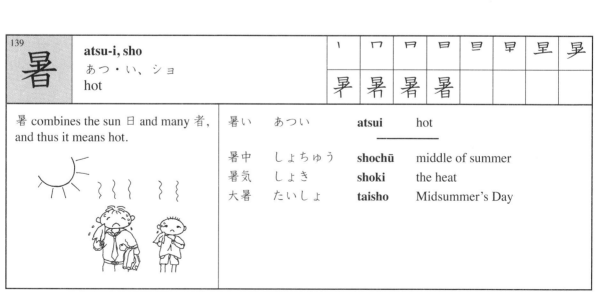

139

暑

atsu-i, sho
あつ・い、ショ
hot

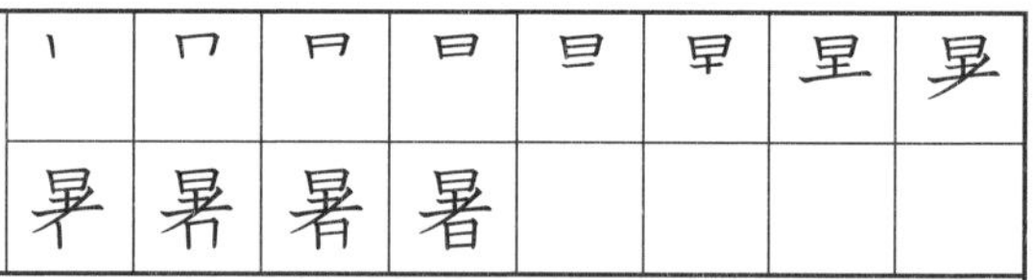

暑 combines the sun 日 and many 者, and thus it means hot.

暑い	あつい	**atsui**	hot
暑中	しょちゅう	**shochū**	middle of summer
暑気	しょき	**shoki**	the heat
大暑	たいしょ	**taisho**	Midsummer's Day

140 寒 samui, kan
さむ・い、カン
cold

`	`	宀	宁	宇	守	审	宭
宭	寒	寒	寒				

A brick 共 house 宀 with icicles 冫 hanging from a roof, means cold.

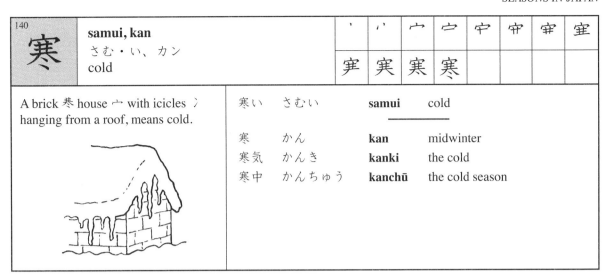

寒い	さむい	**samui**	cold
寒	かん	**kan**	midwinter
寒気	かんき	**kanki**	the cold
寒中	かんちゅう	**kanchū**	the cold season

141 温 atata-kai, atata-meru, on
あたた・かい、あたた・める、オン
warm

`	`	氵	汀	沪	沪	沪	温
温	温	温	温				

Sunshine 日 makes the water 氵 in a dish 皿 warm. Thus 温 means warm.

温める	あたためる	**atatameru**	to warm up
気温	きおん	**kion**	temperature
室温	しつおん	**shitsuon**	room temperature
温室	おんしつ	**onshitsu**	greenhouse
温泉	おんせん	**onsen**	hot spring

142 度 tabi, do
たび、ド
degree, limit, times

`	亠	广	广	庐	庐	庐	庐
度							

Hand 又 combines with 庐 meaning to measure by hand. In ancient China, people measured objects using their hands. Thus 度 means degree.

度	ど	**do**	degree
温度	おんど	**ondo**	temperature
制度	せいど	**seido**	system
今度	こんど	**kondo**	this time, next time
毎度	まいど	**maido**	every time
度々	たびたび	**tabitabi**	often
経度	けいど	**keido**	longitude
度忘れ	どわすれ	**dowasure**	forget for the moment

4 ▶ Practice

I. Write the readings of the following kanji in hiragana.

1. 季節

2. 風

3. 運ぶ

4. 春

5. 秋

6. 寒い

7. 温度

8. スープを温めましょう。

9. 日本の夏はむし暑いです。

10. 暖かい冬を暖冬といいます。

11. 私は、温暖な季節が一番好きです。

12. 日本へ台風が近づいています。

13. 春分の日と秋分の日は、明るい時間と暗い時間が同じです。

II. Fill in the blanks with appropriate kanji.

1.　たい　ふう

［　　　］［　　　］

typhoon

2.　うん　てん　しゅ

［　　　］［　　　］［　　　］

driver

3.　はる

［　　　］

spring

4.　なつ　やす

［　　　］［　　　］み

summer vacation

5.　ふゆ　やす

［　　　］［　　　］み

winter vacation

6.　あき

［　　　］

autumn

7.　おん　だん

［　　　］［　　　］な

warm

8.　あつ

［　　　］い

hot

9.　さむ

［　　　］い

cold

10.　おん　ど

［　　　］［　　　］

temperature

5 ▶ Advanced Placement Exam Practice Questions

You are preparing an article for the student newspaper of your sister school in Japan. Write an article in which you compare and contrast seasons in Japan and your country. Describe at least THREE aspects of each and highlight the similarities and differences between seasons in Japan and your country.

Your article should be 300 to 400 characters or longer. Use the **desu/masu** or **da** (plain) style, but use one style consistently. Also, use kanji wherever kanji from the AP Japanese kanji list is appropriate. You have 20 minutes to write.

LESSON 12 Going to Akihabara

秋葉原へ行きます

A kihabara is one of the most famous towns in Tokyo. It is known as Akihabara Electric Town (**Akihabara Denki-gai**) not only by Japanese but also by foreign people. There are many electronics shops, computer shops and animation shops, large and small, on the main street and on the back streets. They deal in new and used items, from parts to finished goods. Akihabara is always crowded with visitors and buyers. In this lesson, you will learn several kanji written in the user's manual for a digital camera and concerning Akihabara Electric Town.

1 ▶ Introductory Quiz

Look at the illustrations below and refer to the words in **Vocabulary**. Then try the following quiz.

This is a user's manual for a digital camera. Which pages must you refer to for each of the below instructions?

デジタルカメラ
使用説明書

1. (p.　) Taking movies
2. (p.　) Taking pictures
3. (p.　) To see pictures you took
4. (p.　) Preparation for taking pictures
5. (p.　) How to use the basics
6. (p.　) How to use the voice recording feature

秋葉原には多くの電気店が集まっています。店には大量の商品があります。
安いものは半額で売っています。テレビなどの重いものは送ってくれます。

2 ▷ Vocabulary

Study the readings and meanings of these words to help you understand the **Introductory Quiz**.

1. 使用説明書	し よ う せつ めい しょ	**shiyō setsumeisho**	manual
2. 目次	もく じ	**mokuji**	table of contents
3. 撮影	さつ えい	**satsuei**	taking pictures
4. 準備	じゅん び	**jumbi**	preparation
5. 基本的な	き ほん てき な	**kihonteki na**	basic
6. 動画	どう が	**dōga**	moving image
7. 音声	おん せい	**onsei**	voice, sound
8. 再生	さい せい	**saisei**	playback
9. 秋葉原	あき は ばら	**Akihabara**	Akihabara
10. 多い	おお い	**ōi**	a lot of, many
11. 電気店	でん き てん	**denkiten**	electric shop
12. 大量の	たい りょう の	**tairyō no**	a large quantity of
13. 商品	しょう ひん	**shōhin**	goods
14. 半額	はん がく	**hangaku**	half price
15. 重い	おも い	**omoi**	heavy

3 New Characters

Ten characters are introduced in this lesson. Use the explanations to help you understand and remember the characters. Study the compound words to increase your vocabulary.

説　次　画　音　声　再　多　量　額　重

143

説

to-ku, setsu, zei
と・く、セツ、ゼイ
opinion, theory; explain

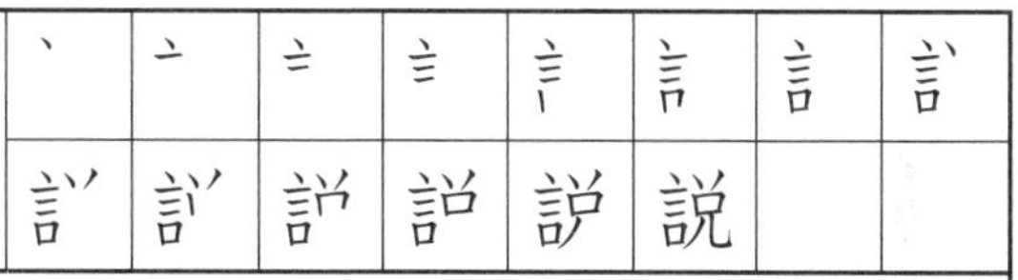

A person with a big mouth 口 is a big brother 兄 who gives advice to his siblings. The words 言 of an older brother 兄 with horns ソ are powerful and assertive. Thus 説 means to explain, persuade, or preach a doctrine.

使用説明書	しよう せつめいしょ	**shiyō setsumeisho**	manual
小説	しょうせつ	**shōsetsu**	novel
学説	がくせつ	**gakusetsu**	theory
社説	しゃせつ	**shasetsu**	editorial
私小説	ししょうせつ	**shishōsetsu**	autobiographical novel

144

次

tsugi, tsu-gu, shi, ji
つぎ、つ・ぐ、シ、ジ
next, the second

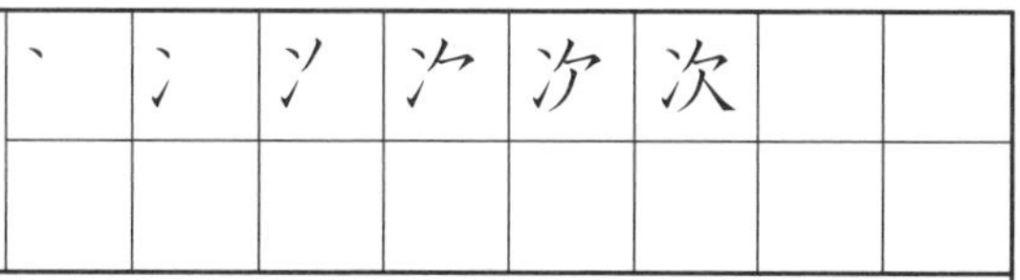

欠 is the pictograph of a man yawning with his mouth wide open. 欠 combined with ice 冫, 次 means next. First water, next ice.

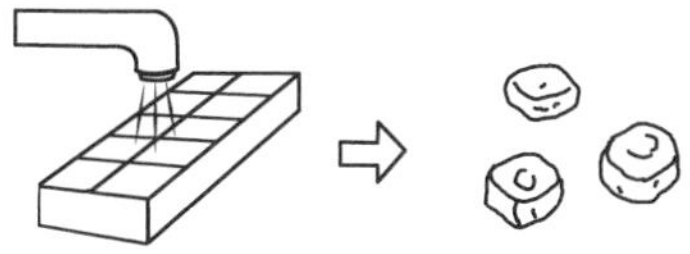

次	つぎ	**tsugi**	next
目次	もくじ	**mokuji**	table of contents
次男	じなん	**jinan**	second son
二次	にじ	**niji**	second
次元	じげん	**jigen**	dimension
次第	しだい	**shidai**	procedure
次期	じき	**jiki**	next term
次回	じかい	**jikai**	next time

145 画

ga, kaku, (ka')
ガ、カク、（カッ）
draw, picture; stroke

一 厂 厂 币 币 币 画 画 画

画 meant to draw a boundary, ⊔ and 一, around a rice paddy 田. Thus 画 means to draw.

日本画	にほんが	**nihonga**	Japanese-style painting
録画する	ろくがする	**rokuga suru**	to record
動画	どうが	**dōga**	animation, movie, moving image
		――――――	
画数	かくすう	**kakusū**	stroke count
画家	がか	**gaka**	painter
計画する	けいかくする	**keikaku suru**	to plan
区画	くかく	**kukaku**	division
画期的	かっきてき	**kakkiteki**	epoch-making

146 音

oto, ne, on, in
おと、ね、オン、イン
sound

丶 亠 六 产 立 产 音 音
音

When a new day 日 arises 立, people begin to make sounds 音.

音	おと	**oto**	sound
発音	はつおん	**hatsuon**	pronunciation
音読み	おんよみ	**on'yomi**	**on**-reading (of kanji)
		――――――	
母音	ぼいん	**boin**	vowel
子音	しいん	**shiin**	consonant
音色	ねいろ	**neiro**	(sound) tone

147 声

koe, (goe), kowa, sei, shō
こえ、（ごえ）、こわ、セイ、ショウ
voice

一 十 士 声 声 声 声

声 depicts a simple Chinese instrument (slate bars hanging on strings).

声	こえ	**koe**	voice
音声	おんせい	**onsei**	voice
大声	おおごえ	**ōgoe**	loud voice
		――――――	
小声	こごえ	**kogoe**	whisper
声楽家	せいがくか	**seigakuka**	vocalist
人声	ひとごえ	**hitogoe**	voice
肉声	にくせい	**nikusei**	natural voice
声明	せいめい	**seimei**	declaration

148 再 — futata-bi, sai, sa / ふたた・び、サイ、サ / once more, again, twice

一	丆	冂	市	再	再		

冉 is a simplified figure of a basket upside down. 一 is added to mean one more time, or again.

再び	ふたたび	**futatabi**	again
再生	さいせい	**saisei**	playback
再開	さいかい	**saikai**	reopen
再発行する	さいはっこうする	**saihakkō suru**	to reissue
再入国する	さいにゅうこくする	**sainyūkoku suru**	to reenter a country
再会する	さいかいする	**saikai suru**	to meet again
再利用	さいりよう	**sairiyō**	recycle
再三	さいさん	**saisan**	again and again
再考する	さいこうする	**saikō suru**	to reconsider

149 多 — ō-i, ta / おお・い、タ / many, much

ノ	ク	タ	夕	多	多		

With double evening, 多 means that many days have passed and means in general many or much.

多い	おおい	**ōi**	many, much
多分	たぶん	**tabun**	probably
多大な	ただいな	**tadai na**	much
多数の	たすうの	**tasū no**	many
多少	たしょう	**tashō**	a little
多額の	たがくの	**tagaku no**	a lot of (money)
多面	ためん	**tamen**	many sides
多用	たよう	**tayō**	busyness
雑多な	ざったな	**zatta na**	various

150 量 — haka-ru, ryō / はか・る、リョウ / scale; quantity

丶	口	戸	日	旦	昙	昙	昙
昌	昌	量	量				

Day 日 and heavy 重 combined, 量 means quantity.

大量の	たいりょうの	**tairyō no**	a large quantity of
音量	おんりょう	**onryō**	volume
重量	じゅうりょう	**jūryō**	weight
分量	ぶんりょう	**bunryō**	amount
大量生産	たいりょうせいさん	**tairyō seisan**	mass production
容量	ようりょう	**yōryō**	capacity
度量	どりょう	**doryō**	generosity

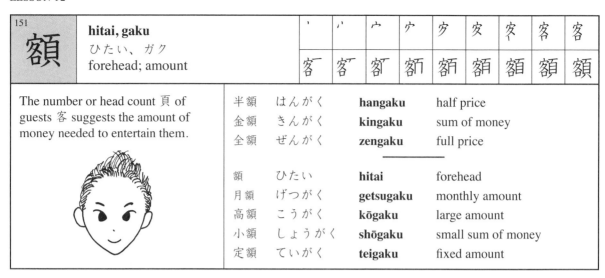

151 額	**hitai, gaku** ひたい、ガク forehead; amount	'	'	宀	ウ	夕	安	安	客	客
		客	客	額	額	額	額	額	額	額

The number or head count 頁 of guests 客 suggests the amount of money needed to entertain them.

半額	はんがく	**hangaku**	half price
金額	きんがく	**kingaku**	sum of money
全額	ぜんがく	**zengaku**	full price
額	ひたい	**hitai**	forehead
月額	げつがく	**getsugaku**	monthly amount
高額	こうがく	**kōgaku**	large amount
小額	しょうがく	**shōgaku**	small sum of money
定額	ていがく	**teigaku**	fixed amount

152 重	**omo-i, kasa-naru, e, jū, chō** おも・い、かさ・なる、え、ジュウ、チョウ heavy; lap; fold	一	二	千	舌	盲	盲	重	重
		重							

重 is the pictograph of a man ノ standing on a pile of heavy things on the ground 土.

重い	おもい	**omoi**	heavy
重要な	じゅうような	**jūyō na**	important
音声多重	おんせいたじゅう	**onsei tajū**	multiplex
重力	じゅうりょく	**jūryoku**	gravity
重工業	じゅうこうぎょう	**jūkōgyō**	heavy industry
重荷	おもに	**omoni**	burden
無重力	むじゅうりょく	**mujūryoku**	zero gravity

4 ▷ Practice

I. Write the readings of the following kanji in hiragana.

1. 使用説明書　　　2. 目次　　　　　3. 動画　　　　　4. 大声
5. 多い　　　　　　6. 大量　　　　　7. 半額
8. となりの部屋でへんな音がします。
9. ビデオを再生します。
10. あのレストランの料理は量が多いです。
11. 重そうですね。持ちましょうか。
12. あなたは、日本語の発音がとてもいいです。
13. 次の番組は重要ですから、よく見てください。

II. Fill in the blanks with appropriate kanji.

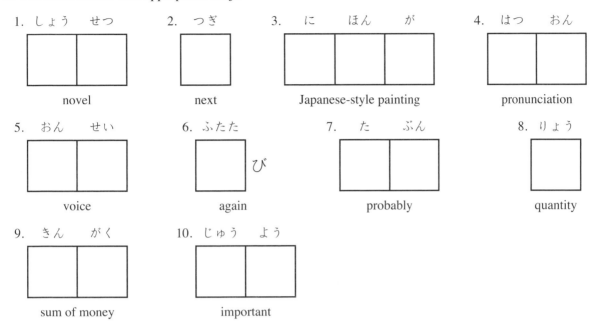

1. しょう せつ

novel

2. つぎ

next

3. に ほん が

Japanese-style painting

4. はつ おん

pronunciation

5. おん せい

voice

6. ふたた

び

again

7. た ぶん

probably

8. りょう

quantity

9. きん がく

sum of money

10. じゅう よう

important

5 ▶ Advanced Placement Exam Practice Questions

You will read several selections in Japanese. For each question, choose the response that is best according to the selections.

Read this set of e-mails.

受信箱

Message #1

差出人： たろう

送信日： 4月5日

件 名： 新しい携帯 (けい たい)

携帯、新しいのにしたんだ。動画もきれいだし、音楽の再生もできるんだ。5人までグループ登録が
できて、¹通話料 (つう わ りょう) が安くなるんだって。グループにならないか。

Message #2

差出人： かおり

送信日： 4月5日

件 名： RE: 新しい携帯

私も買いかえたいな。でも旅行に行って、お金がないのよね。アルバイトしてるんだけど、安いバイ
トだから、お金ぜんぜんたまんないし。でも、通話料が安くなるのはいいわね。

Message #3

差出人：　はじめ

送信日：　4月5日

件　名：　RE: 新しい携帯

おれのも同じ会社のだよ。秋葉原なら学生は半額で買えるんだ。音声ガイドも便利だし。グループ登録に²賛成！

Message #4

差出人：　えみこ

送信日：　4月5日

件　名：　RE: 新しい携帯

私、たくさんバイトしてるから、たろうと同じのに買いかえるわ。携帯番号はそのままでいいんでしょ？グループ登録するわ。

Message #5

差出人：　ひでき

送信日：　4月5日

件　名：　RE: 新しい携帯

ぼくのはテレビが見られるから、このままでいいや。

¹通話料 : the charge for a call
²賛成: agree

1. Which message is from someone who works part-time a lot?
   A. Message #1
   B. Message #2
   C. Message #3
   D. Message #4

2. Which message is from someone who took a trip?
   A. Message #1
   B. Message #2
   C. Message #4
   D. Message #5

3. Which message is from someone who bought a new cell phone?
   A. Message #1
   B. Message #2
   C. Message #3
   D. Message #4

4. Which message is from someone who has no intention of buying a new cell phone?
   A. Message #2
   B. Message #3
   C. Message #4
   D. Message #5

5. Why do they want to form a cellular group?
   A. It is easier.
   B. They can watch TV.
   C. The cost of cell phones is cheaper.
   D. They prefer to gather together.

Events and Fairs in Japan

LESSON 13

日本の年中行事と祭り

There are fifteen national holidays and various festivals in Japan. The biggest of these is **Shōgatsu**, the New Year's holiday. All temples toll a huge bell 108 times on New Year's Eve to atone for the 108 worldly passions of humans. You can go to the nearest temple and join in hitting the bell yourself, too. Then the Japanese start the celebration of beginning a new year. All people, companies, stores, banks, post offices and so on stop work, except for transportation, hospitals, and other essential services. The Japanese don't even clean house during this time, that is, they give a rest to brooms also.

A few examples of the other national holidays, festivals and events held all over Japan are **Seijin no hi** (Coming of Age Day, celebrating those who are turning 20 years old), **Setsubun** (celebrating the start of spring), **Hinamatsuri**, the doll festival (celebrating girls), **Kodomo no hi** (Children's Day, originally celebrating boys), **Tanabata** festival (the Star Festival), **Obon** (a Buddhist festival celebrating one's ancestors), and **Shichigosan** (the "7-5-3" fair celebrating children of those ages).

1 Introductory Quiz

Look at the item below and refer to the words in **Vocabulary**. Then try the following quiz.

Read this diary (日記 にっき) and answer the following question.

> 昨日友だちと神社のお祭りを見てきた。若い人が神輿（みこし）をかついでいた。子どもが太鼓（たいこ）をたたいていて、かわいかった。小さい店がたくさん出ていた。赤と白の幕（まく）をあちらこちらで見た。これは、お祝い（いわい）の時に使うそうだ。昔、日本には、伝統的な祭りがたくさんあったそうだが、少しずつなくなってきたようだ。昔からの文化がなくなるのは、ざんねんだと思う。日本で一番大きな行事というと、正月らしい。昔は、三日間は店も閉まってしまうので、その前に、買い物をして、おせち料理を作っておいたそうだ。大晦日（おおみそか）には、お寺へ行って、除夜（じょや）の鐘（かね）を打つそうだ。そうするとわるい考えが消え去るらしい。正月は、朝から神社へ初もうでに行って、一年間の無事（ぶじ）をいのる。一年の計は元旦（がんたん）にありと言って、その年の計画（けいかく）を立てたが、今は、そんな習慣（しゅうかん）もなくなってきているそうだ。

What did the author see yesterday? Write ○ (correct) or ✕ (wrong) in the spaces provided.

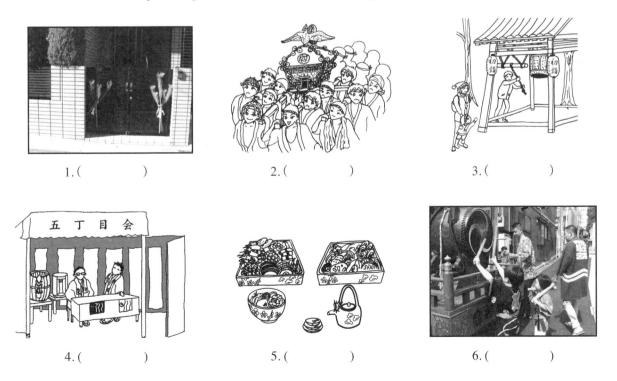

1. (   )   2. (   )   3. (   )

4. (   )   5. (   )   6. (   )

2 Vocabulary

Study the readings and meanings of these words to help you understand the **Introductory Quiz**.

1. 行事	ぎょう じ	**gyōji**	event
2. 昨日	きのう	**kinō**	yesterday
3. 神社	じん じゃ	**jinja**	a shrine
4. 若い	わか い	**wakai**	young
5. 神輿	み こし	**mikoshi**	a portable shrine
6. 太鼓	たい こ	**taiko**	Japanese drum
7. 赤	あか	**aka**	red
8. 幕	まく	**maku**	a curtain
9. 昔	むかし	**mukashi**	a long time ago
10. 伝統的な	でん とう てき な	**dentōteki na**	traditional
11. 少し	すこ し	**sukoshi**	a little
12. 文化	ぶん か	**bunka**	culture
13. 正月	しょう がつ	**shōgatsu**	New Year Day
14. おせち料理	おせち りょう り	**osechi ryōri**	festive food for the New Year
15. 大晦日	おお みそか	**ōmisoka**	the last day of the year, New Year's Eve
16. お寺	おてら	**otera**	temple
17. 除夜の鐘	じょ や の かね	**joya no kane**	a temple bell on New Year's Eve
18. 打つ	う つ	**utsu**	to hit, to strike
19. 消え去る	き え さる	**kie saru**	to disappear, to fade
20. 初もうで	はつ もうで	**hatsumōde**	the first visit of the year to a shrine
21. 無事	ぶ じ	**buji**	safety
22. 一年の計	いち ねん の けい	**ichinen no kei**	plans for the year
23. 元旦	がん たん	**gantan**	New Year's Day (January 1st)
24. 言う	い う	**iu**	to say, to tell
25. 計画	けい かく	**keikaku**	plan
26. 習慣	しゅう かん	**shūkan**	custom

3 New Characters

Eleven characters are introduced in this lesson. Use the explanations to help you understand and remember the characters. Study the compound words to increase your vocabulary.

昨 神 若 赤 昔 伝 的 少 化 打 言

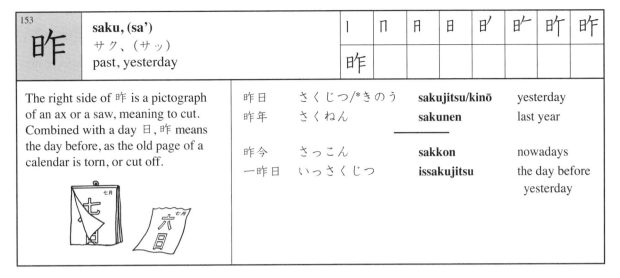

153 昨	**saku, (sa')** サク、(サッ) past, yesterday	一	冂	月	日	日′	旷	旷	昨
		昨							

The right side of 昨 is a pictograph of an ax or a saw, meaning to cut. Combined with a day 日, 昨 means the day before, as the old page of a calendar is torn, or cut off.	昨日	さくじつ/*きのう	**sakujitsu/kinō**	yesterday
	昨年	さくねん	**sakunen**	last year
	昨今	さっこん	**sakkon**	nowadays
	一昨日	いっさくじつ	**issakujitsu**	the day before yesterday

154 神	**kami, kan, shin, jin** かみ、かん、シン、ジン god, shrine	丶	ラ	ネ	ネ	ネ	礻刀	礻刀	神
		神							

神 combines altar ネ and heavenly speech 申.	神	かみ	**kami**	god
	神様	かみさま	**kamisama**	god
	神×輿	*みこし	**mikoshi**	portable shrine
	神父	しんぷ	**shimpu**	Catholic priest
	神経	しんけい	**shinkei**	nerve
	神道	しんとう	**Shintō**	Shinto(ism)
	神社	じんじゃ	**jinja**	shrine
	神主	かんぬし	**kannushi**	a Shinto priest

155 若	**waka-i, jaku, nyaku** わか・い、ジャク、ニャク young	一	十	艹	ヷ	芏	芉	若	若

Young 若 girls put a flower 艹 on the right 右 side of the head.	若い	わかい	**wakai**	young
	若者	わかもの	**wakamono**	young man
	若手	わかて	**wakate**	younger member
	若木	わかぎ	**wakagi**	young tree
	若年	じゃくねん	**jakunen**	young people

156 赤	aka, seki, shaku あか、セキ、シャク red	一	十	土	亍	亣	赤	赤		

赤 combines earth 土 and flame ⺝灬.
The color of burning magma is red.

赤	あか	**aka**	red
赤い	あかい	**akai**	red
赤ちゃん	あかちゃん	**akachan**	baby
赤道	せきどう	**sekidō**	equator
赤字	あかじ	**akaji**	deficit, the red
赤面	せきめん	**sekimen**	blush
赤十字	せきじゅうじ	**sekijūji**	Red Cross

157 昔	mukashi, seki, shaku むかし、セキ、シャク long ago	一	十	卅	艹	艹	苦	昔	昔	

昔 combines many days passed 卅
and days 日.

昔	むかし	**mukashi**	old time
昔話	むかしばなし	**mukashi banashi**	old tale
大昔	おおむかし	**ōmukashi**	ancient times
昔々	むかしむかし	**mukashi mukashi**	once upon a time
昔日	せきじつ	**sekijitsu**	long time ago

158 伝	tsuta-eru, den つた・える、デン convey, transmit	ノ	イ	仁	仁	伝	伝			

伝 combines a person イ and to speak
云, and means to convey a message.

伝える	つたえる	**tsutaeru**	to transmit
伝記	でんき	**denki**	biography
自伝	じでん	**jiden**	autobiography
伝説	でんせつ	**densetsu**	legend
伝言	でんごん	**dengon**	message
伝来	でんらい	**denrai**	being transmitted
以心伝心	いしんでんしん	**ishindenshin**	telepathy
家伝	かでん	**kaden**	family tradition

159 的	**mato, teki** まと、テキ target, attributive suffix	´	´	⺈	白	白	白´	的	的

的 combines a curved spot 勺 and painted white 白, suggesting target.

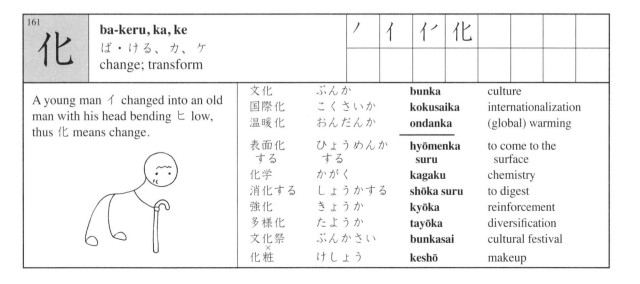

的_×	まと	**mato**	target
伝統的な	でんとうてきな	**dentōteki na**	traditional
目的	もくてき	**mokuteki**	purpose
一時的	いちじてき	**ichijiteki**	temporary
知的	ちてき	**chiteki**	intellectual
私的	してき	**shiteki**	private
自発的	じはつてき	**jihatsuteki**	voluntary
公的	こうてき	**kōteki**	public

160 少	**suko-shi, suku-nai, shō** すこ・し、すく・ない、ショウ few, a little	丿	小	小	少				

小, depicts a stick shaved on both sides to make it slender and small. A knife 丿 is added to suggest a small amount.

少し	すこし	**sukoshi**	a little
少ない	すくない	**sukunai**	few
少年	しょうねん	**shōnen**	boy
少女	しょうじょ	**shōjo**	girl
少々	しょうしょう	**shōshō**	a little
少しずつ	すこしずつ	**sukoshizutsu**	little by little
少数	しょうすう	**shōsū**	minority

161 化	**ba-keru, ka, ke** ば・ける、カ、ケ change; transform	丿	亻	亻´	化				

A young man 亻 changed into an old man with his head bending ヒ low, thus 化 means change.

文化	ぶんか	**bunka**	culture
国際化	こくさいか	**kokusaika**	internationalization
温暖化	おんだんか	**ondanka**	(global) warming
表面化する	ひょうめんかする	**hyōmenka suru**	to come to the surface
化学	かがく	**kagaku**	chemistry
消化する	しょうかする	**shōka suru**	to digest
強化	きょうか	**kyōka**	reinforcement
多様化	たようか	**tayōka**	diversification
文化祭	ぶんかさい	**bunkasai**	cultural festival
化粧_×	けしょう	**keshō**	makeup

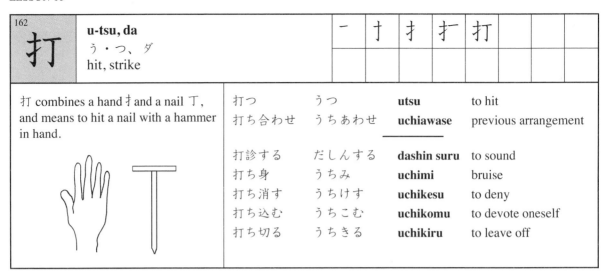

162 打	u-tsu, da う・つ、ダ hit, strike	一	十	扌	打	打			

打 combines a hand 扌 and a nail 丁, and means to hit a nail with a hammer in hand.	打つ	うつ	**utsu**	to hit
	打ち合わせ	うちあわせ	**uchiawase**	previous arrangement
	打診する	だしんする	**dashin suru**	to sound
	打ち身	うちみ	**uchimi**	bruise
	打ち消す	うちけす	**uchikesu**	to deny
	打ち込む	うちこむ	**uchikomu**	to devote oneself
	打ち切る	うちきる	**uchikiru**	to leave off

163 言	i-u, koto, (goto), gen い・う、こと、（ごと）、ゲン speak, word	、	二	亖	言	言	言	言	

言 combines something that comes out from the mouth 亖 and the mouth 口. Thus 言 means to speak.	言う	いう	**iu**	to say
	一言	ひとこと	**hitokoto**	a word
	小言	こごと	**kogoto**	scolding
	言い分	いいぶん	**iibun**	one's say
	発言	はつげん	**hatsugen**	remark
	方言	ほうげん	**hōgen**	dialect
	予言	よげん	**yogen**	prediction

4 ▶ Practice

I. Write the readings of the following kanji in hiragana.

1. 若者　　　　2. 昨年　　　　3. 目的　　　　4. 神

5. 少し　　　　6. 文化　　　　7. 打つ　　　　8. 赤

9. 今は、国際化の時代だと言われています。

10. 昔の伝統は、少なくなりました。

11. 一時から、打ち合わせをしましょう。

12. 一言、申し上げます。

II. Fill in the blanks with appropriate kanji.

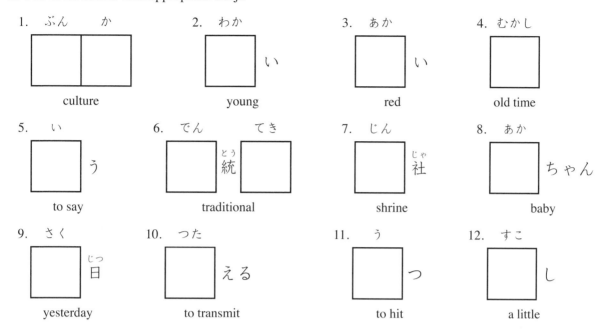

1. ぶん か
☐☐
culture

2. わか
☐ い
young

3. あか
☐ い
red

4. むかし
☐
old time

5. い
☐ う
to say

6. でん てき
☐ 統 ☐
とう
traditional

7. じん
☐ 社
じゃ
shrine

8. あか
☐ ちゃん
baby

9. さく
☐ 日
じっ
yesterday

10. つた
☐ える
to transmit

11. う
☐ つ
to hit

12. すこ
☐ し
a little

5 ▶ Advanced Placement Exam Practice Questions

Read the following conversation.

Akiko: 昨日はひな祭りだったね。皆でちらしずしを食べて、甘酒を飲んで、歌も歌ったりおもし
<small>あまざけ</small> <small>うた</small>
ろかったよ。みんなで若ちゃん、どうして来ないんだろうって言ってたんだよ。

Masako: そうよ。楽しかったよ。どうして若ちゃん来なかったの。

Wakako: 家じゃ、昔から伝わっているひな人形があって、いつも親類が集まることになっている
<small>にんぎょう</small> <small>しんるい</small>
ので、行かれなかったのよ。家の親類には、女が多いからね。

Akiko: そう。伝統的な人形なんだろうね。一度見たいなあ。

Kaori: それはそうと、昔は3月3日は、女の子の祭りで、5月5日は、こいのぼりを立てて、[1]しょ
うぶを入れたお風呂に入って、五月人形をかざって、男の子のお祭りだったのに、どうし
<small>ふろ</small>
て、5月5日が「子どもの日」になったんだろうね。不公平だね。

Wakako: 日本は、昔から男の社会だもの。[2]当たり前よ。
<small>あ</small>

Masako: 昭和の時は、4月29日が[3]天皇誕生日、5月3日が[4]憲法記念日だったから、続けて休み
<small>しょうわ</small> <small>てんのうたんじょうび</small> <small>けんぽうきねんび</small>
たかったんじゃないの。

Akiko: 5月は季節もいいしね。
<small>き</small>

Kaori: そうかなあ。何だか、分かんないな。

[1]しょうぶ: iris

[2]当たり前: natural

[3]天皇誕生日: The Emperor's Birthday

[4]憲法記念日: Constitution Memorial Day

(**Hinamatsuri**, March 3)

According to the conversation,

1. Who could not join the **Hinamatsuri** party?
   A. Akiko
   B. Masako
   C. Wakako
   D. Kaori

2. Who said that Japan is a man-based society as the reason for May 5, Children's Day?
   A. Akiko
   B. Masako
   C. Wakako
   D. Kaori

3. Who said that May 5th is one day of consecutive holidays?
   A. Akiko
   B. Masako
   C. Wakako
   D. Kaori

4. Who could not understand why May 5th is Children's Day?
   A. Akiko
   B. Masako
   C. Wakako
   D. Kaori

(**Kodomo no hi**, May 5)

6 ▶ Supplement

日本の祭日 (Japanese National Holidays)

1月1日	元旦	(**Gantan**)	New Year's Day
1月第2月曜日	成人の日	(**Seijin no hi**)	Coming of Age Day
2月11日	建国記念日	(**Kenkoku Kinembi**)	National Founding Day
3月21日*	春分の日	(**Shumbun no hi**)	Vernal Equinox Day
4月29日	昭和の日	(**Shōwa no hi**)	Showa Day
5月3日	憲法記念日	(**Kempō Kinembi**)	Constitution Memorial Day
5月4日	みどりの日	(**Midori no hi**)	Greenery Day
5月5日	子どもの日	(**Kodomo no hi**)	Children's Day
7月第3月曜日	海の日	(**Umi no hi**)	Marine Day

8月11日	山の日	**(Yama no hi)**	Mountain Day
9月15日	敬老の日	**(Keirō no hi)**	Respect for the Aged Day
9月23日*	秋分の日	**(Shūbun no hi)**	Autumnal Equinox Day
10月第2月曜日	体育の日	**(Taiiku no hi)**	Health and Sports Day
11月3日	文化の日	**(Bunka no hi)**	Culture Day
11月23日	勤労感謝の日	**(Kinrō Kansha no hi)**	Labor and Thanksgiving Day
12月23日	天皇誕生日	**(Tennō Tanjōbi)**	The Emperor's Birthday

*means that the day changes depending on the year.

Other festivals which are not holidays but very popular

(**Setsubun:** the day before the calendrical
beginning of spring, around February 3)

(**Tanabata:** the Star Festival, July 7)

(**Shichigosan:** the festival day
for children aged seven,
five and three, November 15)

Visiting Kyoto

京都へ行きます

Surrounded on three sides by mountains with the Kamo river in the center of the city, Kyoto is one of the most beautiful cities in Japan. Kyoto was established as Japan's capital city in the year 794; there are many old temples and palaces in Kyoto, with some having been selected as World Heritage Sites. In the famous temples and gardens, visitors are greeted by the beautiful work of genius artisans. Kyoto is also the place where many high school students go on their graduation trip. Besides visiting old temples, they often choose to experience wearing old costumes and making crafts. In this lesson, you will learn some of the kanji related to a trip to Kyoto.

1 ▶ Introductory Quiz

Look at the items below and refer to the words in **Vocabulary**. Then try the following quiz.

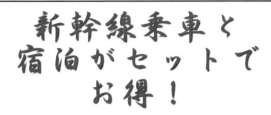

新幹線乗車と
宿泊がセットで
お得！

25000円~

春の旅　　京都＜1泊2日＞

一日目	東京駅 ⟶ 京都駅　京都泊  清水寺　 金閣寺 きれいな庭園と古い寺(世界遺産)をまわり、自由行動 宿泊は京都市内のホテル	夕食は 日本料理
二日目	京都駅 ⟶ 東京駅  龍安寺　石庭　　 二条城 午後はまいこ体験または映画村体験	朝食または 昼食付き
交通	往復東海道新幹線のぞみ号自由席利用	

わたしは　まいこに
なろうかしら。映画村
に行こうかしら。

Referring to the brochure (page 133) from a travel agent, write ○ for true or X for false in the spaces (   ).

1. 京都に二日泊まる。 （   ）
2. 2万5千円は新幹線とホテルの料金が入っている。 （   ）
3. 寺は一つだけ見る。 （   ）
4. 夕食は日本料理がついている。 （   ）
5. 朝食と昼食を食べることができる。 （   ）

2 ▸ Vocabulary

Study the readings and meanings of these words to help you understand the **Introductory Quiz**.

1.	新幹線	しん かん せん	**Shinkansen**	Super Express, bullet train
2.	乗車	じょう しゃ	**jōsha**	getting on a train
3.	宿泊	しゅく はく	**shukuhaku**	stay
4.	セット		**setto**	set
5.	得	とく	**toku**	economical; profit
6.	春の旅	はる の たび	**haru no tabi**	trip in spring
7.	1泊2日	いっ ぱく ふつか	**ippaku futsuka**	two-day trip, overnight trip
8.	泊	はく	**haku**	stay
9.	夕食	ゆう しょく	**yūshoku**	dinner
10.	日本料理	に ほん りょう り	**nihon ryōri**	Japanese food
11.	清水寺	きよ みず でら	**Kiyomizudera**	Kiyomizudera temple
12.	金閣寺	きん かく じ	**Kinkakuji**	Golden Pavilion temple
13.	庭園	てい えん	**teien**	garden
14.	世界遺産	せ かい い さん	**Sekai isan**	World Heritage Site
15.	自由行動	じ ゆう こう どう	**jiyū kōdō**	free time
16.	龍安寺	りょう あん じ	**Ryōanji**	Ryoanji temple
17.	石庭	せき てい	**sekitei**	stone garden
18.	二条城	に じょう じょう	**Nijōjō**	Nijojo Castle
19.	まいこ		**maiko**	apprentice geisha
20.	映画村	えい が むら	**eigamura**	movie village
21.	体験	たい けん	**taiken**	experience
22.	朝食	ちょう しょく	**chōshoku**	breakfast
23.	昼食付き	ちゅう しょく つき	**chūshoku tsuki**	lunch included
24.	交通	こう つう	**kōtsū**	transportation

25.	往復	おう ふく	**ōfuku**	to and from; two-way
26.	東海道	とう かい どう	**Tōkaidō**	Tokaido (railway line name)
27.	自由席	じ ゆう せき	**jiyūseki**	non-reserved seat

3 New Characters

Thirteen characters are introduced in this lesson. Use the explanations to help you understand and remember the characters. Study the compound words to increase your vocabulary.

幹 乗 宿 泊 得 夕 寺 由 石 庭 朝 昼 海

---

164 幹

miki, kan
みき、カン
main part, trunk

| 一 | 十 | 十 | 古 | 吉 | 直 | 草 |
| 卓 | 幹 | 幹 | 幹 | 幹 | | |

Tree trunks 幹 are used to dry 干 the laundry in the morning when the sun 日 is low in the grass 十.

新幹線	しんかんせん	**Shinkansen**	Super Express, bullet train
木の幹	きのみき	**ki no miki**	trunk
幹部	かんぶ	**kambu**	executive
幹事	かんじ	**kanji**	organizer

---

165 乗

no-ru, no-seru, jō
の・る、の・せる、ジョウ
get on, ride

| 一 | 二 | 三 | 千 | 乎 | 垂 | 垂 |
| 乗 | | | | | | |

乗 was originally written with two people 扌 and ヒ on a tree 木, 乗. Thus 乗 means to get on.

乗る	のる	**noru**	to get on
乗車券	じょうしゃけん	**jōshaken**	passenger ticket
乗用車	じょうようしゃ	**jōyōsha**	passenger car
乗り場	のりば	**noriba**	(taxi) stand, (ship) pier, (bus) stop
便乗する	びんじょうする	**binjō suru**	to take advantage of

135

166 宿

yado, yado-ru, shuku, (juku)
やど、やど・る、シュク、（ジュク）
lodging, inn

`	゛	宀	宀	宀	宀	宀	宀
宿	宿	宿					

One hundred 百 people イ in a house 宀 indicates a lodge.

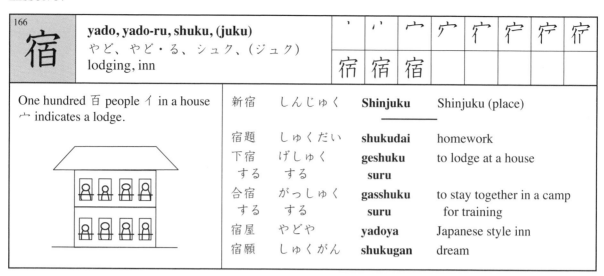

新宿	しんじゅく	**Shinjuku**	Shinjuku (place)
宿題	しゅくだい	**shukudai**	homework
下宿 する	げしゅく する	**geshuku suru**	to lodge at a house
合宿 する	がっしゅく する	**gasshuku suru**	to stay together in a camp for training
宿屋	やどや	**yadoya**	Japanese style inn
宿願	しゅくがん	**shukugan**	dream

167 泊

to-maru, haku, (paku)
と・まる、ハク、（パク）
stay, lodge

`	冫	シ	ジ	汀	泊	泊	泊

A boat anchors in shallow, white 白 water 氵 to stay.

泊まる	とまる	**tomaru**	to put up for the night
一泊	いっぱく	**ippaku**	overnight stay
宿泊	しゅくはく	**shukuhaku**	stay, lodging
泊まり客	とまりきゃく	**tomarikyaku**	houseguest
外泊する	がいはくする	**gaihaku suru**	to stay out over-night

168 得

e-ru, u-ru, toku, (doku)
え・る、う・る、トク、（ドク）
gain

ノ	ク	イ	彳	彳	彳	彳	彳
彳	得	得					

Go 彳 to catch shellfish 旦 by hand 寸, means to catch something valuable, or to gain something.

得る	える	**eru**	to gain
得	とく	**toku**	economical, profit
お買い得	おかいどく	**okaidoku**	bargain
得意な	とくいな	**tokui na**	be good at
不得意な	ふとくいな	**futokui na**	be not good at
所得	しょとく	**shotoku**	income
得点	とくてん	**tokuten**	score
お得意さま	おとくいさま	**otokui sama**	customer
説得	せっとく	**settoku**	persuasion
説得力	せっとくりょく	**settokuryoku**	persuasive

136

169 夕	yū, seki ゆう、セキ evening	ノ	ク	夕					

| | | | | | | | | | |

This is a pictograph of the moon just above a mountain in the evening.

夕食	ゆうしょく	**yūshoku**	supper, dinner
夕方	ゆうがた	**yūgata**	evening
夕日	ゆうひ	**yūhi**	setting sun
朝夕	あさゆう	**asayū**	mornings and evenings
夕立	ゆうだち	**yūdachi**	afternoon shower
夕月	ゆうづき	**yūzuki**	evening moon

170 寺	tera, ji てら、ジ temple	一	十	土	寺	寺	寺		

土 soil and 寸 hand suggest work. A place where priests work is a temple.

寺	てら	**tera**	temple
金閣寺	きんかくじ	**Kinkakuji**	Golden Pavilion temple
清水寺	きよみずでら	**Kiyomizudera**	Kiyomizudera temple
寺社	じしゃ	**jisha**	temples and shrines
山寺	やまでら	**yamadera**	mountain temple
古寺	ふるでら	**furudera**	old temple

171 由	yoshi, yū, yu, yui よし、ユウ，ユ、ユイ reason, cause	l	口	巾	由	由			

由 is the pictograph of a wine jar with the mouth protruding from the center, out of which wine is poured. Thus 由 means a cause of the outcome.

自由	じゆう	**jiyū**	free, freedom
不自由	ふじゆう	**fujiyū**	discomfort; want
自由席	じゆうせき	**jiyūseki**	non-reserved seat
理由	りゆう	**riyū**	reason
由来	ゆらい	**yurai**	origin
自由化	じゆうか	**jiyūka**	liberalization
自由業	じゆうぎょう	**jiyūgyō**	freelance occupation
経由	けいゆ	**keiyu**	by way of

137

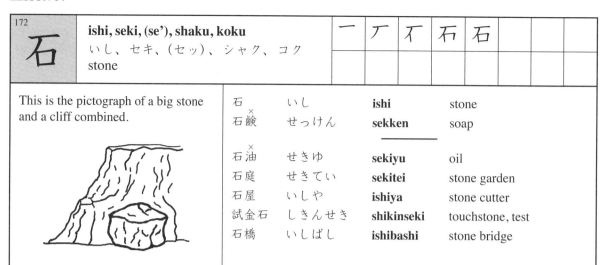

| 172 石 | ishi, seki, (se'), shaku, koku
いし、セキ、（セッ）、シャク、コク
stone | 一 | 丆 | 丆 | 石 | 石 |

This is the pictograph of a big stone and a cliff combined.

石	いし	**ishi**	stone
石鹸	せっけん	**sekken**	soap
石油	せきゆ	**sekiyu**	oil
石庭	せきてい	**sekitei**	stone garden
石屋	いしや	**ishiya**	stone cutter
試金石	しきんせき	**shikinseki**	touchstone, test
石橋	いしばし	**ishibashi**	stone bridge

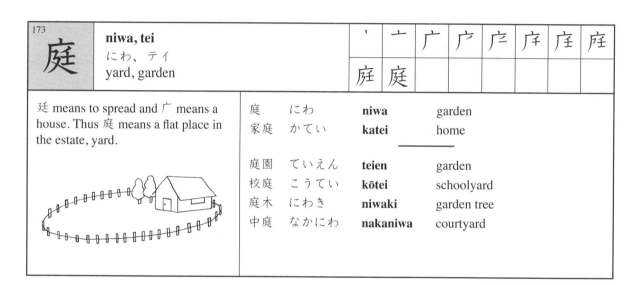

| 173 庭 | niwa, tei
にわ、テイ
yard, garden | 丶 | 亠 | 广 | 疒 | 庐 | 庑 | 庭 | 庭 |
| | | 庭 | 庭 | | | | | | |

廷 means to spread and 广 means a house. Thus 庭 means a flat place in the estate, yard.

庭	にわ	**niwa**	garden
家庭	かてい	**katei**	home
庭園	ていえん	**teien**	garden
校庭	こうてい	**kōtei**	schoolyard
庭木	にわき	**niwaki**	garden tree
中庭	なかにわ	**nakaniwa**	courtyard

| 174 朝 | asa, chō
あさ、チョウ
morning | 一 | 十 | 十 | 古 | 吉 | 卓 | 車 | 卓 |
| | | 軯 | 朝 | 朝 | 朝 | | | | |

In the morning, the sun 日 is between the trees 十 and the moon 月 can still be seen.

朝	あさ	**asa**	morning
今朝	*けさ	**kesa**	this morning
朝食	ちょうしょく	**chōshoku**	breakfast
毎朝	まいあさ	**maiasa**	every morning
朝日	あさひ	**asahi**	morning sun
朝日新聞	あさひしんぶん	**Asahi Shimbun**	Asahi Daily News

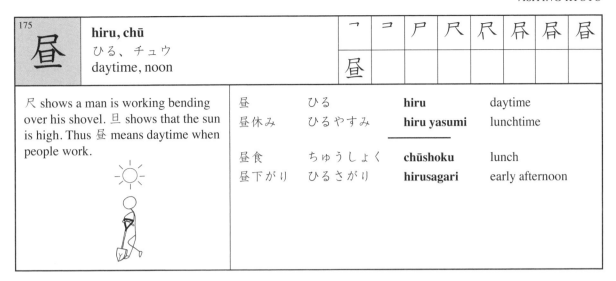

175 昼	**hiru, chū** ひる、チュウ daytime, noon	ㄱ	ㄱ	尸	尺	尺	尽	昼	昼
		昼							

昼	ひる	**hiru**	daytime
昼休み	ひるやすみ	**hiru yasumi**	lunchtime
昼食	ちゅうしょく	**chūshoku**	lunch
昼下がり	ひるさがり	**hirusagari**	early afternoon

尺 shows a man is working bending over his shovel. 旦 shows that the sun is high. Thus 昼 means daytime when people work.

176 海	**umi, kai** うみ、カイ sea	`	⸴	氵	汀	汇	汄	洵	海
		海							

Every 每 river, or water 氵, empties into the sea.

海	うみ	**umi**	sea
海外	かいがい	**kaigai**	overseas
海水	かいすい	**kaisui**	sea water
海面	かいめん	**kaimen**	sea level
日本海	にほんかい	**Nihonkai**	the Sea of Japan
東海道 新幹線	とうかいどう しんかんせん	**Tōkaidō** **Shinkansen**	Tokaido Super Express
大海	たいかい	**taikai**	ocean

4 ▶ Practice

I. Write the readings of the following kanji in hiragana.

1. 木 の 幹 2. 乗 車 券 3. 一 泊 4. 新 宿
5. 石 鹸（けん） 6. 不 自 由
7. 学 校 で 多 く の 友 だ ち を 得 ま し た 。
8. 寺 に 泊 ま る こ と が で き ま す 。
9. 昼 休 み は 海 の 見 え る レ ス ト ラ ン へ 行 き ま し た 。
10. 夕 方 、 庭 を さ ん ぽ し ま す 。
11. 今 朝 、 連 絡 が き ま し た 。

II. Fill in the blanks with appropriate kanji.

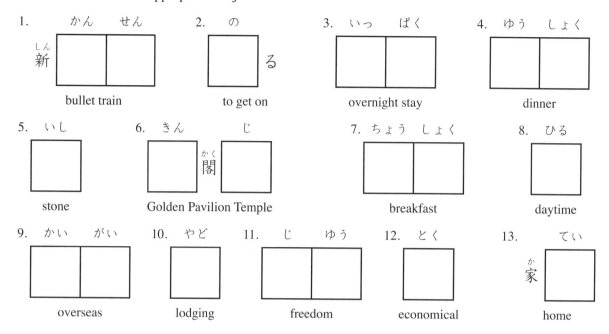

1. かん せん 新□□ bullet train	2. の □る to get on	3. いっ ぱく □□ overnight stay	4. ゆう しょく □□ dinner
5. いし □ stone	6. きん じ □閣□ Golden Pavilion Temple	7. ちょう しょく □□ breakfast	8. ひる □ daytime
9. かい がい □□ overseas	10. やど □ lodging	11. じ ゆう □□ freedom	12. とく □ economical	13. てい 家□ home

5 ▸ Advanced Placement Exam Practice Questions

These are the messages students wrote on the board of a high school's homepage about their trip to Kyoto. Read them and answer the questions.

Message #1

去年は友だちと丸山公園の桜を見ました。すごくきれいだった。今年は、まいこの体験がよかった。見ているときれいだけど、¹カツラが重くて大変な仕事だと思った。

【高3女子　ようこ】

Message #2

京都には何回も行きました。清水寺はいつ行ってもいいなと思います。今回は宿のホテルがよかった。朝食もおいしかったですよ。

【教師】

Message #3

私は²庭園めぐりコースで行った寺の石庭がよかった。石だけで³宇宙を⁴表すなんて、すごい。

【高2女子　まりこ】

Message #4

私は京都は二度目でした。 去年、家族と⁵平安神宮や嵐山の桜をみてとてもよかった。今年は、⁶観光タクシーに乗って映画村へ行った。⁷忍者はおもしろいけど、⁸訓練が大変だろうな。

【高3男子　あきひこ】

Message #5

ぼくは何といっても東海道新幹線。小さいときから鉄道が好きなんだ。

【高2男子　いちろう】

¹カツラ: wig

²庭園めぐりコース: route of garden tour

³宇宙: cosmos

⁴表す: show

⁵平安神宮: Heian shrine

⁶観光タクシー: sightseeing taxi

⁷忍者: ninja, spy

⁸訓練: training

1. Which messages are from people who say "cherry blossoms were good"?
   A. Message #1 and Message #2.
   B. Message #1 and Message #3.
   C. Message #1 and Message #4.
   D. Message #1 and Message #5.

2. Which messages are from people who went to Kyoto more than once?
   A. Message #1, #2 and #3.
   B. Message #1, #2 and #4.
   C. Message #1, #2 and #5.
   D. Message #2, #3 and #4.

3. Which messages are from people who say they were "impressed by the temples"?
   A. Message #1 and Message #2.
   B. Message #1 and Message #3.
   C. Message #1 and Message #4.
   D. Message #2 and Message #3.

4. Based on this message board, which of the following is correct?
   A. The teacher said only the hotel was good.
   B. To experience a real **maiko** costume was good, because the wig was so heavy.
   C. The stone garden was impressive because it expresses the cosmos using only stones.
   D. To train to be a **ninja** may not be difficult.

Going to Onsen

温泉に行きます

As you may know, there are many volcanoes in Japan. In these areas there are natural hot springs, called **onsen**. For centuries, **onsen** have been used to help heal wounded soldiers and relax tired farmers. In more modern times **onsen** visits have been principally thought of as a pastime of the elderly, but more recently, the **onsen** has become more popular among the young. Of course, luxurious hotels in the famous **onsen** areas have their own private **onsen**, but there are also many public baths such as Hakone and around Mt. Fuji, which are approximately an hour and half from Tokyo by car. These public **onsen** tend to be very crowded with young people during national holidays.

1 ▶ Introductory Quiz

Look at the illustrations (page 143) and refer to the words in **Vocabulary**. Then try the following quiz.

Two girls are talking about the short trip to the hot springs. Choose the appropriate dialogue portion (A–G) for each illustration.

Dialogue A

B: なんだか美人になったみたいね。

A: きのう、日帰りで、温泉へ行ってきたの。

Dialogue B

A: きのうは朝早く起きて、河口湖行きのバスに乗ったの。

Dialogue C

B: どんなところだった。

A: とてもきれいな 湖 で、中には小さな島があったわ。

Dialogue D

A: 鳥がないていて、自然がいっぱいだったわ。

Dialogue E

A: そのあと、村営の温泉へ行ったのよ。ろてん風呂から富士山が見えてすごく気分がよかった。

Dialogue F

B: ご飯はどうしたの。

A: 晩ご飯は温泉のレストランで食べたのよ。

Dialogue G

B: 泊まらなかったの。

A: ええ、夜遅く帰って、うちで寝たの。

1. (   )   2. (   )   3. (   )

4. (   )   5. (   )   6. (   )   7. (   )

2 ▶ Vocabulary

Study the readings and meanings of these words to help you understand the **Introductory Quiz**.

1.	美人	び じん	**bijin**	beauty
2.	日帰り	ひ が え り	**higaeri**	day trip
3.	温泉	おん せん	**onsen**	spa; hot springs
4.	朝	あさ	**asa**	morning
5.	早い	はや い	**hayai**	early
6.	起きる	お きる	**okiru**	to get up
7.	河口湖	かわ ぐ ち こ	**Kawaguchiko**	Lake Kawaguchi

143

8.	乗る	のる	**noru**	to take, ride in
9.	湖	みずうみ	**mizuumi**	lake
10.	島	しま	**shima**	island
11.	静かな	しずかな	**shizuka na**	quiet
12.	自然	しぜん	**shizen**	nature
13.	いっぱい		**ippai**	full of
14.	村営	そんえい	**son'ei**	run by a village
15.	ろてん風呂	ろてんぶろ	**rotenburo**	outside bath
16.	富士山	ふじさん	**Fujisan**	Mount Fuji
17.	気分	きぶん	**kibun**	feeling
18.	ご飯	ごはん	**gohan**	meal
19.	晩	ばん	**ban**	evening
20.	泊まる	とまる	**tomaru**	to stay
21.	夜	よる	**yoru**	night
22.	遅い	おそい	**osoi**	late
23.	寝る	ねる	**neru**	to sleep

3 ▶ New Characters

Ten characters are introduced in this lesson. Use the explanations to help you understand and remember the characters. Study the compound words to increase your vocabulary.

早 起 島 静 然 村 飯 晩 夜 寝

177 早	**haya-i, sō, sa'** はや・い、ソウ、サッ early	丶	口	曰	日	旦	早	

The sun 日 is rising just above a field of plants 木 early in the morning.

早い	はやい	**hayai**	early
早春	そうしゅん	**sōshun**	early spring
早々に	そうそうに	**sōsō ni**	early, immediate
早期発見	そうきはっけん	**sōki hakken**	early detection
早めに	はやめに	**hayame ni**	a little early

144

178 起

o-kiru, o-kosu, ki
お・きる、お・こす、キ
awakening, rise, get up

一	十	土	丰	丰	走	走	起
起	起						

起 combines rise 己 and run 走, and means to rise up.

起きる	おきる	**okiru**	to get up
早起き	はやおき	**hayaoki**	early bird
起立する	きりつ	**kiritsu**	to stand up
起用する	きようする	**kiyō suru**	to appoint
起点	きてん	**kiten**	starting point
起工式	きこうしき	**kikōshiki**	ground breaking ceremony

179 島

shima, tō
しま、トウ
island

′	亻	宀	户	白	自	鳥	島
島	島						

鳥 is the pictograph of a bird. Combined with 山 mountain, 島 means island with a mountain where massive birds alight for nesting.

島	しま	**shima**	island
広島	ひろしま	**Hiroshima**	Hiroshima (place)
半島	はんとう	**hantō**	peninsula
島国	しまぐに	**shimaguni**	island country
無人島	むじんとう	**mujintō**	uninhabited island
本島	ほんとう	**hontō**	main island
全島	ぜんとう	**zentō**	the whole island

180 静

shizu-ka, shizu-maru, shizu, sei, jō
しず・か、しず・まる、しず、セイ、ジョウ
quiet

一	十	丰	主	青	青	青	青
青	青	静	静	静	静		

静 combines blue 青 and war 争 and suggests the calm peace after the war.

静かな	しずかな	**shizuka na**	quiet
冷静	れいせい	**reisei**	calmness
安静	あんせい	**ansei**	rest
静物	せいぶつ	**seibutsu**	still life
静止	せいし	**seishi**	stillness
平静	へいせい	**heisei**	calmness
静的	せいてき	**seiteki**	static
静脈	じょうみゃく	**jōmyaku**	vein

181 然	zen, nen ゼン、ネン as, like, correct	ノ	ク	タ	タ	ター	夕	然	然
		然	然	然	然				

然 combines the flesh 月 of dog 犬 and flame 灬, and originally meant to burn. Later it came to mean correct.

自然	しぜん	**shizen**	nature
全然	ぜんぜん	**zenzen**	not at all
		———	
天然	てんねん	**tennen**	natural
平然	へいぜん	**heizen**	calm
公然	こうぜん	**kōzen**	open, frank
必然	ひつぜん	**hitsuzen**	inevitability

182 村	mura, son むら、ソン village	一	十	オ	木	朮	村	村	

村 village combines tree 木 and rule 寸, suggesting a place with trees where people live following the same rules.

村	むら	**mura**	village
村営	そんえい	**son'ei**	run by a village
		———	
村人	むらびと	**murabito**	villager
寒村	かんそん	**kanson**	poor village
村落	そんらく	**sonraku**	village
村有	そんゆう	**son'yū**	village-owned
村道	そんどう	**sondō**	village road

183 飯	meshi, han めし、ハン meal, cooked rice	ノ	ハ	仁	今	今	今	食	食
		飣	飣	飯	飯				

飯 combines opposite 反 and food 食, and means meal, because 反 suggests the returning movement of the hands in eating 食.

ご飯	ごはん	**gohan**	meal, cooked rice
夕飯	ゆうはん	**yūhan**	supper, dinner
		———	
昼ご飯	ひるごはん	**hirugohan**	lunch
赤飯	せきはん	**sekihan**	(festive) rice cooked with red beans
晩飯	ばんめし	**bammeshi**	supper, dinner
昼飯	ひるめし	**hirumeshi**	lunch

184 晩

ban
バン
evening

丨	冂	月	日	日ˊ	日ク	日ク	日免
晚	晚	晚	晚				

晚 combines a woman giving birth 免, which is hard, and a day 日, suggesting evening when it is hard to see.

晚	ばん	**ban**	evening
晩ご飯	ばんごはん	**bangohan**	supper, dinner
毎晩	まいばん	**maiban**	every night
晩年	ばんねん	**bannen**	latter part of one's life
晩秋	ばんしゅう	**banshū**	late fall

185 夜

yoru, yo, ya
よる、よ、ヤ
night

`	亠	广	疒	疒	夜	夜	夜

夜 combines a person イ, a house 亠, and the moon 月, suggesting a person in the house at night.

夜	よる	**yoru**	night
今夜	こんや	**kon'ya**	tonight
昨夜	さくや	**sakuya**	last night
夜間	やかん	**yakan**	during the night
夜学	やがく	**yagaku**	evening class
夜行	やこう	**yakō**	night train
夜明け	よあけ	**yoake**	dawn

186 寝

ne-ru, ne-kasu, shin
ね・る、ね・かす、シン
sleep

`	ˋ	宀	宀	宀	宀	疒	宀
宀	宀	疒	寝	寝			

寝 combines a house 宀, to go to the inner part 㑋 and a bed 丬. Thus 寝 means to sleep.

寝る	ねる	**neru**	to sleep
寝室	しんしつ	**shinshitsu**	bedroom
寝台	しんだい	**shindai**	bed
寝台車	しんだいしゃ	**shindaisha**	sleeping car

4 ▶ **Practice**

I. Write the readings of the following kanji in hiragana.

1. 広 島　　　　　　2. 安 静　　　　　　　3. 毎 晩　　　　　　4. 今 夜
5. 寝 室　　　　　6. 朝 早 く 起 き ま し た 。
7. い そ が し く て 、 テ ス ト の 勉 強 が 全 然 で き ま せ ん で し た 。
8. み な さ ん 、 静 か に し て く だ さ い 。
9. 村 の レ ス ト ラ ン で 夕 飯 を 食 べ ま し た 。

II. Fill in the blanks with appropriate kanji.

1. はや　　　　　2. お　　　　　　3. しま　　　4. しず　　　　5. し　　　ぜん

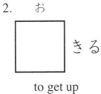
い

きる

か

nature

early　　　　　　　to get up　　　　island　　　　quiet　　　　　nature

6. むら　　　　　7. ばん　　　はん　　　　8. よる　　　　9. ね

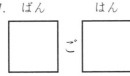
ご

る

village　　　　　　dinner　　　　　　　night　　　　　to sleep

5 ▶ Advanced Placement Exam Practice Questions

This is a letter about a high school trip. Read it and answer the questions.

¹一日スキー教室のお知らせ

父母の皆様へ

　きびしい寒さが続いておりますが、皆様お元気でいらっしゃいますか。
さて、桜高校では春休み、一年生と二年生のために一日スキー教室を計画し
ています。自然がいっぱいの富士山でスキーを楽しんだ後、静かな小川村温泉
で体を休めます。晩ご飯を食べて、夜少し遅く帰って来ます。どうぞ皆さん
²参加してください。

日：	3月10日（土曜）
時間：	集合　午前6時半　出発　午前7時
³解散：	午後9時半ごろ
⁴集合場所：	玄関前
往復：	⁵貸し切りバス
目的地：	富士山ろくスキー場および温泉「ゆったり」
費用：	6,500円　バス代、夕食代、スキーレンタル料⁶含む
	（昼食は各自）

＊父母の皆様が⁷現地へ連れて来られてもいいですが、費用は変わりません。

¹一日スキー教室: one day ski class　　　²参加: participation　　　³解散: breakup
⁴集合場所: meeting place　　　⁵貸し切りバス: chartered bus　　　⁶含む: including　　　⁷現地: the spot

1. When does the bus leave?
   A. 6:00 A.M.
   B. 6:30 A.M.
   C. 7:00 A.M.
   D. 9:30 A.M.

2. The 6,500 yen cost includes
   A. the cost of supper, bus fare, and ski rental.
   B. the cost of supper and ski rental only.
   C. the cost of lunch and bus fare.
   D. the cost of lunch and ski rental.

3. Students will enjoy
   A. only skiing.
   B. only hot springs.
   C. both skiing and hot springs.
   D. either skiing or hot springs.

4. Based on the informational letter, choose the correct sentence from below.
   A. Participating students must take the chartered bus.
   B. If parents drive their children there, they will get back their money.
   C. Parents can drive their children to and from the ski lesson if they wish.
   D. Parents can drive their children there, but they won't get back their money.

What's Wrong?

どこが痛いですか

When you feel sick, it might be best to go to the doctor's office, clinic or nearby hospital. Doctor's offices and clinics usually have a simple system and reception hours tend to be longer, while hospitals require a letter of introduction and are always crowded with patients. If something more serious is found in the examination at the doctor's office, he or she will give you a letter of introduction to the hospital. In this lesson, you will learn several kanji related to the body and illness.

1 ▶ Introductory Quiz

Look at the illustrations below and refer to the words in **Vocabulary**. Then try the following quiz.

I. 体の調子が悪いときは、病院へ行きましょう。そうすれば、早く治ります

Fill in the parentheses with the correct letters (a–f).

1.（　　　　）　　　　2.（　　　　）　　　　3.（　　　　）

4. (   )   5. (   )   6. (   )

a. 頭が痛い   b. 顔色が悪い   c. 鼻水が出る

d. 足が痛い   e. 背中が痛い   f. 熱がある

II. 赤ちゃんは元気がいいと、よく笑います。熱があったり、どこか痛いと泣きます。もちろん、おなかがすいたときも泣きます。

Fill in the parentheses with the correct letters (a–d).

1. (   )   2. (   )   3. (   )   4. (   )

a. 泣いている   b. 笑っている   c. 体が弱い   d. 元気な赤ちゃん

2 ▶ Vocabulary

Study the readings and meanings of these words to help you understand the **Introductory Quiz**.

1. 体	からだ	**karada**	body, health
2. 調子	ちょうし	**chōshi**	condition
3. 悪い	わるい	**warui**	bad
4. 病院	びょういん	**byōin**	hospital
5. 治る	なおる	**naoru**	to get well, to recover
6. 頭	あたま	**atama**	head
7. 痛い	いたい	**itai**	to have a pain
8. 顔色	かおいろ	**kaoiro**	complexion
9. 鼻水	はなみず	**hanamizu**	nasal mucus
10. 足	あし	**ashi**	leg, foot
11. 背中	せなか	**senaka**	back

12. 熱	ねつ	**netsu**	fever
13. 元気	げんき	**genki**	fine, well
14. 笑う	わらう	**warau**	to laugh
15. 泣く	なく	**naku**	to cry
16. 弱い	よわい	**yowai**	weak

3 ▷ New Characters

Thirteen characters are introduced in this lesson. Use the explanations to help you understand and remember the characters. Study the compound words to increase your vocabulary.

悪 治 頭 痛 顔 鼻 足 背 熱 元 笑 泣 弱

| 187 悪 | **waru-i, aku, o**
わる・い、アク、オ
bad | 一 | 厂 | 亓 | 冃 | 更 | 亜 | 亜 | 亜 |
| | | 悪 | 悪 | 悪 | | | | | |

悪 combines to press a heart 心 with a heavy weight 亜. Thus 悪 means bad.

悪い	わるい	**warui**	bad
悪法	あくほう	**akuhō**	bad law
悪用	あくよう	**akuyō**	misuse
悪人	あくにん	**akunin**	villain
悪名	あくめい	**akumei**	notoriety
悪習	あくしゅう	**akushū**	bad habit
悪相	あくそう	**akusō**	evil face
悪寒	おかん	**okan**	chill

| 188 治 | **nao-ru, osa-meru, chi, ji**
なお・る、おさ・める、チ、ジ
healing, govern | ` | 氵 | 氵 | 汀 | 治 | 治 | 治 | 治 |
| | | | | | | | | | |

台 adds a stick to plough with ム and word 口, meaning to do something good with tools and words. Combined with water 氵, 治 means to govern, because to govern the water was to govern the country in ancient times.

治る	なおる	**naoru**	to get well
治安	ちあん	**chian**	security
治水	ちすい	**chisui**	flood control
自治	じち	**jichi**	self government
明治時代	めいじじだい	**Meiji jidai**	Meiji Era
治める	おさめる	**osameru**	to govern

189 頭

atama, kashira, tō, to, zu
あたま、かしら、トウ、ト、ズ
head; leader

一	厂	戸	豆	巨	亘	豆	豆
豆	豇	豇	頭	頭	頭	頭	頭

頭 combines the phonetic sign 豆 and a head 頁, suggesting head.

頭	あたま	**atama**	head
先頭	せんとう	**sentō**	the front
		———	
頭上注意	ずじょうちゅうい	**zujō chūi**	watch your head
頭取	とうどり	**tōdori**	president of a bank
番頭	ばんとう	**bantō**	head clerk

---

190 痛

ita-i, ita-mu, tsū
いた・い、いた・む、ツウ
pain

丶	亠	广	广	疒	疒	疒	疒
疒	疔	痛	痛				

痛 combines sickness 疒 and to go through 甬, suggesting the pain that runs through the body.

痛い	いたい	**itai**	to have a pain, sore
頭痛	ずつう	**zutsū**	headache
		———	
痛み止め	いたみどめ	**itamidome**	painkiller
痛手	いたで	**itade**	severe wound
痛切に	つうせつに	**tsūsetsu ni**	keenly
痛快な	つうかいな	**tsūkai na**	exciting

---

191 顔

kao, (gao), gan
かお、（がお）、ガン
face

丶	亠	立	产	立	产	彦	彦
彦	彦	顔	顔	顔	顔	顔	顔

顔 combines head 頁, which in ancient times meant forehead, and a man 彦, suggesting a person's face.

顔	かお	**kao**	face
顔色	かおいろ	**kaoiro**	complexion
		———	
顔面	がんめん	**gammen**	face
新顔	しんがお	**shingao**	newcomer
丸顔	まるがお	**marugao**	round face
横顔	よこがお	**yokogao**	profile
顔立ち	かおだち	**kaodachi**	countenance

192 鼻	hana, bi はな、ビ nose	´	⺊	冂	白	白	自	自	鳥
		鳥	畠	畠	畠	鼻	鼻		

鼻 combines a nose 自, with the lower part of the character only showing the pronunciation. 自 is a pictograph of a nose.	鼻	はな	**hana**	nose
	鼻水	はなみず	**hanamizu**	nasal mucus
	鼻声	はなごえ	**hanagoe**	nasal voice
	鼻紙	はながみ	**hanagami**	tissue paper
	鼻歌	はなうた	**hanauta**	humming
	鼻炎	びえん	**bien**	rhinitis

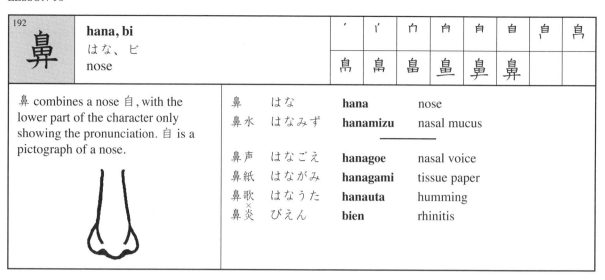

193 足	ashi, ta-riru, ta-su, soku あし、た・りる、た・す、ソク leg, enough	丶	ロ	口	⻊	⻊	⻊	足

足 is a pictograph of a knee 口 and the lower part of the leg 止.	足	あし	**ashi**	leg
	足りる	たりる	**tariru**	enough
	遠足	えんそく	**ensoku**	excursion
	不足	ふそく	**fusoku**	not enough
	一足	いっそく	**issoku**	a pair of (shoes)
	足下	あしもと	**ashimoto**	at one's feet
	土足	どそく	**dosoku**	with shoes on
	発足	ほっそく／ はっそく	**hossoku/ hassoku**	start
	足場	あしば	**ashiba**	footing

194 背	se, sei, somu-ku, hai せ、せい、そむ・く、ハイ back, height, defy	一	⺈	⺌	⽌	北	北	背	背
		背							

背 combines two people sitting back to back 北, and a body 月, suggesting the back of the body.	背	せ	**se**	back; height
	背中	せなか	**senaka**	back
	背広	せびろ	**sebiro**	business suit
	背後	はいご	**haigo**	behind
	背く	そむく	**somuku**	to defy

195 熱

			一	十	土	尹	尹	走	幸	幸
	atsu-i, netsu, (ne')									
	あつ・い、ネツ、（ネッ）		刲	埶	埶	埶	熱	熱	熱	
	heat, fever									

熱 combines the round 丸 earth 土 and flame 灬. The inside of the earth is burning hot.

熱い	あつい	**atsui**	hot
熱	ねつ	**netsu**	fever
熱心な	ねっしんな	**nesshin na**	enthusiastic
高熱	こうねつ	**kōnetsu**	high fever
熱湯	ねっとう	**nettō**	boiling water
熱意	ねつい	**netsui**	enthusiasm
平熱	へいねつ	**heinetsu**	normal temperature
熱気	ねっき	**nekki**	heated atmosphere

196 元

			一	二	テ	元				
	moto, gan, gen									
	もと、ガン、ゲン									
	origin, foundation									

儿 suggests body, emphasizing the legs, and 二 suggests the head. The head is thought to be the origin of human beings.

元気	げんき	**genki**	fine, well
元日	がんじつ	**ganjitsu**	New Year's Day
身元	みもと	**mimoto**	one's background
元本	がんぽん	**gampon**	the capital
親元	おやもと	**oyamoto**	parents' home
元年	がんねん	**gannen**	the first year
三次元	さんじげん	**sanjigen**	three dimensions
元外相	もと	**moto**	former minister of
	がいしょう	**gaishō**	foreign affairs
地元	じもと	**jimoto**	locality

197 笑

			ノ	ト	ト	ヒ	ㄌㄌ	竹	竹	竺
	wara-u, e-mu, shō									
	わら・う、え・む、ショウ		竿	笑						
	laugh, smile									

笑 combines bamboo 竹 and a variation of the character for dog 犬. People laugh to see a dog with a bamboo hat on.

笑う	わらう	**warau**	to laugh
笑顔	えがお	**egao**	smiling face
大笑い	おおわらい	**ōwarai**	loud laughter
冷笑	れいしょう	**reishō**	scornful laugh
ほほ笑む	ほほえむ	**hohoemu**	to smile

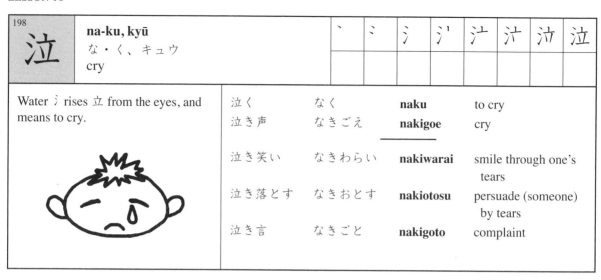

198 泣	na-ku, kyū な・く、キュウ cry	丶	丶	氵	氵	汁	汁	汁	泣

Water 氵 rises 立 from the eyes, and means to cry.

泣く	なく	**naku**	to cry
泣き声	なきごえ	**nakigoe**	cry
泣き笑い	なきわらい	**nakiwarai**	smile through one's tears
泣き落とす	なきおとす	**nakiotosu**	persuade (someone) by tears
泣き言	なきごと	**nakigoto**	complaint

199 弱	yowa-i, jaku よわ・い、ジャク weak	⁊	⁊	弓	弓	弓	弔	弔	弱
		弱	弱						

弱 means a decorative bow not as strong as an ordinary bow. Therefore, 弱 means weak.

弱い	よわい	**yowai**	weak
弱風	じゃくふう	**jakufū**	weak wind
弱気	よわき	**yowaki**	faintheartedness
弱者	じゃくしゃ	**jakusha**	the weak

4 ▶ Practice

I. Write the readings of the following kanji in hiragana.

1. 悪 い   2. 治 る   3. 先 頭   4. 顔
5. 鼻 水   6. 熱 い   7. 元 気   8. 笑 う
9. 泣 く   10. 弱 い
11. 頭 が 痛 い で す 。
12. 時 間 が 足 り ま せ ん 。
13. 父 は 背 が 高 い で す 。

156

II. Fill in the blanks with appropriate kanji.

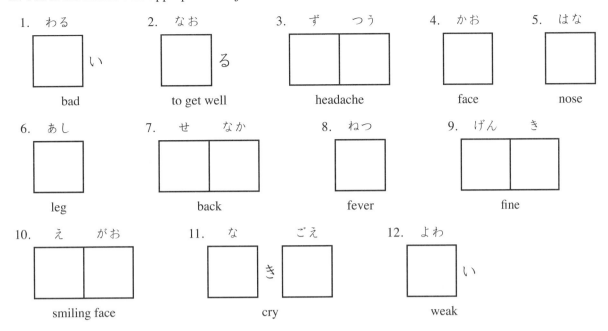

1. わる
□ い
bad

2. なお
□ る
to get well

3. ず　つう
□□
headache

4. かお
□
face

5. はな
□
nose

6. あし
□
leg

7. せ　なか
□□
back

8. ねつ
□
fever

9. げん　き
□□
fine

10. え　がお
□□
smiling face

11. な　ごえ
□ き □
cry

12. よわ
□ い
weak

---

5 ▶ Advanced Placement Exam Practice Questions

Read this dialogue between a doctor and a patient named Taro, and answer the questions.

Doctor: どうしましたか。

Taro: 頭が痛いんです。それに熱もあります。

Doctor: いつからですか。

Taro: 頭痛は三日前からです。熱は昨日からです。

Doctor: せきは出ますか。

Taro: せきは出ませんが、鼻水が夕べから止まりません。ずっと鼻をかんでいたので、鼻のまわりが赤くなってしまいました。

Doctor: どれどれ、そうですね。赤くなっていますね。それでは、口を大きく開けてください。のども赤いですね。おなかはどうですか。

Taro: [1] 食欲がなくて、困っています。何も食べたくないんです。

Doctor: 風邪でしょう。薬を[2] 二種類出しますから、一日三回飲んでください。かならず2種類いっしょに食後に飲んでください。

Taro: お風呂に入ってもいいですか。

Doctor: シャワーやお風呂は熱がさがってからにしたほうがいいでしょう。

今、インフルエンザがはやっていますから、家へ帰ったら[3] うがいをして、早く休んでください。

Taro: はい、ありがとうございます。

Doctor: お大事に。

¹食 欲: appetite

²二種 類: two kinds of

³うがいをする: to gargle

1. Taro has
   A. a stomachache.
   B. a headache.
   C. a cough.
   D. an appetite.

2. Taro has had a runny nose since
   A. this morning.
   B. yesterday morning.
   C. yesterday afternoon.
   D. last night.

3. Taro is suffering from
   A. a headache and a fever.
   B. a headache and a cough.
   C. a stomachache and a fever.
   D. a stomachache and a cough.

4. Taro has to take medicine
   A. twice a day before eating.
   B. twice a day after eating.
   C. three times a day before eating.
   D. three times a day after eating.

5. The doctor advised Taro
   A. to take a shower.
   B. to go to bed early.
   C. to take a bath.
   D. not to blow his nose too much.

How About the Weather?

天気はどうですか

The weather in Japan is so changeable that it is a common conversation point. Nowadays, a newer profession called certified weather forecaster has become increasingly popular in Japan, since of course the weather conditions have a significant effect on agriculture and the navigation of ships and planes. Knowing the local weather conditions is useful to people for many reasons. Many young people register to receive weather reports by PC or smartphone. In this lesson you will learn some of the kanji used in weather reports.

1 ▶ Introductory Quiz

Look at the illustrations (page 160) and refer to the words in **Vocabulary**. Then try the following quiz.

What will the weather be tomorrow in the five cities listed? Write the correct city's letter (a–e) on page 160 in the spaces below.

1. あした雪が降るでしょう。　　（　　　） 　 2. あした雨が降るでしょう。　　　　　（　　　）

3. あしたは晴れでしょう。　　　（　，　） 　 4. あしたの最低気温は5℃でしょう。（　　　）

5. 来週、台風が接近するでしょう。（　　　）

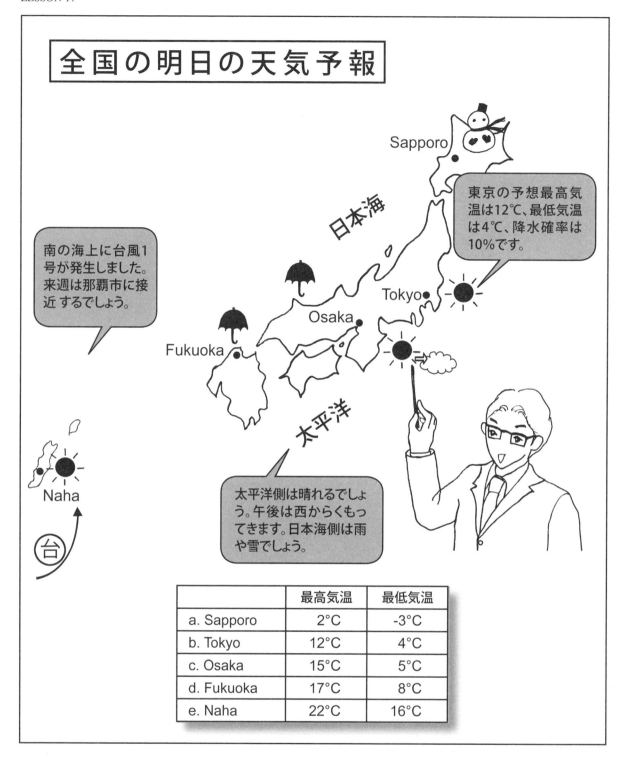

a. Sapporo (さっぽろ)   b. Tokyo (とうきょう)   c. Osaka (おおさか)

d. Fukuoka (ふくおか)   e. Naha (なは)

2 ▶ Vocabulary

Study the readings and meanings of these words to help you understand the **Introductory Quiz**.

1.	全国	ぜん こく	**zenkoku**	the whole country
2.	天気予報	てん き よ ほう	**tenki yohō**	weather forecast
3.	太平洋側	たい へい よう がわ	**taiheiyō gawa**	the Pacific Ocean side
4.	晴れる	は れる	**hareru**	to clear up
5.	西	にし	**nishi**	west
6.	くもる		**kumoru**	to be cloudy
7.	日本海	に ほん かい	**Nihonkai**	the Sea of Japan
8.	雨	あめ	**ame**	rain
9.	雪	ゆき	**yuki**	snow
10.	予想	よ そう	**yosō**	expectation
11.	最高気温	さい こう き おん	**saikō kion**	highest temperature
12.	最低気温	さい てい き おん	**saitei kion**	lowest temperature
13.	降水	こう すい	**kōsui**	precipitation
14.	確率	かく りつ	**kakuritsu**	percentage
15.	南	みなみ	**minami**	south
16.	海上	かい じょう	**kaijō**	on the sea
17.	台風1号	たい ふう いち ごう	**taifū ichigō**	typhoon No. 1
18.	発生する	はっ せい する	**hassei suru**	to appear
19.	来週	らい しゅう	**raishū**	next week
20.	那覇市	な は し	**Nahashi**	Naha city
21.	接近する	せっ きん する	**sekkin suru**	to approach, be on its way
22.	降る	ふ る	**furu**	to rain, snow

3 ▶ New Characters

Nine characters are introduced in this lesson. Use the explanations to help you understand and remember the characters. Study the compound words to increase your vocabulary.

天　側　晴　雨　雪　最　低　降　接

200 天

ame, ama, ten
あめ、あま、テン
heaven

| 一 | 二 | 天 | 天 | | | | |

A big 大 person is holding the sky 一 above him/her.

天気	てんき	**tenki**	weather
天気予報	てんきよほう	**tenki yohō**	weather forecast
雨天	うてん	**uten**	rainy weather
天国	てんごく	**tengoku**	paradise
天使	てんし	**tenshi**	angel
天体	てんたい	**tentai**	heavenly body
天文学的	てんもんがくてき	**temmongaku-teki**	astronomical
天下	てんか	**tenka**	the world

201 側

kawa, (gawa), soku, (so')
かわ、（がわ）、ソク、（ソッ）
side

| ノ | イ | 仔 | 仍 | 俱 | 但 | 但 | 俱 |
| 俱 | 側 | 側 | | | | | |

A cooking vessel 貝 and a knife 刂 attached to a man イ, means 側 nearby or side.

側	がわ	**gawa**	side
日本海側	にほんかいがわ	**Nihonkai gawa**	the Japan Sea side
右側	みぎがわ	**migigawa**	right side
両側	りょうがわ	**ryōgawa**	both sides
向こう側	むこうがわ	**mukōgawa**	other side
右側通行	みぎがわつうこう	**migigawa tsūkō**	Keep to the right
側近	そっきん	**sokkin**	close advisor
山側	やまがわ	**yamagawa**	mountainside
側面	そくめん	**sokumen**	side

202 晴

ha-reru, sei
は・れる、セイ
clear up

| 丨 | 冂 | 月 | 日 | 日一 | 日十 | 日キ | 日キ |
| 晴 | 晴 | 晴 | 晴 | | | | |

晴 is a combination of the sun 日 and 青 transparent. This is how the sky looks on a fine day.

晴れ	はれ	**hare**	fine
晴れる	はれる	**hareru**	to clear up
晴天	せいてん	**seiten**	fine weather
快晴	かいせい	**kaisei**	clear

203 雨

ame, ama, u
あめ、あま、ウ
rain

一 厂 厅 币 币 雨 雨 雨

雨 is the pictograph of rain as raindrops fall from the clouds.

雨	あめ	**ame**	rain
大雨	おおあめ	**ōame**	heavy rain
雨期	うき	**uki**	rainy season
梅雨	*つゆ／ばいう	**tsuyu/baiu**	rainy season
雨天中止	うてんちゅうし	**uten chūshi**	to be canceled in case of rain
小雨	こさめ	**kosame**	drizzle

204 雪

yuki, setsu
ゆき、セツ
snow

一 厂 厂 干 干 雪 雪 雪
雪 雪 雪

The falling rain 雨 combined with a picture of a broom ヨ means snow, because a broom was used to sweep the snow away.

雪	ゆき	**yuki**	snow
新雪	しんせつ	**shinsetsu**	new-fallen snow
大雪	おおゆき	**ōyuki**	heavy snowfall
初雪	はつゆき	**hatsuyuki**	the first snow

205 最

motto-mo, sai
もっと・も、サイ
the most, highest

丶 冂 日 日 旦 早 昗 昗
昗 昗 最 最

取 combines ear 耳 and hand 又. Ancient Chinese warriors used to cut the ears off their conquered enemies. Now 取 means to take. To take the sun 日 is the most 最 difficult thing to do.

最高気温	さいこうきおん	**saikō kion**	highest temperature
最新	さいしん	**saishin**	newest
最後	さいご	**saigo**	last
最初	さいしょ	**saisho**	first
最大	さいだい	**saidai**	biggest
最近	さいきん	**saikin**	recently
最も	もっとも	**mottomo**	the most
最終	さいしゅう	**saishū**	last

206 低	**hiku-i, tei** ひく・い、テイ low	ノ	イ	イ′	化	仟	低	低	

氏 means family and thus means a person by emphasizing the lower part. In addition, combined with イ, 低 means a short person. Thus 低 means low.

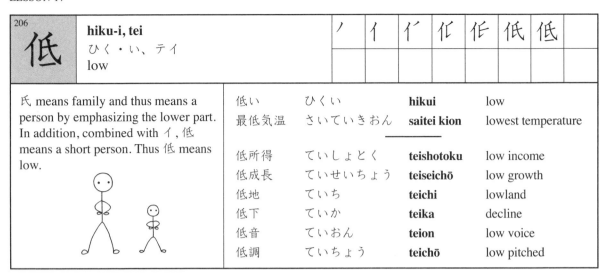

低い	ひくい	**hikui**	low
最低気温	さいていきおん	**saitei kion**	lowest temperature
低所得	ていしょとく	**teishotoku**	low income
低成長	ていせいちょう	**teiseichō**	low growth
低地	ていち	**teichi**	lowland
低下	ていか	**teika**	decline
低音	ていおん	**teion**	low voice
低調	ていちょう	**teichō**	low pitched

207 降	**fu-ru, o-riru, kō** ふ・る、お・りる、コウ descend, get off	⁊	⻖	⻖	⻖′	⻖⁊	隆	隆	降
		隆	降						

A stone wall ⻖ and the switching right and left feet 夊, 丰, suggest to descend.

降る	ふる	**furu**	to rain, to snow, to fall
降りる	おりる	**oriru**	to descend
降水	こうすい	**kōsui**	rainfall, precipitation
以降	いこう	**ikō**	since
乗り降り	のりおり	**noriori**	getting on and off

208 接	**tsu-gu, setsu, (se')** つ・ぐ、セツ、(セッ) join, touch, contact	一	十	扌	扌′	扩	扩	扩	挟
		挟	接	接					

接 combines a girl 女, stand up 立, and hand 扌. A girl stands up with a drink in her hand and serves the guest.

接する	せっする	**sessuru**	to touch
接近する	せっきんする	**sekkin suru**	to approach
面接	めんせつ	**mensetsu**	interview
直接	ちょくせつ	**chokusetsu**	direct
間接	かんせつ	**kansetsu**	indirect
接続	せつぞく	**setsuzoku**	connection
接待	せったい	**settai**	reception

164

4 ▶ Practice

I. Write the readings of the following kanji in hiragana.

1. 天気予報(ほう)　　2. 日本海側　　3. 晴れ　　　　4. 新雪
5. 降水　　　　6. 夜になって雨が強く降ってきました。
7. 最近、気温の低い日が続いています。
8. 仕事の面接に行きました。
9. アメリカはカナダと接しています。

II. Fill in the blanks with appropriate kanji.

1. てん　　き

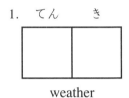

weather

2. 　　がわ

右(みぎ)

right side

3. は

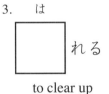 れる

to clear up

4. おお　　あめ

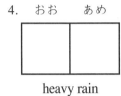

heavy rain

5. おお　　ゆき

heavy snowfall

6. さい　　てい

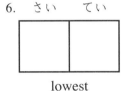

lowest

7. お

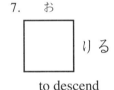 りる

to descend

8. せっ

 近(きん)する

to approach

5 ▶ Advanced Placement Exam Practice Questions

Read the article, and answer the questions.

異常気象　世界で!

　世界(せかい)各地で[1]異常気象(いじょうきしょう)が起きている。これは「[2]エルニーニョ現象(げんしょう)」のためとみられるが、[3]地(ち)球温暖化(きゅうおんだんか)の[4]影響(えいきょう)もあるといわれる。20××年の気象(きしょう)は以下のようであった。

　(日本)[5]気象庁(きしょうちょう)によると、1990年以降(いこう)、平均(へいきん)気温の高い年が続いている。昨年は平年に比べて平均気温が0.44℃高く、12月になっても雪が少なく、雪不足のスキー場が多かった。大きな台風も発生し、[6]被害(ひがい)が広がった。

　(米国)昨年は平均気温、最高気温の高い一年だった。空気が[7]乾燥(かんそう)して山火事で失われた面積(めんせき)は[8]過去最悪(かこさいあく)だった。

　(オーストラリア)オーストラリア南東部では数ヶ月間雨がまったく降らないなど最も乾燥(かんそう)した一年だった。しかし、西部ではサイクロンにより大雨が降り、大きな被害(ひがい)がでた。

¹異 常 気 象 : extraordinary (abnormal) weather

²エルニーニョ 現象 : El Niño

³地 球 温 暖 化: global warming

⁴影 響 : impact; influence

⁵気 象 庁 : the Meteorological Agency

⁶被害: damage, loss

⁷乾燥 : dry

⁸過 去 最 悪: worst ever

According to this article:

1. Last year, in Japan,
    A. the average temperature was low and there was much rainfall.
    B. the average temperature was low and there was much snowfall.
    C. the average temperature was high and there was little rainfall.
    D. the average temperature was high and there was little snowfall.

2. Last year, in the U.S.A.,
    A. the average temperature was low and there were many forest fires.
    B. the average temperature was high and there were many forest fires.
    C. the average temperature was low and there was much snowfall.
    D. the average temperature was high and there was much snowfall.

3. Last year, in Australia,
    A. there was a flood in the Southeast and there was also a flood in the West.
    B. there was a flood in the Southeast and it was dry in the West.
    C. it was dry in the Southeast and there was a flood in the West.
    D. it was dry in the Southeast and it was also dry in the West.

4. The weather of the world
    A. is abnormal due to the impact of typhoons.
    B. is abnormal because of cyclones and forest fires.
    C. is abnormal because of El Niño and global warming.
    D. is abnormal because of El Niño, but not due to the impact of global warming.

Writing a New Year's Card

年賀状を書きましょう

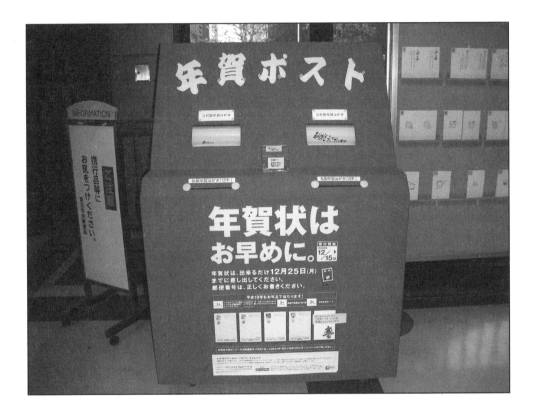

The Japanese have a custom of sending New Year's cards, **Nengajō**. A New Year's card is similar to a Christmas card, but the big difference is the date of its arrival. New Year's cards have to be mailed within a specified period in December, in order to be delivered on the first of January precisely. Therefore, at the end of the year, Japanese people are kept busy writing tens or hundreds of cards to their relatives, friends and colleagues, to ensure timely delivery of their greetings. In this lesson, you will learn some kanji appearing on New Year's cards.

1 ▶ Introductory Quiz

Look at the illustrations below and refer to the words in **Vocabulary**. Then try the following quiz.

I. Read the cards below and write the appropriate letters (a–d) in the parentheses.

1. 成人 （　　　　）

新年おめでとうございます

成人しました。

どうぞよいお年をお迎えください。

平成二十八年一月一日

青山　花子

2. 喪中・失礼 （　　　　）

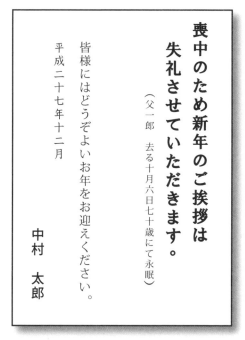

喪中のため新年のご挨拶は
失礼させていただきます。

皆様にはどうぞよいお年をお迎えください。

平成二十七年十二月

（父一郎　去る十月六日七十歳にて永眠）

中村　太郎

3. 結婚 （　　　　）

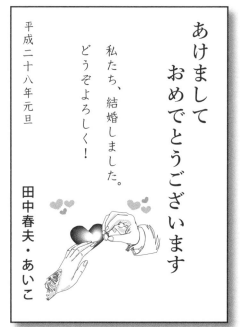

あけまして
おめでとうございます

私たち、結婚しました。

どうぞよろしく！

平成二十八年元旦

田中春夫・あいこ

4. 卒業 （　　　　）

迎春

大学を卒業して、社会人になりました。

どうぞよろしくお願いいたします。

平成二十八年元旦

長田　あや

a. We got married.　b. I turned 20 years old.　c. I graduated from the University.　d. My father passed away.

II. 年賀状は元旦に配達されます。しかし、若い人のなかには、はがきではなく電子メールで
新年のあいさつをする人もふえています。

When you get a new year's e-mail and send a return mail, which mark (A, B, C) do you click? Circle the correct letter.

A. 返信　　B. 全員へ返信　　　　　C. 転送

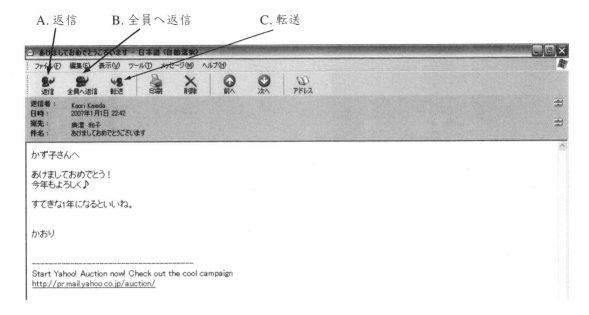

2 ▶ Vocabulary

Study the readings and meanings of these words to help you understand the **Introductory Quiz**.

1. 新年	しん ねん	**shinnen**	new year
2. 成人	せい じん	**seijin**	grown-up
3. 迎える	むか える	**mukaeru**	to greet, welcome
4. 平成	へい せい	**heisei**	Heisei (era)
5. 喪中	も ちゅう	**mochū**	in mourning
6. 挨拶	あい さつ	**aisatsu**	greeting
7. 失礼する	しつ れい する	**sitsurei suru**	to apologize
8. 永眠する	えい みん する	**eimin suru**	to die, pass away
9. 皆様	みな さま	**minasama**	everyone (very polite)
10. 結婚	けっ こん	**kekkon**	marriage
11. 元旦	がん たん	**Gantan**	New Year's Day (January 1st)
12. 迎春	げい しゅん	**geishun**	A happy new year
13. 卒業	そつ ぎょう	**sotsugyō**	graduation
14. 社会人	しゃ かい じん	**shakaijin**	(working) member of society

15. よろしくお願い 　　いたします	よろしく お ねが い 　　いたします	**yoroshiku onegai 　itashimasu**	polite formal ending
16. 年賀状	ねん が じょう	**nengajō**	New Year's card
17. 配達	はい たつ	**haitatsu**	delivery
18. 電子メール	でん し メール	**denshi mēru**	e-mail
19. 返信	へん しん	**henshin**	reply
20. 全員	ぜん いん	**zen'in**	all
21. 転送	てん そう	**tensō**	forward, transfer

3 ▶ New Characters

Ten characters are introduced in this lesson. Use the explanations to help you understand and remember the characters. Study the compound words to increase your vocabulary.

失　結　婚　卒　賀　状　配　達　返　信

---

209 失	**ushina-u, shitsu, (shi')** うしな・う、シツ、（シッ） lose	ノ　ヒ　ヒ　失　失

失 is a pictograph of something dropping ヽ from the hand 手.	失う	うしなう	**ushinau**	to lose
	失礼する	しつれいする	**shitsurei 　suru**	to be sorry
	失言	しつげん	**shitsugen**	a slip of the tongue
	失明	しつめい	**shitsumei**	blindness
	失意	しつい	**shitsui**	despair
	失神 (失心)	しっしん	**shisshin**	faint
	消失	しょうしつ	**shōshitsu**	disappearance

210

結

musu-bu, yu-u, ketsu, (ke')
むす・ぶ、ゆ・う、ケツ、(ケッ)
conclude; tie, bind

吉 is the pictograph of a pot tightly covered with a lid. Combined with 糸 thread, 結 means that a pot is covered and tied with a cord. Thus 結 means to tie, to bind, to conclude or to end.

結ぶ	むすぶ	**musubu**	to tie
結婚	けっこん	**kekkon**	marriage
結局	けっきょく	**kekkyoku**	after all
結成する	けっせいする	**kessei suru**	to organize
結語	けつご	**ketsugo**	concluding remarks
終結	しゅうけつ	**shūketsu**	conclusion

211

婚

kon
コン
marriage

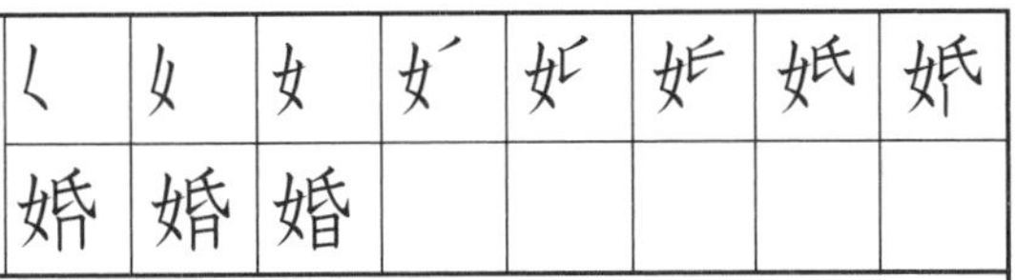

The day to become Mr. 氏 and Mrs. 女 is a wedding day 日.

結婚式	けっこんしき	**kekkonshiki**	wedding ceremony
婚約	こんやく	**kon'yaku**	engagement
新婚	しんこん	**shinkon**	newly married
新婚旅行	しんこんりょこう	**shinkon ryokō**	honeymoon
婚期	こんき	**konki**	marriageable age
銀婚式	ぎんこんしき	**ginkonshiki**	silver wedding anniversary
再婚	さいこん	**saikon**	remarriage
晩婚	ばんこん	**bankon**	late marriage

212

卒

sotsu
ソツ
end, graduate

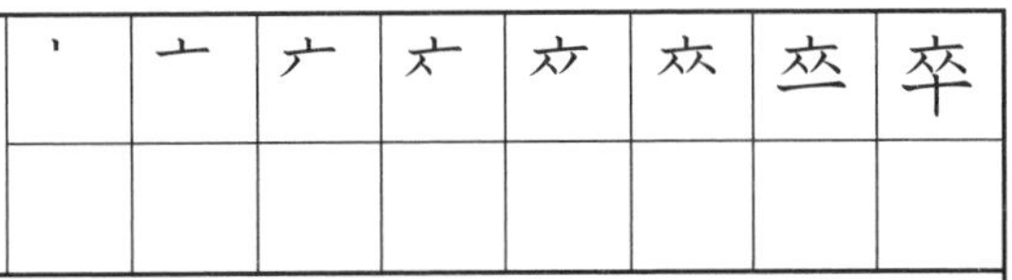

卒 combines a hat 亠, people 人人, and ten 十, suggesting a graduation ceremony.

卒業	そつぎょう	**sotsugyō**	graduation
新卒	しんそつ	**shinsotsu**	newly graduated
卒業式	そつぎょうしき	**sotsugyōshiki**	graduation ceremony
卒業生	そつぎょうせい	**sotsugyōsei**	graduate

213

賀

ga
ガ
congratulations

ラ	カ	カ	加	加	加	加	賀
賀	賀	賀	賀				

加 means to add. 貝 once was used as money. 賀 combines add 加 and money 貝, and thus means congratulations.

年賀状	ねんがじょう	**nengajō**	New Year's card
賀状	がじょう	**gajō**	New Year's card
賀正	がしょう	**gashō**	New Year's greetings
祝賀	しゅくが	**shukuga**	celebration
祝賀会	しゅくがかい	**shukugakai**	celebration party

214

状

jō
ジョウ
letter, condition

丨	丬	丬	壮	壮	状	状	

Slender and a dog 犬 combined, 状 first meant the appearance of a dog and now it means appearance or condition in general.

礼状	れいじょう	**reijō**	letter of thanks
現状	げんじょう	**genjō**	present situation
白状	はくじょう	**hakujō**	confession
免状	めんじょう	**menjō**	diploma
実状	じつじょう	**jitsujō**	actual state

215

配

kuba-ru, hai, (pai)
くば・る、ハイ、（パイ）
distribute

一	厂	兀	丙	酉	酉	酉	酉
酉	配						

酉 depicts a wine jar and 己 is a kneeling man. 配 shows a man kneeling by a wine jar, suggesting to allot, to distribute or pass out the jar's contents.

配る	くばる	**kubaru**	to distribute
心配	しんぱい	**shimpai**	worry
支配	しはい	**shihai**	control
配分	はいぶん	**haibun**	distribution
配送	はいそう	**haisō**	delivery
配下	はいか	**haika**	followers
配置	はいち	**haichi**	placement
手配	てはい	**tehai**	preparation
遅配	ちはい	**chihai**	delay in delivery

172

216 達	tatsu, (datsu), (ta'), tachi, (dachi) タツ、（ダツ）、（タッ）、タチ、（ダチ） reach, animate; plural suffix	一	十	土	耂	坴	圥	坴	坴
		幸	達	達	達				

土 land, sheep or something good 羊, and come 辶, all combine to suggest that something good (like a sheep) will be delivered to you.

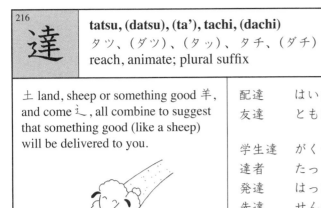

配達	はいたつ	**haitatsu**	delivery
友達	ともだち	**tomodachi**	friend
学生達	がくせいたち	**gakusei tachi**	students
達者	たっしゃ	**tassha**	be going strong
発達	はったつ	**hattatsu**	development
先達	せんだつ	**sendatsu**	pioneer

217 返	kae-su, hen かえ・す、ヘン to return	一	厂	万	反	反	返	返	

Road 辶 and 反 curved combined, 返 means to return.

返す	かえす	**kaesu**	to return
返事	へんじ	**henji**	reply
返品する	へんぴんする	**hempin suru**	to return goods
返送	へんそう	**hensō**	send back
返金	へんきん	**henkin**	repayment
引き返す	ひきかえす	**hikikaesu**	to turn back
返上	へんじょう	**henjō**	send back
返答	へんとう	**hentō**	reply

218 信	shin シン faith, trust, belief	ノ	イ	イ゙	亻゙	信	信	信	信
		信							

亻 a man accepts 言 the word of others. Thus 信 means to believe.

信じる	しんじる	**shinjiru**	to believe
返信	へんしん	**henshin**	reply
信用	しんよう	**shinyō**	trust
信号	しんごう	**shingō**	signal
自信	じしん	**jishin**	self-confidence
通信	つうしん	**tsūshin**	communication
信心	しんじん	**shinjin**	faith
不信	ふしん	**fushin**	distrust, suspicion
赤信号	あかしんごう	**akashingō**	red (traffic) light
背信	はいしん	**haishin**	betrayal, disloyalty

173

4 **Practice**

I. Write the readings of the following kanji in hiragana.

1. 失う　　　　2. 結婚　　　　3. 卒業　　　　4. 年賀状
5. 配る　　　　6. 友達　　　　7. 失礼します。
8. 年賀状は一月一日に配達されます。
9. 図書館の本は2週間以内に返してください。
10. あなたを信じます。

II. Fill in the blanks with appropriate kanji.

1. しつ　れい
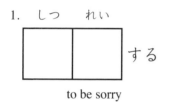
する
to be sorry

2. けっ　こん

marriage

3. そつ　ぎょう
graduation

4. ねん　が　じょう
New Year's card

5. はい　たつ
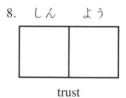
delivery

6. とも　だち
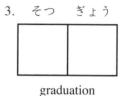
friend

7. へん　じ
reply

8. しん　よう
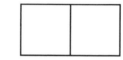
trust

9. しん　ぱい
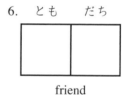
worry

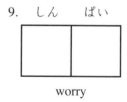

5 **Advanced Placement Exam Practice Questions**

Read the text and answer the following questions.

　日本には古くから年賀状の習慣(しゅうかん)がありました。最初は一部の人のものでしたが、18[1]世紀(せいき)には普通の人も年賀状を出すようになりました。日本中に広まったのは、1873年に郵便はがきが発売されてからです。1899年には年賀状に「1月1日」の[2]消印(けしいん)が押されるようになりました。初めて年賀はがきが発売されたのは1949年です。この年賀はがきは[3]お年玉(としだま)付だったので、大ヒットしてたくさんの年賀状が出されるようになりました。今では子どもから[4]お年寄(としよ)りまで多くの人が年賀状を書きます。

　前もって出しておいた年賀状は元旦に配達されます。新年になって友達や親類、会社や趣味(しゅみ)の[5]仲(なか)

間、知人から届く年賀状を読むのは楽しいものです。一年に一度、年賀状だけであいさつをし、10年以上も会わない人もいます。しかし、家族の写真や一年のできごとが書いてある年賀状を読めば、会わなくてもその人たちのことを知ることができます。遠くに住んでいてなかなか会えない人たちといつまでも友達でいられるのは年賀状のおかげだと思う人は多いはずです。

1世紀: century
2消印: postmark
3お年玉付: with lottery numbers
4お年寄り: the elderly
5仲間: friends

1. The first New Year's cards were sold in
   A. 1873.
   B. 1899.
   C. 1840.
   D. 1949.

2. New Year's cards are delivered
   A. on January 1st.
   B. before New Year's Day.
   C. after New Year's Day.
   D. every day.

3. Who writes New Year's cards nowadays?
   A. A few people do.
   B. Only young people do.
   C. Almost all kinds of people do.
   D. Only the elderly do.

4. To whom do Japanese write New Year's cards?
   A. Only to relatives
   B. Only to friends
   C. To people with whom they can't meet
   D. To the people they know

5. Japanese think that a New Year's card is
   A. a new tradition.
   B. good and useful.
   C. good but out-of-date.
   D. an old and bad tradition.

Shopping at a Department Store

LESSON 19

デパートで買い物します

Department stores have existed in Japan since 1673. There are many chains now, and they have many branches all over Japan and around the world. Japanese department stores specialize in clothing and household goods and have a wide range of stock. They sell fancy, expensive, high-quality goods, and imported goods, too. You may request the department store to deliver an item to your home or to the home of someone else, if it is a gift; you may have to pay a delivery charge. In the department stores, big signs direct you to floors with specific merchandise. Store clerks, some of whom speak English, may assist you, but it is always helpful to know some kanji at the department store.

1 ▶ Introductory Quiz

Look at the illustrations below and refer to the words in **Vocabulary**. Then try the following quiz.

When you want to buy a present for your friend, the best place to go is the department store. Review the department store directory below, and answer the questions.

		本 館 の ご 案 内	
屋上		●日本庭園　●ペットコーナー	
7	リビングフロア 美術・家庭用品・ 食堂		
6	本・絵本・ おもちゃ 人形・文房具・ 色紙		
5	ベビー用品・ 子ども服・ きもの		
4	メンズフロア		
3	ヤングズフロア		
2	レディスフロア		
1	ファショングッズ フロア		
B1	食料品 世界のワイン 地下鉄連絡口		
B2	駐車場		

I. On which floor will you find the goods you want to buy? Refer to the information above.

1. にんぎょうを買いたいです。 ＿＿＿＿＿＿＿＿＿＿ 階に行けばいいです。

2. 子どもふくは、 ＿＿＿＿＿＿＿＿＿ 階にあります。

3. イタリアのワインは、 ＿＿＿＿＿＿＿＿＿ 階にあります。

4. えほんは、 ＿＿＿＿＿＿＿＿＿ 階にあります。

II. Read each conversation between two people. Which floor should they go to? Insert the floor's number in the spaces provided.

2 ▸ Vocabulary

Study the readings and meanings of these words to help you understand the **Introductory Quiz**.

1.	本館	ほん かん	**honkan**	main building
2.	屋上	おく じょう	**okujō**	roof
3.	庭園	てい えん	**teien**	garden
4.	美術	び じゅつ	**bijutsu**	art
5.	家庭用品	か てい よう ひん	**katei yōhin**	household articles
6.	絵本	え ほん	**ehon**	picture book
7.	おもちゃ		**omocha**	toys
8.	人形	にん ぎょう	**ningyō**	doll
9.	文房具	ぶん ぼう ぐ	**bumbōgu**	stationery
10.	色紙	しき し	**shikishi**	square piece of fancy paper
11.	ベビー用品	ベビー よう ひん	**bebī yōhin**	goods for baby
12.	子ども服	こ ども ふく	**kodomofuku**	children's wear
13.	食料品	しょく りょう ひん	**shokuryōhin**	food
14.	世界	せ かい	**sekai**	the world
15.	地下鉄連絡口	ち か てつ れん らく ぐち	**chikatetsu renrakuguchi**	exit for subway
16.	駐車場	ちゅう しゃ じょう	**chūshajō**	parking lot
17.	母の日	はは の ひ	**haha no hi**	Mother's Day
18.	贈り物	おく り もの	**okurimono**	present, gift
19.	決める	き める	**kimeru**	to decide
20.	黒い	くろ い	**kuroi**	black
21.	忙しい	いそが しい	**isogashii**	busy

3 ▸ New Characters

Ten characters are introduced in this lesson. Use the explanations to help you understand and remember the characters. Study the compound words to increase your vocabulary.

絵 形 色 服 世 界 贈 決 黒 忙

179

219 絵	**e, kai** エ、カイ painting	く	纟	纟	纟	糸	糸	糸	紒
		紒	絵	絵	絵				

絵 combines to gather 会 and thread 糸, meaning embroidered picture made with threads of various colors.	絵	え	**e**	picture, painting
	絵本	えほん	**ehon**	picture book
			———————	
	絵画	かいが	**kaiga**	picture
	口絵	くちえ	**kuchie**	frontispiece
	絵文字	えもじ	**emoji**	pictograph
	絵心	えごころ	**egokoro**	artistic eye

220 形	**kata, katachi, kei, gyō** かた、かたち、ケイ、ギョウ form, shape	一	二	于	开	开	形	形	

A square frame □ and decoration 彡 combined, 形 means shape.	形	かたち	**katachi**	shape
	人形	にんぎょう	**ningyō**	doll
			———————	
	円形	えんけい	**enkei**	circle
	形式	けいしき	**keishiki**	form
	図形	ずけい	**zukei**	figure
	正方形	せいほうけい	**seihōkei**	square

221 色	**iro, shoku, shiki** いろ、ショク、シキ color, erotic passion	ノ	ク	ク	各	各	色		

色 combines a bending person ク, and a kneeling person 巴, to suggest the idea of erotic passion and complexion. It later came to mean color.	色	いろ	**iro**	color
	色えんぴつ	いろえんぴつ	**iro empitsu**	color pencil
	色紙	しきし	**shikishi**	square piece of fancy paper
	色々な	いろいろな	**iroiro na**	various
			———————	
	茶色	ちゃいろ	**chairo**	brown
	特色	とくしょく	**tokushoku**	characteristic
	配色	はいしょく	**haishoku**	color scheme
	単色	たんしょく	**tanshoku**	single color
	難色	なんしょく	**nanshoku**	disapproval

222 服

fuku
フク
clothes, obey

ノ	刀	月	月	肝	肌	肥	服

A man is kneeling 又 to his standing master 卩 to show obedience. Clothes 服 obey the body 月.

子ども服	こどもふく	**kodomofuku**	children's clothes
制服	せいふく	**seifuku**	uniform
婦人服	ふじんふく	**fujinfuku**	women's wear
和服	わふく	**wafuku**	Japanese clothing
洋服	ようふく	**yōfuku**	Western clothing
平服	へいふく	**heifuku**	plain clothes
式服	しきふく	**shikifuku**	ceremonial dress

223 世

yo, se, sei
よ、セ、セイ
world, era

一	十	卅	丗	世			

世 means thirty years 十十十. Thirty years is a long time, like an era. Later 世 came to mean the world.

世話する	せわする	**sewa suru**	to take care of
世の中	よのなか	**yononaka**	world, society
世代	せだい	**sedai**	generation
世間	せけん	**seken**	society
出世	しゅっせ	**shusse**	succeed in life/get ahead
二世	にせい	**nisei**	second generation
後世	こうせい	**kōsei**	later years
中世	ちゅうせい	**chūsei**	Middle Ages
近世	きんせい	**kinsei**	modern times

224 界

kai
カイ
world

ﾉ	口	田	田	田	界	界	界
界							

介 means to be in between. Combined with a rice field 田, 界 means the boundary of a rice field and thus meant an enclosed area. By extension, it means world.

世界	せかい	**sekai**	world
学界	がっかい	**gakkai**	academic world
外界	がいかい	**gaikai**	external world
下界	げかい	**gekai**	this world
社交界	しゃこうかい	**shakōkai**	high society
新世界	しんせかい	**shinsekai**	the New World
銀世界	ぎんせかい	**ginsekai**	snowy scene

225 贈	**oku-ru, zō, sō** おく・る、ゾウ、ソウ give, present	丨	冂	冃	目	目	目	貝	貝`	貝´
		貝´	貯	贮	贈	贈	贈	贈	贈	贈

贈 combines layered 曽 and money 貝. Thus, 贈 means to give someone valuable things or money.

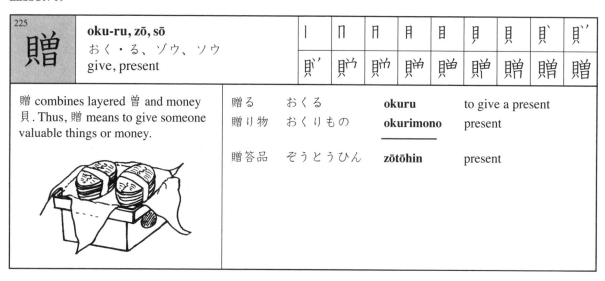

贈る	おくる	**okuru**	to give a present
贈り物	おくりもの	**okurimono**	present
贈答品	ぞうとうひん	**zōtōhin**	present

---

226 決	**ki-meru, ki-maru, ketsu, (ke')** き・める、き・まる、ケツ、（ケッ） decide	丶	冫	氵	沪	沪	決	決		

This is a combination of water 氵, washed out dune ユ, and person 人.

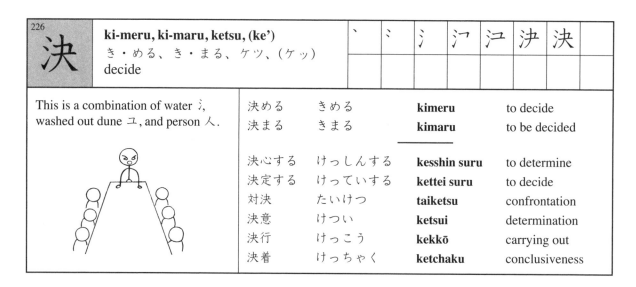

決める	きめる	**kimeru**	to decide
決まる	きまる	**kimaru**	to be decided
決心する	けっしんする	**kesshin suru**	to determine
決定する	けっていする	**kettei suru**	to decide
対決	たいけつ	**taiketsu**	confrontation
決意	けつい	**ketsui**	determination
決行	けっこう	**kekkō**	carrying out
決着	けっちゃく	**ketchaku**	conclusiveness

---

227 黒	**kuro, kuro-i, koku, (ko')** くろ、くろ・い、コク、（コッ） black	丨	冂	冃	日	甲	甲	里	里`
		黒	黒	黒					

里 combines a rice paddy 田 and the land 土, meaning a village. Flame 灬 is added to suggest a burnt down village which looks black.

黒い	くろい	**kuroi**	black
黒字	くろじ	**kuroji**	(in the) black
黒海	こっかい	**kokkai**	the Black Sea
暗黒	あんこく	**ankoku**	darkness
大黒	だいこく	**daikoku**	God of Wealth

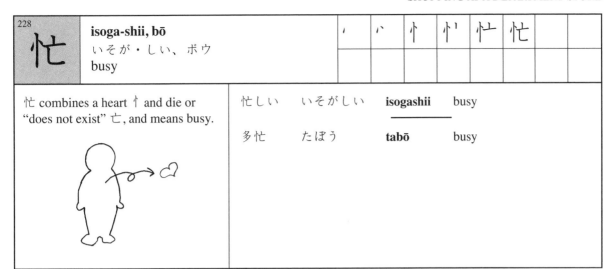

228 忙	isoga-shii, bō いそが・しい、ボウ busy	ヽ	ハ	忄	忙	忙	忙		

忙 combines a heart 忄 and die or "does not exist" 亡, and means busy.

忙しい	いそがしい	**isogashii**	busy
多忙	たぼう	**tabō**	busy

4 ▶ Practice

I. Write the readings of the following kanji in hiragana.

1. 人 形
2. 絵 本
3. 色 紙
4. 色
5. 洋 服
6. 世 話
7. 贈 る
8. 黒
9. 私 は 、 毎 日 忙 し い で す 。
10. 日 本 の 文 化 を 勉 強 し よ う と 決 め ま し た 。
11. 世 界 は 、 だ ん だ ん 近 く な っ て い ま す 。
12. そ の 服 は 、 形 が い い で す ね 。

II. Fill in the blanks with appropriate kanji.

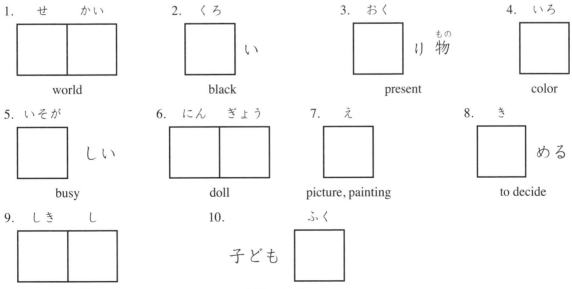

1. せ　かい
　世界
　world

2. くろ
　□ い
　black

3. おく
　□ り 物 (もの)
　present

4. いろ
　□
　color

5. いそが
　□ しい
　busy

6. にん　ぎょう
　□□
　doll

7. え
　□
　picture, painting

8. き
　□ める
　to decide

9. しき　し
　□□
　square piece of fancy paper

10. ふく
　子ども □
　children's clothes

5 Advanced Placement Exam Practice Questions

Read the article about department stores in Japan. Then answer the following questions.

　日本のデパートは、百貨店と言われるように、色々なものが売られている。日用品から電気1製品、絵や2家具など買うことができる。世界各地のものがそろっていて、有名ブランドがずらりと店を出している。デパートは地下鉄の地下道や電車の駅から直接入ることもでき、3気軽に立ちよることができる。デパートの地下（デパ地下）では、料理された食料品が一人分から買える。有名店やホテルのお弁当やおかずが売られていて、夕方は、会社帰りの人々でこむ。それを持ち帰って家族で食べる。忙しい時にとても便利である。また、どのデパートにも喫茶室や食堂があって、つかれたら休めるし、食事もできる。デパートの最上階には、レストラン街もあり、いろいろな料理を楽しむこともできる。4お中元や5お歳暮の時期は、客であふれる。セールの時も、たくさんの人が集まる。スーパーやコンビニにくらべると6値段は少し高いが、特に贈り物をする時など、日本人はデパートを利用する人が多い。贈り物をする相手に届けてくれるサービスもある。もちろん大きいものを買った時は、家まで届けてくれる。地下には、駐車場があって車で行くこともできる。

1製品: product

2家具: furniture

3気軽に: light-heartedly

4お中元: a midyear present

5お歳暮: a year-end present

6値段: price

1. According to this article, what can you buy at the department store?
   A. a few things
   B. several things
   C. almost everything
   D. only goods made in other countries

2. According to this article, how do you go to a department store?
   A. only by subway
   B. only by train
   C. only by car
   D. by any vehicle

3. According to this article, what can you buy at the basement?
   A. various kinds of food
   B. only food from famous hotels
   C. only food from famous restaurants
   D. only food for a special event

4. According to this article, when do Japanese especially go to the department store?
   A. whenever they need to buy anything
   B. when they need to buy a present for their friends or family
   C. when they need to buy food
   D. whenever they want to buy things from other countries

5. According to this article, which type of store is comparatively expensive?
   A. convenience store
   B. supermarket
   C. department store
   D. other small store

Meeting People

いろいろな人に会います

When you meet new people in Japan, it is common to exchange business cards, on which the person's name and business information are printed. To read the business cards, it is helpful to know some of the common kanji for names. It is also useful to know kanji related to persons' positions. In this lesson, you will learn some Japanese surnames and terminology related to positions.

1 ▶ Introductory Quiz

Look at the illustrations below and refer to the words in **Vocabulary**. Then try the following quiz.

These are sample business cards.

a.

やまと大学
　工学部教授

工学博士　　**大　野　和　夫**

　　　　勤務先　〒999-9999　上山市文京町1-1-1
　　　　　　　　　TEL & FAX: 11-111-1111
　　　　自　宅　〒999-9999　　上山市東町2-2-2

b.

国際出版株式会社

製作部　部長

小林　進

東京都品川区大崎○-○-○
電話 99-9999-9999

185

c.

エネルギー研究所

研究員 森 千代

〒000-0000 東京都文京区中駒込一—一—一〇〇

電話99—9999—9999

d.

Ｔ 東都旅行

第五課
係長 青 山 正 子

東都旅行　東京旅行支店
〒111-11 11 東京都東区南町3-3-3
TEL: 03-5555-5555　FAX: 03-3333-3333

Which name card belongs to whom? Fill in the spaces with the correct letters (a–d) of the business cards.

私は旅行会社につとめています。1月には
ハワイツアーに出かける予定です。

1. (　　　　)

私は、出版社の製作部長です。英語の本を
作っています。

2. (　　　　)

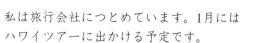

私は、研究員です。毎日実験ばかりして
います。

3. (　　　　)

私は、大学の教授です。専門は、コンピュータ
サイエンスです。

4. (　　　　)

2 ▶ Vocabulary

Study the readings and meanings of these words to help you understand the **Introductory Quiz**.

1. 名刺	めい し	**meishi**	name card, business card
2. 旅行会社	りょ こう がい しゃ	**ryokō gaisha**	travel agent
3. 東都旅行	とう と りょ こう	**Tōto Ryokō**	Toto Travel Agent
4. 第五課	だい ご か	**dai go ka**	the fifth section
5. 係長	かかり ちょう	**kakarichō**	section chief
6. 青山正子	あお やま まさ こ	**Aoyama Masako**	Aoyama, Masako
7. 出版株式会社	しゅっ ぱん かぶ しき がい しゃ	**shuppan kabushiki gaisha**	publishing company
8. 製作部	せい さく ぶ	**seisakubu**	production department
9. 部長	ぶ ちょう	**buchō**	general manager
10. 小林進	こ ばやし すすむ	**Kobayashi Susumu**	Kobayashi, Susumu
11. エネルギー研究所	エネルギー けん きゅう しょ／じょ	**enerugī kenkyū sho/jo**	Energy Research Institute
12. 研究員	けん きゅう いん	**kenkyūin**	researcher
13. 実験	じっ けん	**jikken**	experiment
14. 森千代	もり ち よ	**Mori Chiyo**	Mori, Chiyo
15. 教授	きょう じゅ	**kyōju**	professor
16. 大野和夫	おお の かず お	**Ōno Kazuo**	Ono, Kazuo
17. 勤務先	きん む さき	**kimmusaki**	place of work
18. 自宅	じ たく	**jitaku**	home, residence

3 ▶ New Characters

Eleven characters are introduced in this lesson. Use the explanations to help you understand and remember the characters. Study the compound words to increase your vocabulary.

社 係 長 青 作 林 進 員 森 授 夫

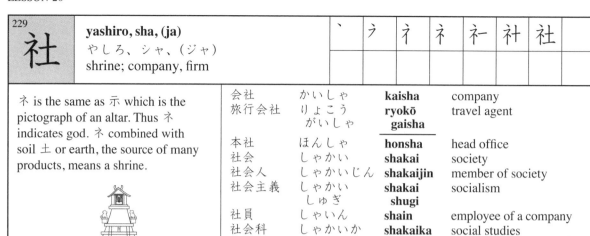

229 社	yashiro, sha, (ja) やしろ、シャ、（ジャ） shrine; company, firm	丶	ラ	ネ	ネ	ネ	ネ	社	社

ネ is the same as 示 which is the pictograph of an altar. Thus ネ indicates god. ネ combined with soil 土 or earth, the source of many products, means a shrine.

会社	かいしゃ	**kaisha**	company
旅行会社	りょこう がいしゃ	**ryokō gaisha**	travel agent
本社	ほんしゃ	**honsha**	head office
社会	しゃかい	**shakai**	society
社会人	しゃかいじん	**shakaijin**	member of society
社会主義	しゃかい しゅぎ	**shakai shugi**	socialism
社員	しゃいん	**shain**	employee of a company
社会科	しゃかいか	**shakaika**	social studies
商社	しょうしゃ	**shōsha**	trading company
神社	じんじゃ	**jinja**	shrine

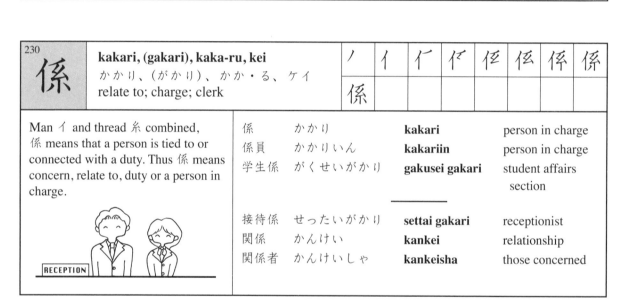

230 係	kakari, (gakari), kaka-ru, kei かかり、（がかり）、かか・る、ケイ relate to; charge; clerk	ノ	イ	伫	仔	仔	伔	係	係
		係							

Man イ and thread 糸 combined, 係 means that a person is tied to or connected with a duty. Thus 係 means concern, relate to, duty or a person in charge.

係	かかり	**kakari**	person in charge
係員	かかりいん	**kakariin**	person in charge
学生係	がくせいがかり	**gakusei gakari**	student affairs section
接待係	せったいがかり	**settai gakari**	receptionist
関係	かんけい	**kankei**	relationship
関係者	かんけいしゃ	**kankeisha**	those concerned

231 長	naga-i, chō なが・い、チョウ long, chief	丨	厂	F	F	長	長	長	長

This is the pictograph of an old man with long hair.

長い	ながい	**nagai**	long
係長	かかりちょう	**kakarichō**	section chief
会長	かいちょう	**kaichō**	chairman
社長	しゃちょう	**shachō**	president
部長	ぶちょう	**buchō**	general manager
長男	ちょうなん	**chōnan**	the oldest son
特長	とくちょう	**tokuchō**	strong point
長期	ちょうき	**chōki**	long term
長方形	ちょうほうけい	**chōhōkei**	rectangle

232 青	ao, ao-i, sei, shō あお、あお・い、セイ、ショウ blue, green; unripe	一	十	キ	主	主	青	青	青

青 is a combination of green bud 生 and the moon 月, suggesting blue and green.

青い	あおい	**aoi**	blue
青信号	あおしんごう	**aoshingō**	green (traffic) light
青年	せいねん	**seinen**	youth
青山	あおやま	**Aoyama**	Aoyama (place, surname)
青年会	せいねんかい	**seinenkai**	youth association
青春	せいしゅん	**seishun**	youth
青空	あおぞら	**aozora**	blue sky
青少年	せいしょうねん	**seishōnen**	youth

233 作	tsuku-ru, (zuku-ru), saku, (sa'), sa つく・る、(づく・る)、サク、(サッ)、サ make	ノ	イ	イ	仁	作	作	作

Man 亻 and hacksaw (indicating to cut) 乍 combined, 作 means to cut and make things.

作る	つくる	**tsukuru**	to make
作り方	つくりかた	**tsukurikata**	how to make
作文	さくぶん	**sakubun**	essay
作者	さくしゃ	**sakusha**	author
作物	さくもつ	**sakumotsu**	crops
手作り	てづくり	**tezukuri**	handmade
作業	さぎょう	**sagyō**	work
作家	さっか	**sakka**	writer
合作	がっさく	**gassaku**	joint work
作品	さくひん	**sakuhin**	work

234 林	hayashi, (bayashi), rin はやし、(ばやし)、リン wood	一	十	オ	木	杧	村	材	林

Two trees signify a wood.

林	はやし	**hayashi**	wood
小林	こばやし	**Kobayashi**	Kobayashi (surname)
山林	さんりん	**sanrin**	mountains and forests
林道	りんどう	**rindō**	forest road
林間学校	りんかんがっこう	**rinkan gakkō**	outdoor school
雑木林	ぞうきばやし	**zōkibayashi**	thicket of miscellaneous trees
林業	りんぎょう	**ringyō**	forestry

189

235 進	**susu-mu, shin** すす・む、シン advance, proceed, promote	ノ	イ	イ´	广	什	件	隹	隹
		´隹	進	進					

進 combines a bird 隹 and to proceed 辶, and means to go forward.	進む	すすむ	**susumu**	to proceed
	進歩	しんぽ	**shimpo**	progress
	進	すすむ	**Susumu**	Susumu (first name, male)
	進学	しんがく	**shingaku**	entrance to higher school
	進行	しんこう	**shinkō**	onward movement
	進化	しんか	**shinka**	evolution
	先進	せんしん	**senshin**	advance
	後進	こうしん	**kōshin**	successors
	進言	しんげん	**shingen**	advice

236 員	**in** イン member	ヽ	冂	口	尸	吊	尉	冐	冒
		員	員						

Mouth 口 and money 貝 together means to count money and other things. Thus 員 means an employee or a staff member to carry out the work.	研究員	けんきゅういん	**kenkyūin**	research fellow
	店員	てんいん	**ten'in**	clerk
	会社員	かいしゃいん	**kaishain**	employee of a company
	定員	ていいん	**teiin**	capacity, number of persons
	会員	かいいん	**kaiin**	member
	全員	ぜんいん	**zen'in**	all members
	教員	きょういん	**kyōin**	teacher
	工員	こういん	**kōin**	worker
	乗務員	じょうむいん	**jōmuin**	crew (train, plane)

237 森	**mori, shin** もり、シン forest	一	十	オ	木	木	杧	杰	森
		杰	森	森	森				

Three trees 森 means many trees and thus a forest.	森	もり	**mori**	forest
	森林	しんりん	**shinrin**	forest

238 授	**sazu-keru, ju** さず・ける、ジュ give, grant, teach	一	十	扌	扩	扩	扩	扩	扩
		护	扲	授					

To extend a hand 扌 to a receiver 受 means to give.	教授	きょうじゅ	**kyōju**	professor
	授業	じゅぎょう	**jugyō**	class
	伝授	でんじゅ	**denju**	induction

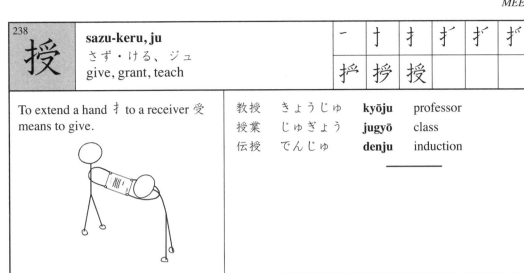

239 夫	**otto, fu, fū, pu** おっと、フ、フウ、プ husband	一	二	卉	夫				

This is the pictograph of a big 大 tall man with a topknot ⼇ on his head. 夫 means an adult man.	夫	おっと	**otto**	husband
	夫人	ふじん	**fujin**	wife
	夫婦	ふうふ	**fūfu**	Mr. and Mrs.
	夫妻	ふさい	**fusai**	Mr. and Mrs.
	工夫	くふう	**kufū**	device
	水夫	すいふ	**suifu**	sailor
	車夫	しゃふ	**shafu**	rickshaw puller
	前夫	ぜんぷ	**zempu**	former husband

4 ▶ Practice

I. Write the readings of the following kanji in hiragana.

1. 係長　　　　　2. 部長　　　　　3. 社長　　　　　4. 青年

5. 長い　　　　　6. 教授　　　　　7. 研究員　　　　8. 夫婦

9. 林　　　　　10. 青い

11. 森の中を、どんどん進んで行きます。

12. 夫は、会社員です。朝、9時から午後5時まで働いています。

13. この問題については、係員に聞いてください。

191

II. Fill in the blanks with appropriate kanji.

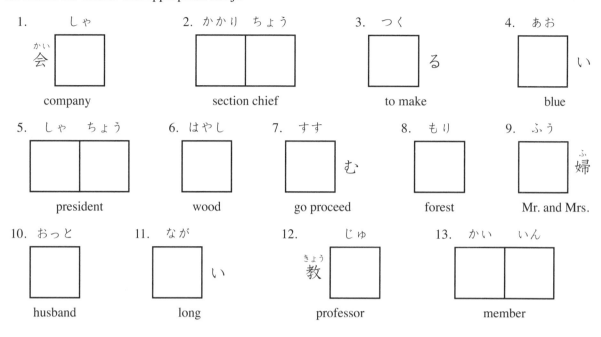

1. しゃ
かい 会 ☐
company

2. かかり ちょう
☐ ☐
section chief

3. つく
☐ る
to make

4. あお
☐ い
blue

5. しゃ ちょう
☐ ☐
president

6. はやし
☐
wood

7. すす
☐ む
go proceed

8. もり
☐
forest

9. ふう
☐ 婦ふ
Mr. and Mrs.

10. おっと
☐
husband

11. なが
☐ い
long

12. じゅ
教きょう ☐
professor

13. かい いん
☐ ☐
member

▶5 Advanced Placement Exam Practice Questions

The four people who were introduced in the Introductory Quiz and Aoyama's colleague met at a party. Read this conversation and answer the following questions.

大野： あっ、森さん、しばらくですね。

森： ああ、大野教授、おひさしぶりです。お元気ですか。

大野： ええ、元気ですが、毎日忙しいです。コンピュータ関係の分野はどんどん進歩していきますからね。研究におわれています。

森： そうでしょうね。私も、毎日実験で大変たいへんです。あ、小林さん、本の出版しゅっぱんの際は、お世話様になりました。大野先生、こちらは出版社の小林さんです。

小林： 小林です。初めまして。国際出版に[1]勤つめております。

大野： やまと大学の大野です。初めまして。出版社の方ですか。今度、本を作る時は、よろしくお願いします。あ、青山さん、こちらへ来ませんか。皆さん、こちらは、東都旅行の係長青山さんです。外国へ出る時、いつもお世話になっています。

青山： みなさん、初めまして。東都旅行の青山です。ご旅行の際は、ぜひお世話させてください。いっしょに仕事をしている山田です。

山田： 初めまして、どうぞよろしくお願いします。

[1]勤つとめております: to be working for (humble ending)

1. Who introduced Mr. Kobayashi?
   A. Ono
   B. Mori
   C. Aoyama
   D. Yamada

2. Who knows each other already?
   A. Ono and Aoyama
   B. Mori and Aoyama
   C. Ono and Kobayashi
   D. Kobayashi and Yamada

3. Who knows Ms. Mori?
   A. Ono and Aoyama
   B. Aoyama and Yamada
   C. Ono and Kobayashi
   D. Kobayashi and Yamada

4. Who works for the publishing company?
   A. Ono
   B. Mori
   C. Aoyama
   D. Kobayashi

5. Who works for the travel agency?
   A. Ono and Mori
   B. Mori and Aoyama
   C. Aoyama and Yamada
   D. Yamada and Kobayashi

What are Your Weekend Plans?

週末は何をしますか

On the weekends, many office workers in Japan tend to go to the gym, to the movies, or to museums. There are about 90 concert halls and 70 museums in Tokyo, which is comparable to the numbers found in London and New York. As for high school students, many spend their weekends participating in club activities. Four times as many students belong to sports clubs, such as baseball, basketball and soccer, compared to non-sports-related clubs, like bands, art clubs or photography clubs.

1 ▶ Introductory Quiz

Look at the illustrations below and refer to the words in **Vocabulary**. Then try the following quiz.

十月

月	火	水	木	金	土	日
		1 水泳 16:00	**2**	**3** 体育館 16:00	**4** 歌の練習 16:00	**5** 遊園地 11:00
6	**7**	**8** 水泳 16:00	**9**	**10**	**11** 歌の練習 16:00	**12** 美術館 13:00
13	**14**	**15** 水泳 16:00	**16**	**17**	**18** 歌の練習 14:00 （時間変更）	**19** 音楽会
20	**21**	**22** 水泳 16:00	**23**	**24** 体育館 16:00	**25** ボランティア 13:00	**26** 映画 （時間未定）
27	**28**	**29** 水泳 16:00	**30**	**31**		

a. 走る

b. 遊ぶ

c. 映画

d. 絵を見る

e. 歌う

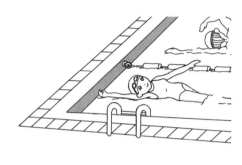

f. 泳ぐ

What is the schedule of each given day? Write the correct letter (a–f) in the below spaces, and choose the appropriate word for questions 7 and 8.

1. 10月5日（　　　　）　　2. 10月8日（　　　　）　　3. 10月12日（　　　　）

4. 10月18日（　　　　）　　5. 10月24日（　　　　）　　6. 10月26日（　　　　）

7. 10月18日 歌の練習の時間は（A.決定　B.未定　C.変更）です。

8. 10月26日 映画の時間は（A.決定　B.未定　C.変更）です。

2　Vocabulary

Study the readings and meanings of these words to help you understand the **Introductory Quiz**.

1. 週末	しゅう まつ	**shūmatsu**	weekend
2. 水泳	すい えい	**suiei**	swimming
3. 体育館	たい いく かん	**taiikukan**	gymnasium, gym
4. 歌	うた	**uta**	song
5. 遊園地	ゆう えん ち	**yūenchi**	amusement park
6. 美術館	び じゅつ かん	**bijutsukan**	art museum
7. 変更	へん こう	**henkō**	change
8. 音楽会	おん がく かい	**ongakukai**	concert

9.	ボランティア		**borantia**	volunteer work
10.	映画	えいが	**eiga**	movie
11.	未定	みてい	**mitei**	undecided
12.	走る	はしる	**hashiru**	to run
13.	遊ぶ	あそぶ	**asobu**	to play
14.	歌う	うたう	**utau**	to sing
15.	泳ぐ	およぐ	**oyogu**	to swim
16.	決定	けってい	**kettei**	decision

3 ▶ New Characters

Eleven characters are introduced in this lesson. Use the explanations to help you understand and remember the characters. Study the compound words to increase your vocabulary

末 泳 体 歌 遊 術 変 楽 映 未 走

240 末	**sue, matsu** すえ、マツ end	一 二 キ 才 末

末 combines a tree 木 and a longer horizontal line 一, to emphasize the end part of the tree, and means end.

週末	しゅうまつ	**shūmatsu**	weekend
月末	げつまつ	**getsumatsu**	end of the month
年末	ねんまつ	**nemmatsu**	year-end
期末	きまつ	**kimatsu**	end of the term
終末	しゅうまつ	**shūmatsu**	end
末期	まっき	**makki**	the final (last) stage
歳末	さいまつ	**saimatsu**	year end
始末する	しまつする	**shimatsu suru**	to dispose of
年度末	ねんどまつ	**nendomatsu**	end of the fiscal year

---

241 泳

oyo-gu, ei
およ・ぐ、エイ
swim

`丶 冫 氵 氵 氵 汀 泳 泳`

永 is a pictograph of water flowing in all directions. The rivers are long, and thus 永 means a long time. 泳 combines water 氵 and 永 a long time, and means to swim.

泳ぐ	およぐ	**oyogu**	to swim
水泳	すいえい	**suiei**	swimming
水泳着	すいえいぎ	**suieigi**	swimming suit
泳法	えいほう	**eihō**	swimming style
横泳ぎ	よこおよぎ	**yoko oyogi**	side stroke
平泳ぎ	ひらおよぎ	**hira oyogi**	breast stroke
背泳	はいえい	**haiei**	back stroke
遠泳	えんえい	**en'ei**	long-distance swim

---

242 体

karada, tai, tei
からだ、タイ、テイ
body

`ノ イ 亻 什 休 休 体`

A person's 亻 basic 本 part is the body 体.

体	からだ	**karada**	body
体育館	たいいくかん	**taiikukan**	gymnasium
体験	たいけん	**taiken**	experience
全体	ぜんたい	**zentai**	whole
体重	たいじゅう	**taijū**	body weight
体力	たいりょく	**tairyoku**	physical strength
気体	きたい	**kitai**	gas
体制	たいせい	**taisei**	system
体温	たいおん	**taion**	body temperature
体温計	たいおんけい	**taionkei**	clinical thermometer

---

243 歌

uta, uta-u, ka
うた、うた・う、カ
song, sing

`一 厂 冂 冋 可 哥 哥 哥`
`哥 哥 哥 哥 歌 歌 歌`

可 combines a throat 丁 and voice 口, and means voice. 可可 two voices, combined with an opened mouth 欠, suggests song.

歌	うた	**uta**	song
歌う	うたう	**utau**	to sing
歌手	かしゅ	**kashu**	singer
国歌	こっか	**kokka**	national anthem
和歌	わか	**waka**	waka (31-syllable Japanese poem)
短歌	たんか	**tanka**	tanka (synonym for waka)
歌声	うたごえ	**utagoe**	singing voice

244	**aso-bu, yū, yu** あそ・ぶ、ユウ、ユ play, be idle	`	ユ	方	方	ガ	汸	坊	斿
		斿	斿	遊	遊				

The swing of a child				

Flag 方 and child 子 suggest to shake, or to swing. Road 辶 is added and 遊 means to play, enjoy, or to be idle.

遊ぶ	あそぶ	**asobu**	to play
遊園地	ゆうえんち	**yūenchi**	amusement park
遊歩道	ゆうほどう	**yūhodō**	promenade

245	**jutsu** ジュツ art, means	`	⼓	彳	彳	犲	秫	休	術
		術	術	術					

朮, the pictograph of a plant with grain, suggests the fixed order as plants grow following the natural order. To go 行 is combined, thus 術 means to do something following tradition.

美術館	びじゅつかん	**bijutsukan**	art museum
学術	がくじゅつ	**gakujutsu**	science
美術品	びじゅつひん	**bijutsuhin**	work of art
手術	しゅじゅつ	**shujutsu**	operation
技術	ぎじゅつ	**gijutsu**	technology

246	**ka-eru, ka-waru, hen** か・える、か・わる、ヘン change	`	亠	亠	亣	亦	亦	亦	変
変		変							

The upper part 亦 shows tangled thread, compared to the straight warp of a loom, suggesting an unusual situation. 夂 is a trailing leg. If the legs get tangled when walking, it is not an ordinary condition. Thus 変 means change or strange.

変える	かえる	**kaeru**	to change (vt.)
変わる	かわる	**kawaru**	to change (vi.)
大変な	たいへんな	**taihen na**	terrible, hard
変化	へんか	**henka**	change
変な	へんな	**hen na**	peculiar
不変	ふへん	**fuhen**	permanence
変心	へんしん	**henshin**	change of mind
変色	へんしょく	**henshoku**	discoloration
変容	へんよう	**hen'yō**	transfiguration

247 楽

tano-shii, tano-shimu, gaku, raku
たの・しい、たの・しむ、ガク、ラク
music; enjoyable

′	′	′	′	′	′	′	′
	楽	楽	楽	楽	楽		

This is the pictograph of a tree with nuts on it. The nuts make a delightful sound when they are shaken in a basket. Thus 楽 means music, pleasure, easy and comfortable.

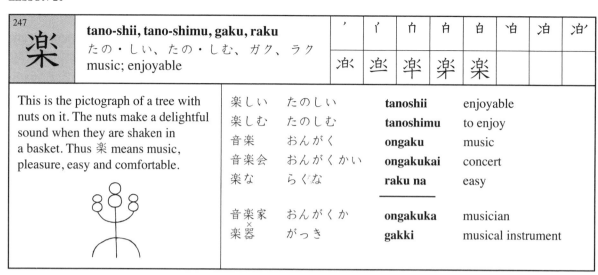

楽しい	たのしい	**tanoshii**	enjoyable
楽しむ	たのしむ	**tanoshimu**	to enjoy
音楽	おんがく	**ongaku**	music
音楽会	おんがくかい	**ongakukai**	concert
楽な	らくな	**raku na**	easy
音楽家	おんがくか	**ongakuka**	musician
楽器	がっき	**gakki**	musical instrument

248 映

utsu-ru, ha-eru, ei
うつ・る、は・える、エイ
reflect, project

丨	冂	月	日	旦	肛	旺	映
映							

Sunlight 日 directed at the center 央 of an object projects a figure on a screen behind the object.

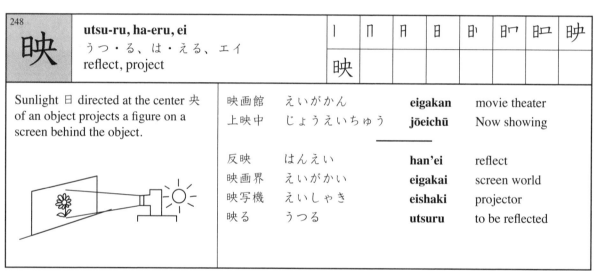

映画館	えいがかん	**eigakan**	movie theater
上映中	じょうえいちゅう	**jōeichū**	Now showing
反映	はんえい	**han'ei**	reflect
映画界	えいがかい	**eigakai**	screen world
映写機	えいしゃき	**eishaki**	projector
映る	うつる	**utsuru**	to be reflected

249 未

mi
ミ
not yet

一	二	キ	丰	未			

未 combines a tree 木 and short horizontal line 一, to emphasize the growing part of the tree, and means not yet.

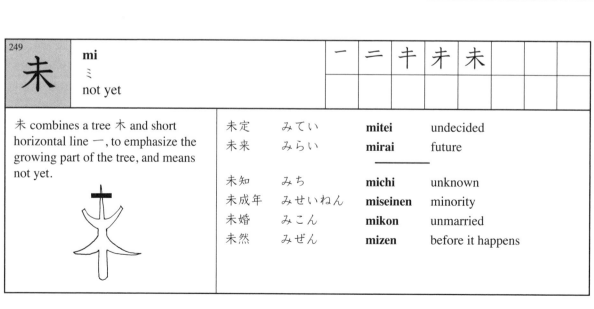

未定	みてい	**mitei**	undecided
未来	みらい	**mirai**	future
未知	みち	**michi**	unknown
未成年	みせいねん	**miseinen**	minority
未婚	みこん	**mikon**	unmarried
未然	みぜん	**mizen**	before it happens

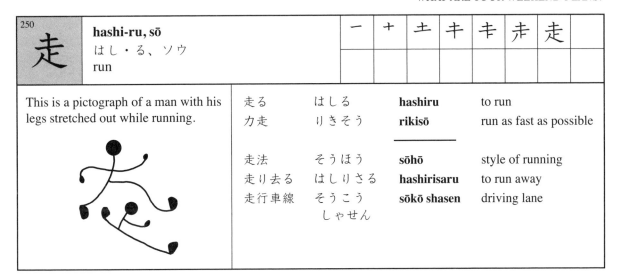

250 走	**hashi-ru, sō** はし・る、ソウ run	一	十	土	キ	キ	走	走

This is a pictograph of a man with his legs stretched out while running.

走る	はしる	**hashiru**	to run
力走	りきそう	**rikisō**	run as fast as possible
走法	そうほう	**sōhō**	style of running
走り去る	はしりさる	**hashirisaru**	to run away
走行車線	そうこう しゃせん	**sōkō shasen**	driving lane

4 ▶ Practice

I. Write the readings of the following kanji in hiragana.

1. 遊ぶ 　 2. 美術館 　 3. 上映中 　 4. 未来

5. 歌手 　 6. 末の妹は歌が 上手 です。

7. 泳ぐことは楽しいです。 　 8. 10kmを力走しました。

9. 最近、体の調子がいいです。

10. 練習の時間が変わりました。

II. Fill in the blanks with appropriate kanji.

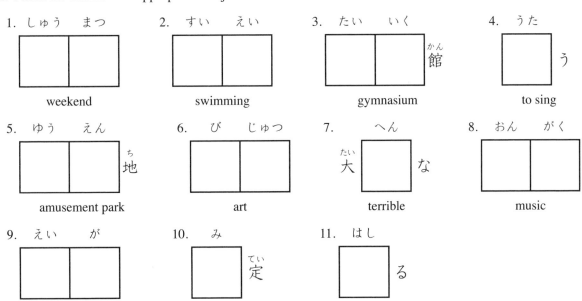

1. しゅう まつ — weekend

2. すい えい — swimming

3. たい いく 館 — gymnasium

4. うた う — to sing

5. ゆう えん 地 — amusement park

6. び じゅつ — art

7. 大 へん な — terrible

8. おん がく — music

9. えい が — movie

10. み 定 — undecided

11. はし る — to run

5 ▶ Advanced Placement Exam Practice Questions

Read this set of e-mails, then respond to the questions.

受信箱

Message #1

差出人：　のりこ

送信日：　10月16日

件　名：　土曜日の映画

あさって、土曜日、映画へ行かない？「未来II」すごくおもしろいらしい。

Message #2

差出人：　田中

送信日：　10月16日

件　名：　時間変更

18日金曜日、歌の練習時間は14時からに変更です。まちがえないように。

音楽会の前日なので講堂で練習します。

Message #3

差出人：　なおき

送信日：　10月16日

件　名：　土曜日カラオケ

水泳の練習はいつも通り、来週水曜日4時。土曜日、音楽会が終わったらカラオケいかない？[1]久^{ひさ}しぶ
りに歌って[2]発散^{はっさん}しよう。みんなもさそっておくから。

Message #4

差出人：　ひろみ

送信日：　10月17日

件　名：　RE: 土曜日の映画

私は、カラオケのほうがいいな。歌うと気分が変わるし、「未来I」あまりおもしろくなかったよ。画
面も暗くて寝ちゃった。カラオケなら　アツシも　行きたいって。

Message #5

差出人：　あい

送信日：　10月17日

件　名：　RE: 土曜日カラオケ

私は、歌ってぱーっと　ストレスを発散したい。

カラオケずっと行ってなかったからね。4人で駅前に4時かな。

Message #6

差出人：　なおき

送信日：　10月20日

件　名：　昨日の件

昨日は楽しかったね。このところ、忙しくて遊べなかったし。人数も4人ぐらいがちょうどいいね。でも、次はのりこもいっしょに遊べるといいね。

1 久^{ひさ}しぶりに: after a long time

2 発散^{はっさん}: blow off, give vent to

1. Which message is from someone who thought "Future I" was not interesting?
   A. Message #1
   B. Message #3
   C. Message #4
   D. Message #5

2. Which message is from someone who didn't go to karaoke?
   A. Message #1
   B. Message #3
   C. Message #4
   D. Message #5

3. Which message is from someone who enjoyed the karaoke?
   A. Message #1
   B. Message #4
   C. Message #5
   D. Message #6

4. Why did they go to karaoke?
   A. Because one of them has seen the movie already.
   B. Because not all of them like a love story.
   C. Because they wanted to relieve their stress.
   D. Because they didn't want to go to choir practice anymore.

5. Mr. Tanaka says that
   A. the choir practice will be held in the music room 2:00 P.M. on Friday.
   B. the concert will be held in the hall 2:00 P.M. on Saturday.
   C. the choir practice will be held in the auditorium 2:00 P.M. on Friday.
   D. the concert and the choir practice will be held in the hall.

APPENDICES
ANSWERS
AP JAPANESE KANJI LIST
ON-KUN INDEX
VOCABULARY INDEX

APPENDIX A

Main Radicals

Below are the main radicals presented in this book, and some examples.

I.   へん (left part) ▮▯
    1.   氵   water   活、港、酒、池、漢、温、泊、海、治、泣、決、泳
    2.   イ   man, people   働、仕、個、伝、化、側、低、信、係、作、体
    3.   糸   thread   経、続、組、紙、練、結、絵
    4.   木   tree   相、校、機、枚、横、橋、村、林、森
    5.   彳   step   待、得、術
    6.   言   speech   調、課、試、読、説
    7.   扌   hand   持、指、打、接、授
    8.   日   sun   暖、昨、晩、晴、映
    9.   女   woman   好、姉、婦、妹、婚
    10. 冫   ice   冷、次

II. つくり (right part) ▯▮
    1.   刂   sword, knife   利、制、別
    2.   頁   head   類、額、頭、顔、願

III. かんむり (top part) ▬
    1.   艹   plant   花、荷、英、落、若
    2.   宀   roof, house   家、客、容、字、宿、寒、寝

IV. あし (bottom part) ▬
    1.   儿   human legs   兄、免、元

V.   かまえ (enclosing part) ▣ ▬
    1.   門   gate   関、聞、問
    2.   囗   enclosure   園、困

VI. にょう (left and bottom part) ▙
    1.   辶   move ahead   遠、近、送、遅、選、運、達、返、進、遊

VII. たれ (top and left part) ▛
    1.   广   slanting roof 広、庭、度
    2.   厂   cliff   石、反

APPENDIX B

Kanji Compounds

I. Main Types of Compounds and Some Examples

Type I. Adjective + Noun

赤信号、悪名、大雨、温室、高熱、好物、初夏、新春、雑音、難問、白線、初荷、丸顔

Type 2. Verb (Modifier) + Noun

笑顔、願書、祝辞、洗剤、動画、旅客

Type 3. Adverb + Verb

悪用、遠泳、快晴、外泊、再会、自習、常駐、多読、予言、予想

Type 4. Verb + Noun (Objective)

禁酒、決心、作文、指名、集金、出荷、点火、返信、転校、発音、分類、冷房、録画

Type 5. Pair of Synonyms

絵画、会合、河川、関係、記録、教育、結成、支持、宿泊、主要、消化、配達、発育、変化

Type 6. Pair of Antonyms

朝夕、往復、親子、強弱、公私、高低、姉妹、夫婦、父母

II. Kanji Commonly Used in Compounds and Some Examples

以： 以下、以外、以後、以前

園： 公園、動物園、庭園、開園、学園、田園

家： 大家、音楽家、画家、家族、家庭、家内、作家、家賃、家主

化： 温暖化、化学、強化、国際化、自由化、消化、正常化、多様化、文化、変化

公： 公園、公開、公式、公表、公平、公約、公用、公立

交： 外交、交通、交番、交付、国交

校： 校正、校庭、校風、小学校、転校、母校

合： 会合、合計、組合、待合室、合意、都合

再： 再生、再発行、再会、再開、再利用、再入国

最： 最近、最後、最終、最初、最新、最大

私： 私見、私語、私生活、私小説、私費、私立

集： 集会室、集金、集中、集落、全集、特集

重： 重工業、重体、重量、重要、重力、体重

心： 安心、関心、初心者、心身、真心

真: 写真、真空、真実、真理、真上、真夏、真冬

制: 制度、税制、強制、申込制、制止、制約、制作

税: 税関、税金、無税、免税、免税店

然: 公然、自然、全然、天然、必然、平然

送: 送信、送料、運送、返送、回送

町: 一番町、大手町、下町、町内会、町家、港町、横町

的: 一時的、公的、私的、自発的、知的、伝統的、天文学的、目的

風: 強風、校風、弱風、台風、洋風、和風

変: 大変、不変、変化、変色、変容

力: 強力、重力、人力、水力、全力、電力、動力、風力、無力、力士

AP JAPANESE KANJI LIST

For the AP Japanese Language and Culture course and exam, students are expected to be able to interpret and produce texts using the kanji on this list. It is based on a survey of commonly used textbooks and represents expectations typical of college courses that represent the point at which students complete approximately 300 hours of college-level classroom instruction. This list is organized by JIS code, but, of course, the kanji need not be presented in this particular order. Kanji should be presented according to students' communicative needs, as characterized by the topic, purpose, and other aspects of their reading and writing.

悪安暗以意医育一員引
飲院右雨運映泳英駅円

親身進人図水数世制成
晴正生西青静昔石赤切

園遠横屋温音下化何夏
家科歌火花荷画会回海

接節説雪先千専川洗線
選前然全組早相走送贈

界皆絵開階外学楽活寒
漢間関館顔願期機帰気

側足速族続卒村多太打
体対待貸台大第題達単

記起休急泣究牛去魚京
強教橋業局近金九空係

短男知地池置遅茶着中
昼注朝町調長鳥痛通低

兄形経計決結月犬見験
元現言個古五午後語公

定庭弟的天店転点伝田
電登都度土冬島東答頭

口向好工広校港考行降
高号合国黒今困婚左最

働動同道特読内南難二
肉日入熱年背配買売白

歳祭際作昨雑三山残仕
使四始姉子市思指止私

八発半反飯晩番非飛美
鼻必百氷表病品不付夫

紙試事字寺持時次治自
辞式七失室実写社者車

婦父部風服払物分文聞
平別変便勉歩母方法忘

若主取手酒受授州秋終
習週集住十重宿出術春

忙北本妹枚毎末万味未
無名明面木目問門夜野

初所暑書女商小少笑上
乗場色食信寝心新森神

薬友有由遊夕予曜様洋
用要来絡落利理立留旅
両料力林冷礼練六和話

ANSWERS TO THE INTRODUCTORY QUIZZES AND ADVANCED PLACEMENT EXAM PRACTICE QUESTIONS

Answers to the Introductory Quizzes

Lesson 1
1. B
2. A

Lesson 2
1. ○
2. ×
3. ×
4. ○
5. ×
6. ○

Lesson 3
1. ×
2. ○
3. ×
4. ×
5. ○
6. ○
7. ×
8. ○
9. ×
10. ○

Lesson 4
I. 1. c
　2. d
　3. b
　4. e
　5. f
　6. a
II. 1. b
　2. e
　3. f
　4. c
　5. d
　6. a

Lesson 5
1. g
2. b

3. d
4. c
5. a
6. e
7. f
8. h

Lesson 6
1. c, d
2. g
3. f
4. h
5. b, d
6. a
7. i
8. e

Lesson 7
省略 (Omitted)

Lesson 8
1. j
2. h
3. i
4. a
5. g
6. b
7. c

Lesson 9
1. a
2. h
3. e
4. f
5. g
6. d

Lesson 10
1. f
2. a
3. c

4. k
5. j
6. h
7. e
8. i
9. d
10. g
11. b

Lesson 11
1. c, f
2. a, g
3. d, h
4. b, e

Lesson 12
1. 4
2. 3
3. 6
4. 1
5. 2
6. 5

Lesson 13
1. ×
2. ○
3. ×
4. ○
5. ×
6. ○

Lesson 14
1. ×
2. ○
3. ×
4. ○
5. ×

Lesson 15
1. C
2. F

3. B
4. D
5. G
6. A
7. E

Lesson 16
I. 1. b
　2. e
　3. c
　4. f
　5. a
　6. d
II. 1. b
　2. a
　3. d
　4. c

Lesson 17
1. a
2. d
3. b, e
4. c
5. e

Lesson 18
I. 1. b
　2. d
　3. a
　4. c
II. 　A

Lesson 19
I. 1. 6
　2. 5
　3. B1 (or 地下 1)
　4. 6
II. 1. 1
　2. B1 (or 地下 1)
　3. 6

Lesson 20
1. d
2. b
3. c
4. a

Lesson 21
1. b
2. f
3. d
4. e

5. a
6. c
7. C
8. B

Answers to the Advanced Placement Exam Practice Questions

Lesson 1
省略 (Omitted)

Lesson 2
1. C
2. D
3. B
4. B
5. A

Lesson 3
1. B
2. B
3. D
4. C
5. B

Lesson 4
省略 (Omitted)

Lesson 5
省略 (Omitted)

Lesson 6
省略 (Omitted)

Lesson 7
1. A
2. B
3. A
4. B
5. D

Lesson 8
1. C
2. B
3. A
4. D

Lesson 9
1. D
2. C
3. D
4. C
5. A

Lesson 10
1. C
2. B
3. A
4. B
5. D

Lesson 11
省略 (Omitted)

Lesson 12
1. D
2. B
3. A
4. D
5. C

Lesson 13
1. C
2. C
3. B
4. D

Lesson 14
1. C
2. B
3. D
4. C

Lesson 15
1. C
2. A
3. C
4. D

Lesson 16
1. B
2. D
3. A
4. D
5. B

Lesson 17
1. D
2. B
3. C
4. C

Lesson 18
1. D
2. A
3. C
4. D
5. B

Lesson 19
1. C
2. D
3. A
4. B
5. C

Lesson 20
1. B
2. A
3. C
4. D
5. C

Lesson 21
1. C
2. A
3. D
4. C
5. C

ON-KUN INDEX

The words in this index are taken from the kanji charts. **On-yomi** in katakana and **kun-yomi** in hiragana are followed by the kanji, the lesson number where it's found, and its serial number in this book. Hiragana after "•" indicates **okurigana**. Modified readings, enclosed in ( ), follow after original readings.

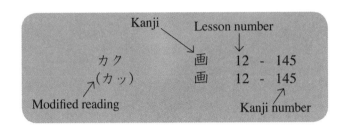

━━【 あ　ア 】━━

あい	相	2	18
あ・う	合	4	52
あお	青	20	232
あお・い	青	20	232
あか	赤	13	156
あき	秋	11	136
あきな・う	商	6	68
アク	悪	16	187
あさ	朝	14	174
あざ	字	9	113
あし	足	16	193
あじ	味	5	60
あじ・わう	味	5	60
あそ・ぶ	遊	21	244
あたた・かい	暖	11	138
あたた・かい	温	11	141
あたた・める	温	11	141
あたま	頭	16	189
あつ・い	暑	11	139
	熱	16	195
あつ・まる	集	2	24
あつ・める	集	2	24
あに	兄	3	33
あね	姉	3	29
あま	天	17	200
	雨	17	203
あめ	天	17	200
	雨	17	203
あらわ・す	現	8	91
あらわ・れる	現	8	91
あ・わす	合	4	52
あ・わせる	合	4	52

━━【 い　イ 】━━

イ	以	7	82
い・う	言	13	163
いえ	家	1	5
イク	育	8	101
いけ	池	8	94
いし	石	14	172
いそが・しい	忙	19	228
いた・い	痛	16	190
いた・む	痛	16	190
いぬ	犬	2	22
いま	今	3	38
いもうと	妹	3	40
い・る	要	9	109
いろ	色	19	221
イン	音	12	146
	員	20	236

━━【 う　ウ 】━━

ウ	雨	17	203
うい	初	9	106
うしな・う	失	18	209
うた	歌	21	243
うた・う	歌	21	243
う・つ	打	13	162
うつく・しい	美	6	75
うつ・す	写	6	69
うつ・る	映	21	248
うみ	海	14	176
う・る	得	14	168
ウン	運	11	133

━━【 え　エ 】━━

え	重	12	152
エ	絵	19	219
エイ	英	9	105
	泳	21	241
	映	21	248
え・む	笑	16	197
えら・ぶ	選	9	110
え・る	得	14	168
エン	遠	2	13
	園	8	99

━━【 お　オ 】━━

オ	悪	16	187
オウ	横	6	74
おお・い	多	12	149
おおやけ	公	8	98
お・きる	起	15	178
お・く	置	8	97
おく・る	送	5	67
	贈	19	225
おく・れる	遅	7	83
お・こす	起	15	178
おさ・める	治	16	188
おそ・い	遅	7	83
お・ちる	落	6	78
おっと	夫	20	239
おと	音	12	146
おとうと	弟	3	37
お・とす	落	6	78
おな・じ	同	3	35
おも	主	3	30
おも・い	重	12	152
おも・う	思	9	114
おや	親	2	17
およ・ぐ	泳	21	241
お・りる	降	17	207
オン	温	11	141
	音	12	146

━━【 か　カ 】━━

カ	家	1	5
	荷	4	54
	花	6	73
	課	10	116
	夏	11	135
	化	13	161
	歌	21	243
ガ	画	12	145
	賀	18	213
カイ	皆	2	26
	海	14	176
	絵	19	219
	界	19	224
かえ・す	帰	4	53
	返	18	217
かえ・る	帰	4	53
(がえ・る)	帰	4	53
か・える	変	21	246
かお	顔	16	191
(がお)	顔	16	191
かかり	係	20	230
(がかり)	係	20	230
かか・る	係	20	230
カク	客	4	46
カク	画	12	145
(カッ)	画	12	145
ガク	額	12	151
	楽	21	247
かざ	風	11	132
かさ・なる	重	12	152
かしら	頭	16	189
かず	数	3	42
かぜ	風	11	132
かぞ・える	数	3	42
かた	形	19	220
かた・い	難	10	123
かたち	形	19	220
カツ	活	1	3
(カッ)	活	1	3
ガッ	合	4	52
かなら・ず	必	9	108
かみ	紙	7	85
(がみ)	紙	7	85
かみ	神	13	154
からだ	体	21	242
かわ	川	8	93
(がわ)	川	8	93
かわ	側	17	201
(がわ)	側	17	201

VOCABULARY INDEX

The words in this index are taken from the vocabulary lists and kanji charts in Lessons 1 through 21.